Lifelong Learning Book Series

Volume 36

Competing visions and paradigms for lifelong learning co-exist at national as well as international levels. The fact that one 'official' discourse may be dominant at any one time does not mean that other ways of thinking about learning throughout the life course have disappeared. They are alive and well in a range of critical traditions and perspectives that retain their power to engage and persuade.

Lifelong learning is presented in this Series in all its versatility. Accordingly, lifelong learning is referred to as an idea, a concept, an approach, a method, a programme, a strategy, even a philosophy or worldview. Similarly, the approaches to lifelong learning presented in the Series are sometimes philosophical, sociological, economic, psychological or educational, and frequently multi-disciplinary. Common foci are the practices of individual, organisational and collective learning as well as the development of people, communities and societies.

The Series promotes critical, evidence-informed exploration of problems, themes and issues in the evolving field of lifelong learning. Each volume is firmly based on high quality scholarship and a keen awareness of both emergent and enduring issues in practice and policy. Our mission is to engage scholars, practitioners, policy makers and professionals with new insights from international research and practice, and to provoke fresh thinking and innovation in lifelong learning. Contributions that highlight previously under-researched groups, countries and territories are strongly encouraged.

The Lifelong Learning Series aims to bring together established authors building on a strong platform of previous work to develop their themes and positions, with new generation authors bringing novel ideas and perspectives. We welcome contributions from multi-disciplinary research collaborations that approach contemporary and emerging global and local challenges in creative ways.

Through advocacy of broad, diverse and inclusive approaches to learning throughout the life course, the series aspires to be a leading resource for researchers and practitioners who seek to rethink lifelong learning to meet the challenges and opportunities of the 21st Century.

The Lifelong Learning Book Series complements the Third International Handbook of Lifelong Learning https://link.springer.com/referencework/10.1007/978-3-031-19592-1 with an elaboration of specific topics, themes and case studies in greater depth than is possible in the Handbook.

Tania Zittoun • Fabienne Gfeller
Editors

Ageing, Learning and Development

Sociocultural and Psychoanalytical Perspectives on Growing Older

Springer

Editors
Tania Zittoun
Institute of Psychology and Education
Université de Neuchâtel
Neuchâtel, Switzerland

Fabienne Gfeller
Institute of Psychology and Education
Université de Neuchâtel
Neuchâtel, Switzerland

ISSN 1871-322X ISSN 2730-5325 (electronic)
Lifelong Learning Book Series
ISBN 978-3-032-11056-5 ISBN 978-3-032-11057-2 (eBook)
https://doi.org/10.1007/978-3-032-11057-2

This Springer imprint is published by the registered company Springer Nature Switzerland AG
The registered company address is: Gewerbestrasse 11, 6330 Cham, Switzerland

Foreword

We are delighted to introduce this new volume on Ageing, Learning and Development, as a timely and important addition to the Lifelong Learning Book Series. The Series promotes critical, evidence-informed exploration of problems, themes and contemporary issues in the evolving field of lifelong learning. Each volume is firmly based on high quality scholarship and a keen awareness of both emergent and enduring issues in practice and policy. Our mission is to engage scholars, practitioners, policy makers and professionals with new insights from international research and practice and to stimulate fresh thinking and innovation where societal challenges are demanding creative responses.

The changes in global demography caused by population ageing are producing multiple challenges across the globe. Between 1974 and 2024, the worldwide share of people aged over 65 has almost doubled. While medical advances have increased overall life expectancy worldwide, achieving healthier lives into the later years is now at the forefront of policy debates. There has been no shortage of high-profile initiatives launched to raise awareness and stimulate action, yet problems are proving intractable in low- and middle-income contexts where older people face hardships, gender discrimination and a host of social and economic barriers. According to the World Health Organisation, there is an enduring disconnect between international calls to action and the implementation of effective programmes and interventions contributing to healthy ageing and well-being. Most significantly from the perspective of lifelong learning and development, evaluations of progress have indicated that life course approaches towards healthy ageing have not been fully recognised and incorporated in interventions.

Learning throughout the adult life course and into later life has become an important focus for the *Springer Lifelong Learning Book Series* in the past decade. It has also featured strongly in our related major reference work, the *Third International Handbook of Lifelong Learning (2023)*. Previous books dedicated to better understandings of later life learning and development have included the anthology *International Perspectives on Older Adult Education* (Volume 22, 2017) and *Taiwan's Senior Learning Movement* (Volume 28), with authors in the Third International Handbook also extending their reach to questions of intergenerational learning and 'fourth age' learning for people living with dementia. Approaches to these topics have included conceptual analysis, historical patterns of provision, policy developments, theoretical perspectives, research studies, challenges faced by countries and 'success stories' of later life learning, giving contextualised insights into the learning that occurs in later life in contrasting social and cultural contexts across the globe.

The editors of *Ageing Learning and Development*, Tania Zittoun and Fabienne Gfeller, start with the observation that 'the diversity and length of trajectories of ageing means that we cannot consider 'the old person' in an isolated, static and undifferentiated way'. This new multi-authored book, subtitled *Sociocultural and Psychoanalytical Perspectives on Growing Older*, brings a completely new approach to understanding learning and development in strategies to support adults' well-being in later life. The book's originality stems from the way in which it brings together two perspectives, drawing from both French and Anglo-Saxon traditions. These traditions are often treated as competing, or as inhabiting irreconcilable realms of thought and understanding. Their combination here generates rich understandings of the complexities of the ageing process. The focus is on how adults, as they grow older, keep developing, uniquely and reflexively, in social, cultural, material and symbolic environments that are themselves constantly changing. New methodological strategies are introduced, in ways that indicate possible future routes for applied research and interventions.

This book is intended for researchers working in the field of ageing, scholars, healthcare professionals, policy makers and social workers. The researchers in the field of ageing who can benefit from this book include many working in the field of educational gerontology who are striving to enrich resources in gerontology for the education professional. Adult learning professionals worldwide are searching for new ways to collaborate in the co-design of strategies to support learning and well-being in later life.

The editors Tania Zittoun and Fabienne Gfeller have expertly curated a collection of chapters that revitalise a core lifelong learning theme. Inspirational ideas and approaches are elegantly explained in ways that respect the richness of lived experiences of people as they grow older. The authors' reflections on research promise to deepen and enrich long-standing debates about interventions, programmes and practices that can better meet the challenges of changing times. At the same time, this book contributes to the Series mission of increasing the circuitry of the wider lifelong learning field, by connecting scholars and practitioners from different traditions and introducing fresh inter-disciplinary insights. We commend it to all our readers.

October 2025

UCL Institute of Education
University College London,
London, UK

Karen Evans
Natasha Kersh

Contents

1 Introduction: Toward an Integrative Approach to Learning and Development in Older Age 1
Tania Zittoun

2 Cognitive Adaptation, Hybrid Minds and Ageing: Epistemic Practices in Cumulative Cultures 19
Roger Säljö

3 Taking Care of Oneself as an Elderly Person While Being Interested in the Future of the Younger Generation: Incompatible Concerns? 37
Benoît Verdon

4 On Being an Oxymoron: A Sociocultural Psychology of Development with Older Age 63
Tania Zittoun

5 Developmental Processes and Meaning-Making in Volunteering Activity 85
Nathalie Muller Mirza

6 Moving House in Older Age: Challenges and Resources for the Sense of Self-continuity 107
Fabienne Gfeller and Michèle Grossen

7 The Dynamics of Dependency in Old Age: Psychoanalytic Perspectives 137
Céline Racin

8 The Paradoxes of Ageing and Its Future 159
Tania Zittoun and Michèle Grossen

Index 173

Contents

Index

Chapter 1
Introduction: Toward an Integrative Approach to Learning and Development in Older Age

Tania Zittoun

> There's no doubt that old age is a journey into a foreign country, so that one is being astonished by what is not possible. Or by what is different from anything that has gone before.
> (Sarton, 1993, p. 72)

Psychologists have still much to discover and understand about learning and development in older age. The ageing of the population has started to be a concern for policy makers and international organisations at the turn of the millennium (World Health Organization, 2002). It has been made possible thanks to the massive increase of general hygiene standards and health care, and, in heavily industrialised countries, the diminution of birthrate (Säljö, 2022); it is however still unequally spread along the world. Over the last century, intellectuals and scientists have become the first explorers of this "foreign country" (Sarton, 1993, p. 72) that is old age, and have often shown an area under-understood, whose inhabitants are silenced and often put aside (de Beauvoir, 1970; Hall, 1922). In less than a century, the country has been mapped out, village have been built, organisations established. Medical doctors, social workers, nurses have been in the frontline of the experience of the older population, and in most industrialised countries, policies have been created and adjusted to transform the conditions of living of the oldest. With the risk of being extremely schematic, the place of older persons has known three main phasis: first, in many countries, the few older persons have (or are still) been long maintained in the community or in the family; second, with urbanisation and the build-up of social welfare, older persons have tendentially been placed into specific institutions, usually out of sight, at the periphery of villages or cities; and third, both under the increasing number of older persons, their relative better health, but also, the pressure on social and health insurances, older persons are, in many countries,

T. Zittoun (✉)
Institute of Psychology and Education, Université de Neuchâtel, Neuchâtel, Switzerland
e-mail: tania.zittoun@unine.ch

T. Zittoun, F. Gfeller (eds.), *Ageing, Learning and Development*, Lifelong Learning Book Series 36, https://doi.org/10.1007/978-3-032-11057-2_1

encouraged and/or demanding to "age in place"—to keep their place, if not their role, in society.

Social scientists and psychologists have, as often, tried to describe the best and optimal conditions of ageing, often also blind to their own very specific and situated focus, or the economical constraints its responds to—whether on active ageing or disengagement—two models of ageing competing in the US led social sciences, or more recently and widespread, on "successful ageing". It is only marginally and progressively that authors have, on the one hand, tried to account for older persons' living environments, and on the other, for people's firsthand experience of becoming older. This introduction recalls these three tendencies as first recalled, before presenting the present volume.

1.1 Psychologies of Ageing: Main Approaches

Psychology of ageing developed out of various lines. The two main ones are a cognitive strand, and a more humanistic one, both born in Europe. On the cognitive side, a rapidly progressing developmental psychology historically rejoined gerontology as theory and methods enabled systematic lifespan enquiries. Paul and Margaret Baltes' seminal study of an 80-years-plus old cohort in Germany was thus a landmark in the field (Baltes & Mayer, 1999), pushing on the one hand the enquiry of the lifespan into the specificity of older age cognition and memory, and on the other hand, showing the importance of cultural resources as compensation for biological losses (Baltes, 1997; Baltes & Baltes, 1990; Säljö, 2025). They also opened the route into the study of experiences specific to the oldest around the idea of wisdom (Baltes, 2004; Baltes & Kunzmann, 2004), although that specific notion was later questioned. On the side of the more humanistic tradition, research focused more on achievements specific to the ages of life, and so both Charlotte Bühler and Erik Erikson examined issues of meaning-making in older age as part of their enquiries into the unfolding of lives (Bühler, 1961; Erikson et al., 1986).

At the boundary between a humanistic approach and the access to systematic longitudinal data, a series of authors created the terms of the debates on ageing. Pursuing an enquiry into age-specific tasks, Robert Havighurst identified the "needs" of older persons (Havighurst, 1952), which led him increasingly to define the conditions of "successful" ageing (Havighurst, 1961). He eventually promoted "active ageing" (Havighurst, 1968; Neugarten, 1972), as opposed to the hypothesis that ageing was synonymous of progressive social disengagement (Cumming & Henry, 1961). During the same period, Robert Butler developed his method of "life review" (Butler, 1963, 1981), an invitation to explore the biography of older persons, initially a diagnostic tools, then seen as having therapeutic effects. These studies, all led by America based authors and on samples of middle-class citizens, set the norms on what ageing should be. More recent studies have mainly pursued their enquiry into cognitive ageing (Thomas, 2020; Verhaeghen, 2011), at times—yet rarely—paying a specific attention to affects and meaning-making in older age (Carstensen, 2019, 2021). These studies led to what has been largely accepted as a standard of "successful ageing" at world level. Mainly, the image of older persons coming out of this dominant stream of studies is that of a responsible, yet lone person, taking care of their physical and cognitive health, so as not only to strive in a youthful mode, but also, to limit social and health costs. This tendency is for instance reflected at the level of the World Health Organization, where the theme "active ageing" (World Health Organization, 2002) was recently replaced by a priority on "healthy ageing" (World Health Organization, 2021, 2024).

1.2 Alternatives Approaches to Ageing

There are alternative to this individualist, normative and ethnocentric view of ageing. First, in parallel to the aforementioned studies, a fertile field of "environmental gerontology" paid attention to the social, material and symbolic environment of people's lives (Lawton, 1977, 1985). If these studies have importantly shown how trajectories of aging could be shaped and enabled by their environment, they somehow disappeared—apparently because they failed to ground their work theoretically and to communicate the importance of their findings (Schwarz, 2012; Wahl & Weisman, 2003). However, notions such as these of "landscape of care" (Bigonnesse & Chaudhury, 2020; Milligan & Wiles, 2010), describing the fields and networks in which the ageing person is situated, and of "convoy of care" (Antonucci & Ajrouch, 2022; Kemp et al., 2013), underlying the dynamics nature of what accompanies the ageing person, as well as various ecological approaches (Moore, 2014; Oswald, 2024), kept such environmental attention alive—even though they may not fully account for developmental dynamics.

Second, at times inspired by the idea of life review and the humanistic approach to ageing, as well as more critical perspectives in psychology, more hermeneutic trends to ageing focused on older person's narratives. Narrative studies of ageing indeed emphasise the first person perspective of ageing persons, and their meaning making (Coleman et al., 2015; Gubrium, 2011; Lieblich, 2014b). If these studies present the great advantage to make us see and hear the experience of older age, they also uncritically admit that narrating is "good" for people, and at times, that some modes of narrative are more developmental than others: thus, some narrative would keep the future open, while others, with "foreclosure", would be more indicative of people's lack of engagement in life (Freeman, 2011)—an implicit normativity questioned since (K. J. Gergen & Gergen, 2010; Lieblich, 2014a).

1.3 Still Wanted: The Singularity of Developing, Situated Older Persons

Appreciating the contributions of these various fields of enquiry, we however also felt some of their limitations to account for the lives of older persons as they unfold in their environment: first, the essentialisation associated to research on "ageing"; second, the unquestioned normativity of many approaches to older age; and third, the lack of an integrative approach that considers the person's experience in their environment.

In effect, ageing implies that interpersonal differences, due to contexts of living, lifestyles, cultural subsystems traversed during one's lives, the hazard of collective and individual events, idiosyncratic specificities and choices, just become larger and wider over time. Critical authors thus note that one of the first tendencies of an ageist outlook is to homogenise older persons, as a group or as a generation (Angus & Reeve, 2006; T. D. Nelson, 2005; White, 2013). Yet without critically question who is "old" (is it an institutional decision, an arbitrary scientific decision, a subjective experience?), or without admitting that one is only always the old of someone else (after Bourdieu, 1978) and that most of us will become older one day too, it is impossible to account for the great diversity of lives of older persons—persons ranging, depending on the literature, between 60 and 115, of all gender and orientation, family status, past and present activities and occupations, modes of life, and social, geographic and symbolic environment. Some authors have thus shown the anger of some persons to find themselves suddenly "othered", and often silenced, as old (Caissie, 2011; Woodward, 2002). Hence, against the risks of essentialising and othering an indistinct group of the "elderly", it seems of primary importance of accounting for the diversity of modes and conditions of developing with age.

Another tendency to erase the diversity of modes of ageing comes from earlier attempts to categorise typical trajectories of ageing and to prioritize some. If authors have long shown the lack of relevance of the old "active ageing" vs "disengagement" fight (M. M. Gergen & Gergen, 2001; Henry, 1998; Wanka, 2018), or its sociocultural situatedness, only few have shown the negative consequences of the notion of active ageing. Social scientists thus start showing how such discourses generate social pressures made on older persons that should be active to cost less to society, or how older persons may interpret and internalise social discourse on ageing (Stenner et al., 2011). Others show that policy makers tend to neglect, if not hide the important and invisible work made by the older population, in terms of social cohesion and care, notably (Carney, 2018; Repetti & Fassa, 2024; Ziegler, 2012). Finally, few authors have questioned the normativity of the assumptions that older persons like to, and should, reminisce and narrate their past (Lieblich, 2014a, 2014b). Again, social discourses, reflecting dominant social sciences, tend to make invisible the diversity of modes of ageing, and the active, often future oriented social role of older persons.

In effect, and third, still few approaches fully consider the situatedness and the singularity of ageing persons. As mentioned, the most convincing lines of work developed so as to account for the importance of the environment of people's ageing, environmental or ecological gerontology, and later, the landscape of care approach, consider mainly the pressing, or supportive, or caring nature of the context of living (Lawton, 1977; Moore, 2014). It is rarer that they also examine how people experience these environments, or how, and in what respects, they contribute to the shaping of these environments, for instance though voluntary work or childcare (Carney, 2018; Muller Mirza, 2025). In addition, given the theoretical effort made on qualifying environments of living, theorising the life of persons themselves has fallen in the background (Hugentobler, 2024). On the other hand, there is one stream that has recently expanded and developed in the landscape of studies of the older person: that of the psychoanalytical approaches to ageing. If psychoanalysis has been long reluctant to consider the specificities of the older person, mainly by fear that people over 50s would be both too rigid to change, and already too complex to be analysed (S. Freud, 1905; Segal, 1958), the demographic shift of the population has led more and more clinicians to work with older persons. At first, authors have tended to focus on intrapsychic tensions and people's reactivations of older conflicts (Assoun, 1983; Ferenczi, 1974; Gutton, 2016; Gutton & Maïdi, 2020); yet soon, other have realised, first, that there is a specific psychic work of ageing (Quinodoz, 2009; Talpin, 2017b; Verdon, 2016; Villa, 2010), and second, that even a more person-centred perspective needs to consider the ageing person in their context, that is, in relationship with others and the world (Talpin, 2020; Villa, 2015), and with it, the conflict raised by the fact that older person are exposed to the multiplicity of social discourses on ageing.

Obviously, then, there is room for approaches that would go beyond social discourses on ageing, yet consider their role, while integrating a developmental understanding of the unique trajectories of people becoming older, in their evolving environments. In this volume, we selected therefore two approaches which we think are good candidates to develop such an integrative effort.

1.4 Approaching Aging from Sociocultural Psychology and Psychoanalysis

Sociocultural, or cultural psychology, has established itself as a field since the 1990s, as reaction to too-cognitive reductions of mind in psychology, and drawing on the newly accessible Russian tradition inaugurated by the work of Lev Vygotsky. It developed as a field with a rich philosophical underpinning, finding in American pragmatism (William James, Charles Peirce, John Dewey) and pre-WWII European psychology (the *Ganzheit psychology*, Pierre Janet, at times even Giambatisto Vico) as well as in further Russian works, such as Bakhtin's dialogism, its groundings. It has become a deeply developmental (or genetic, or historical) psychology focusing on the changing person's transactions with an evolving world. It focuses particularly on human activity and the centrality of sense-making as dialogical process; it considers the key mediating role of human interactions as well as cultural signs and tools in human becoming. In other words, it assumes that humans would not be what they are, think or act, without the transformation of their capacities—thinking, feeling, acting—by culture, itself resulting from the thoughts, experience and actions of other humans. These key assumptions have of course been carried on by authors along diverse branches of studies, often permeable to each other. Jerome Bruner and Katherine Nelson have emphasised the role of narrative and discourse in the becoming of humans and the expansion of culture (Bruner, 2003; K. Nelson, 2007); James Wertsch and Michael Cole have focused more on activities, in a wider diversity of setting—school, works—in which the mediating role of culture becomes key to learning and development (Cole, 1996; Wertsch, 1998); Jaan Valsiner has explored foremost the processes of semiotic mediation, in everyday life, as well as carried out through aesthetic artefacts (Valsiner, 2019, 2021); and Ivana Marková has demonstrated the fundamental dialogical nature of most of these dynamics (Marková, 2003, 2016; Shotter & Billig, 1998). These authors have durably inspired an important and worldwide field of enquiries.

Within it, it is only relatively recently that room has been given for ageing as sociocultural and psychological processes. Notably inspired by Vygotsky's idea that it is life as a whole that should be studied (Zavershneva & Van der Veer, 2018), authors started to expand an enquiry dominantly still focused on childhood and youth, and more rarely, adulthood. After all, if the common-sense organisation of the lifecourse into specific phases is a product of social representations, institutional needs and social and cultural values and norms, then there is no reason to consider ageing simply as a process of progressive decline (Zittoun et al., 2013). "Ageing" itself can be questioned, and one may more simply examine how older persons learn and develop. The progress of the field of sociocultural psychology and of the studies of ageing thus invite to consider learning and development in older age as dynamic processes which are always socially, materially and symbolically situated. It requests us to consider the mediations that shape ageing trajectories, themselves made possible by tools and artefacts existing in specific evolutive environments, and by the semiotic artefacts circulating. It also invited to consider both the "reality" of social, material and symbolic environments, and the modes in which these are experienced by people themselves. Hence, a sociocultural and dialogical outlook on older persons invites us to consider the transformations of the sociocultural environments in which people live, the nature of the transactions between people and these environments, and the unique perspectives of people developing within (Videnović & Baucal, 2025; Brinkmann, 2024; Grossen et al., 2020; Muller Mirza, 2024; Säljö, 2022; Zittoun & Baucal, 2021). If this perspective presents the great advantage of inviting to document these dynamics both from a third-person (the world as it appears to an observer) and a first-person perspective (Fossa & Cortés-Rivera, 2023; Zittoun, 2019), if it has established the importance of accounting not only for what is the case, but also, for what once was, or what could be (Glaveanu, 2020; Josephs, 1998; Zittoun & Gillespie, 2016), that is, to reinstall the key importance of the symbolic world and imagination in human life, and if it is progressively accounting for the role of affects in human experience (Valsiner, 2019), it still focuses on what is accessible to the informed observer, and to people's self-scrutiny—that is, what is accessible through conscious thinking (Gfeller & Grossen, 2025; Muller Mirza, 2025; Zittoun, 2025).

However, living and especially ageing in a changing environment also brings about existential questions, physical transformations, experiences of the time past and the time left, and the inescapable question of finitude. Especially when it comes to development in older age, it is very important to be able to capture feelings just sketched, fears and doubts usually silenced, and thoughts hardly thought and often unspoken—because semiotic means fail or because they are socially or culturally difficult to share, reflect or admit. Suffering, regrets, the fear or the longing for death, as well as mostly simultaneously, an appetite for life and love in older age, are often difficult to articulate for oneself and for others, and more than that, are often inaudible in our sociocultural contexts.

Luckily, this is where the work of psychoanalytically trained clinical psychologists plays an irreplaceable role. Psychoanalysis was developed by Sigmund Freud as theory of the psyche, as a method of research, and as a therapeutic method (S. Freud, 1957). His main contribution to sciences is its formal recognition of unconscious psychic dynamics, and his identification of their origins, variations and effects, as well as the means by which these could be acknowledged and used as developmental dynamics (S. Freud, 1900, 1933). His work, and that of authors he inspired over the decades, further explored this field, in the development of children (A. Freud, 1967; Klein, 1975), in people with war trauma (Abraham & Torok, 1972; W. R. Bion, 1997; Winnicott, 1942), in the life of adults (Green, 2005), in groups and in institutional dynamics (W. R. Bion, 1968; Kaës, 2010, 2012), and in some sociocultural transformations, linked to political violence (Beradt, 2004; Berger, 2016; Puget, 1989) and migration (Moro, 2001; Nathan, 2001).

Although there has been a long resistance in psychoanalysis to address ageing, with the ageing of consulting patients, and the increasing population in institutions for older persons, clinicians have started to develop new understandings of the specificities of development in older age (Assoun, 2021; Bergeret-Amselek, 2016; Bianchi, 2020; Quinodoz, 2009). In France, for instance, new networks address the issues met by older person, as the crossing of their own unique trajectories and the social, material and symbolic realities in which they live (Fernandez & Sagne, 2013; Noël, 2012; Talpin, 2005, 2017a). These approaches have historically been more focused on the singularity of persons, and their intrapsychic dynamics. Yet the evolution of the field has brought authors to acknowledge the multiple "causalities" participating in people's experience—social, biological, temporal, etc.—(Green, 1995; Verdon, 2016). In turn, anchored in an actual therapeutic practice, they bring to social sciences an unique acknowledgement of the complexity of the psyche, the richness of people's apprehension of time (Assoun, 2021; Quinodoz, 2009), the evolution of thinking brought by very old age (Bonnet & Louchard Chardon, 2024) and the depth of the questions addressed by the ageing person (Alric, 2016; Verdon, 2014; Villa, 2010), to themselves and to their environment (Ardeven, 2022; Quinodoz, 2013) (Racin, 2025; Verdon, 2025).

Hence, in the current landscape of approaches to ageing, sociocultural psychology of the lifecourse and psychoanalysis of ageing seem to offer the possibility of a unique complementarity. The former has theorised the development of thinking and learning in all kind of formal and informal situations, accounting for the deep social and cultural grounding of the psyche, yet without much consideration for affects and none of the unconscious determination of human activity—including, in particular, the fear of loneliness, pain and death; psychoanalysis, on the other hand, has a long experience in accounting for these thoughts and dimensions more difficult to name and handle, as they appear to people in various sociomaterial environment, but with less means to theorise complex social and cultural dynamics.

Combining fields of research that have developed along different traditions, with different methods and different purposes can be a risky endeavour. However, historically, sociocultural psychology and psychoanalysis have worked with comparable epistemological choices and in opposition with other fields of psychology. Without adventuring into a complex history of psychologies across continents, it suffices to say that, first, sociocultural psychology as well as psychoanalysis share a developmental, genetic or dynamic understanding of human psyche and societies, and that both admit that temporalities are not simply chronological and linear (Cole, 2016; Gillespie, 2007; Green, 2000; Pontalis, 2001; Valsiner, 2011). Second, both work with the hypothesis of a fundamental relationality of human beings, or in other words, the centrality of dialogicality, or the mutual dependency of intersubjective, or interpsychological, and intrapsychic dynamics—due to their ontogenesis, as condition for semiotic processes, as ethical concern—even though some emphasise the reality and alterity of the other, while other emphasise alterity as already part of one's inner psychic reality (Green, 1999; Marková, 2016; Muller Mirza & Dos Santos Mamed, 2021). Third, both assume the centrality and specificity of sense or meaning in human life, and with it, of the symbolic and the imaginary realm; both address it through a form of semiotic understanding (Neuman, 2009; Roncancio-Moreno et al., 2023; Salvatore & Zittoun, 2011), and both admit, consequently, that human experience is not only cognitive, but also affective, and that thinking is more than reasoning (de Mijolla-Mellor, 1992; Winnicott, 1945; Zittoun, 2023). Fourth, both consider that, at the junction of social, biological and personal trajectories, people develop as singular, unique and complex beings (Winnicott, 1991; Zavershneva & Van der Veer, 2018). And fifth, both have historically developed through the analysis of complex case studies, progressing through abduction and theoretical generalisation (Valsiner, 2017; Visentini, 2021; Zittoun, 2015). As corollary, both disciplines refuse biological, (neuro)cognitive, behavioural or social reductionisms, the atomisation of human life in sub-functions, and statistic generalisations as in nomothetic sciences; both prefer deep descriptions and the search for explanation, that may lead to conceptual tools that enable to better apprehend the complexity of human conduct, rather than prediction (Green, 2005; Valsiner, 2021).

Thus, given sociocultural psychology and psychoanalysis' recent advances in the studies of persons becoming older, in their social, symbolic and material environments, and their deeply compatible epistemologies, this volume is conceived of as a dialogue between authors working within these two traditions. Although each chapter is anchored in one or the other field, authors have developed an attention and interest in what the others said, notably through a workshop that took place in 2024 in Switzerland, and by authors reading and commenting each other's chapters. In the remnants of this chapter each of the contributions is briefly outlined.[1] The final chapter of this book will attempt to reunite, if not integrate, these contributions, so as to open new routes for this exploration of this country that awaits us all.

1.5 Overview of the Volume

Adopting a sociogenetic, or sociohistorical perspective to approach learning, Roger Säljö recalls that humans are the only species that transforms their own living environment. He proposes to consider learning and development from a perspective that assumes the hybrid nature of mind: we can act and think thanks to the tools made possible by previous generations and our social interactions with others. The complexity and evolution of our environment are such that they require constantly renewed epistemic practices—that is, capacities to find new information to access services, to draw on knowledge which are complex, mediated and distributed. This has two consequences: one is still the risk of leaving behind groups and people who do not have access to these epistemic practices. The other implication is that older people are necessarily to keep learning and developing as their environment keeps changing; however, they also may be the one that have the memory of older epistemic practices, and in some cases, the skills to understand the origins of some of current ones: through this, they may also and still participate in the transformation of their environment.

It is the core assumptions that older persons necessarily keep learning and developing, that their development is mediated by cultural tools and social dynamics which they contribute creating, and that they are part of transforming the society, that this book further explores. The chapters then examine the power of older person's engagement in learning and developing, from the most visible forms into political engagement, to its manifestation in everyday life and in various forms of social and institutional settings meant to support them.

Benoît Verdon, a clinical psychologist and psychoanalyst, brings to the fore the paradoxical dynamics in which some older persons engage: they can be fully aware of their age and the limitations it imposes on their life, while also be fully actively committed to society and its future, drawing on their experience of past wars and social fights. He thus explores "the potential to expand possibilities despite the diminishing of one's strength" (p. 49). Drawing on the examples of Sigmund Freud and various French intellectuals, scientists and writers aged between 83 and over 100, Verdon demonstrates the richness and the strength of these positions, engaging

[1] Thanks to the grant HomAge supported by the Swiss national fund (2019–2024) (dir. Tania Zittoun).

their intelligence, humour and creativity, to be fully turned toward others and the collective future. They thus avoid the two pitfalls of ageing—resignation and withdrawal, or focusing on performance and activity so as to deny age. From that perspective, learning and development appear as possible in old and very old age; but these are deeply social activities, requiring the love and support for and by others, and identification with and by them.

The paradoxical nature of learning and development in older age is also present in the chapter by Tania Zittoun. Adopting a developmental perspective, she proposes to examine the transformation of modalities of sense-making in older age. Her theoretical frame examines the many spheres of experience of older persons—their daily activities and long-term engagements. Based on two longitudinal case studies of a married couple in their 90s and of a woman in her mid-80s, Zittoun retraces how these persons progressively reconfigure their spheres of experience, and how, doing so, their main engagements and dynamic patterns come to the fore. Notably, they precisely express some paradoxes of ageing: feeling young while being old, having learned that one has to fight for one's right while helping others, or deeply wanting that one's experience acquired in a gone past may inspire young persons in the future.

In her chapter, Nathalie Muller Mirza observes the learning and developmental opportunities given by voluntary work in older persons. Grounded in sociocultural psychology, her theoretical frame brings to the fore Erikson's views on identity development, and especially the centrality of integrity in older age, attainable, according to her, by their engagement into meaningful pleasurable activities. Nathalie Muller Mirza and her colleagues have devised a research method which they call narrativo-explicative interviews, which enables to focus and makes explicit "acted competencies"—the many skills and knowledge mobilised and used by persons in their voluntary activities. A careful analysis of these interviews shows how much people's acted competences seem to draw on skills and expertise acquired earlier, in their earlier professional trajectories or in other domains of life, and how much these skills can be expanded, transferred, or further enriched. Thus, older persons engaged in volunteering work do much more than fill their time or do something useful: they actually reknit the diversity of their experience, bring more consistency to their life trajectory, and amplify their "melodies of living" (Zittoun et al., 2013). The paper also shows the importance of this type of research and intervention, which creates a dialogical setting fostering reflexivity in people's undertaking of this living experience.

Other aspects of learning appear in the chapter by Fabienne Gfeller and Michèle Grossen, who approach from a dialogical and developmental perspective the experience of older persons moving to a form of intermediary housing called "flats with referents", which enables independent living in an environment adjusted to the needs of older persons. This chapter focuses on in-depth interviews carried out before people moved in a smaller flat, which requires them to get rid of many objects. Moving home challenges people's social relationship, their relationship to their geographical environment and their routines; it obliges them to part with objects that have a special meaning for them and link them to their former activities.

In preparation for this important transition, people are confronted to many contradictions, that can be identified through the various opposing voices echoed in their discourse. Hence their sense of self-continuity is put to the test and requires them to develop new competence to live in this new material and social environment. Taking action, and especially, sorting out objects and furniture, which requires measuring, planning and often dialoguing with others, becomes an important dynamic of re-examining one's life and past commitments and values, and possibly reorganising them, in the light of the upcoming future. Voluntary moving involves thus both confronting oneself to one's ageing and threatening one's balance, as well as learning and development.

Learning and development can take place in very diverse modalities. As a clinical psychologist working in institutions for older persons, Céline Racin examines the question of dependency in older age. Critical of the discourses of ageing as decline as well as success, she underscores that dependency is a process, on a continuum, that starts from birth on, and that can come back to the fore at various moments of one's lifecourse. How an older person experiences it can thus depend on former experiences of dependency. Fragility is, in that respect, not the necessary consequence of dependency, but simply an attractor, while independency always remains a possibility. A clinical vignette following the entry in a nursing home of an 85 year old man shows how this transition enables him to transform the modalities by which he can live independently—from a man proud of his critical capacities and concerned by the loss of his physical autonomy, he became a person actively creating social relations in this new home, happily using a rollator to support his mobility. Thus, even in situations where older persons may appear the most fragile and requiring support, learning and deep developmental transformations may occur.

Hence, the volume proposes a series of chapters examining learning and development in various social settings in which persons becoming older live—their social engagement, their daily activities, their new homes, or the institutions. Each chapter highlights some of the specificities of learning and development in older age, and notably, the social, relational, symbolic, and affective nature of the dynamics involved—and perhaps, also, their paradoxicality. Based on these rich contributions, combining sociocultural, educational, clinical and psychoanalytical perspectives, the final chapter of the volume attempts to integrate these contributions, and highlights the theoretical, empirical and methodological implications of the volume.

References

Abraham, N., & Torok, M. (1972). Mourning or melancholia: Introjection versus incorporation. In N. T. Rand (Ed.), *The Shell and the kernel. Renewals of psychoanalysis* (pp. 125–138). The University of Chicago Press; pdf.

Alric, J. (with Gori, R.). (2016). *Fin de vie & Psychanalyse: Menace de disparition et relance désirante*. Sauramps Médical.

Angus, J., & Reeve, P. (2006). Ageism: A threat to "aging well" in the 21st century. *Journal of Applied Gerontology, 25*(2), 137–152. https://doi.org/10.1177/0733464805285745

Antonucci, T., & Ajrouch, K. (2022). Convoys of care. *Innovation in Aging, 6*(Suppl_1), 435. https://doi.org/10.1093/geroni/igac059.1706
Ardeven, F. (2022). Il est interdit de vieillir. *Topique, 154*(1), 51–59. https://doi.org/10.3917/top.154.0053
Assoun, P.-L. (1983). Le vieillissement saisi par la psychanalyse. *Communications, 37*(1), 167–179. https://doi.org/10.3406/comm.1983.1559
Assoun, P.-L. (2021). Le retour à l'inconscient du vieillissement. Le désir à l'épreuve du temps. In C. Racin, C. Caleca, & P. Gutton (Eds.), *Le vieillissement saisi par le soin* (pp. 41–63). Editions In press.
Baltes, P. B. (1997). On the incomplete architecture of human ontogeny. Selection, optimization and compensation of developmental psychology. *American Psychologist, 52*(4), 266–380.
Baltes, P. B. (2004). *Wisdom as orchestration of mind and virtue*. Max Planck Institute/unpublished manuscript.
Baltes, P. B., & Baltes, M. M. (Eds.). (1990). Psychological perspectives on successful aging: The model of selective optimization with compensation. In *Successul aging. Perspectives from the behavioral sciences* (pp. 1–34). Cambridge University Press.
Baltes, P. B., & Kunzmann, U. (2004). The two faces of wisdom: Wisdom as a general theory of knowledge and judgment about excellence in mind and virtue vs. Wisdom as everyday realization in people and products. *Human Development, 47*(5), 290–299.
Baltes, P. B., & Mayer, K. U. (Eds.). (1999). *The Berlin aging study: Aging from 70 to 100*. Cambridge University Press.
Beradt, C. (2004). *Rêver sous le IIIe Reich*. Payot.
Berger, M. (2016). *De l'incivilité au terrorisme—Comprendre la violence sans l'excuser*. Dunod.
Bergeret-Amselek, C. (2016). Qui sont ces nouveaux analysants de plus de 70 ans? Quel est leur désir? In M.-F. Fuchs (Ed.), *Comment l'esprit vient aux vieux. Penser et vivre un vieillissement durable* (pp. 103–112). érès.
Bianchi, H. (2020). Travail du vieillir et 'travail du trépas'. In *Fragilité et force du lien* (pp. 35–43). In Press. https://doi.org/10.3917/pres.verdo.2020.01.0035
Bigonnesse, C., & Chaudhury, H. (2020). The landscape of "aging in place" in gerontology literature: Emergence, theoretical perspectives, and influencing factors. *Journal of Aging and Environment, 34*(3), 233–251. https://doi.org/10.1080/02763893.2019.1638875
Bion, W. R. (1968). *Experiences in groups and other papers* (New edition). Routledge.
Bion, W. R. (1997). In F. Bion (Ed.), *War Memoirs 1917-1919*. Karnac Books.
Bonnet, M., & Louchard Chardon, C. (Eds.). (2024). *Vieillissement et enveloppes psychiques*. In Press.
Bourdieu, P. (1978). La 'jeunesse' n'est qu'un mot. In *Questions de sociologie* (pp. 143–154). Les éditions de minuit.
Brinkmann, S. (2024). Lili's life: Being summoned as a researcher. *Human Arenas, 7*(1), 198–211. https://doi.org/10.1007/s42087-021-00264-5
Bruner, J. S. (2003). *Making stories: Law, literature, life*. Harvard University Press.
Bühler, C. (1961). Old age and fulfilment of life with considerations of the use of time in old age. *Vita Humana, 4*(3), 129–133.
Butler, R. N. (1963). The life review: An interpretation of reminiscence in the aged. *Psychiatry, 26*, 65–76.
Butler, R. N. (1981). The life review: An unrecognized bonanza. *International Journal of Aging & Human Development, 12*(1), 35–38. https://doi.org/10.2190/WC4T-V05J-40G5-3M7E
Caissie, L. (2011). The raging grannies: Narrative construction of gender and aging. In G. Kenyon, E. Bohlmeijer, & W. L. Randall (Eds.), *Storying later life: Issues, investigations, and interventions in narrative gerontology* (pp. 126–142). Oxford University Press.
Carney, G. M. (2018). Toward a gender politics of aging. *Journal of Women & Aging, 30*(3), 242–258. https://doi.org/10.1080/08952841.2017.1301163

Carstensen, L. L. (2019). Integrating cognitive and emotion paradigms to address the paradox of aging. *Cognition & Emotion, 33*(1), 119–125. https://doi.org/10.1080/02699931.2018.1543181

Carstensen, L. L. (2021). Socioemotional selectivity theory: The role of perceived endings in human motivation. *The Gerontologist, 61*(8), 1188–1196. https://doi.org/10.1093/geront/gnab116

Cole, M. (1996). *Cultural psychology. A once and future discipline*. The Belknap Press of Harvard University Press.

Cole, M. (2016). Designing for development: Across the scales of time. *Developmental Psychology, 52*(11), 1679–1689. https://doi.org/10.1037/dev0000156

Coleman, P. G., Ivani-Chalian, C., & Robinson, M. (2015). *Self and meaning in the lives of older people*. Cambridge University Press.

Cumming, E., & Henry, W. E. (1961). *Growing old, the process of disengagement*. Basic Books.

de Beauvoir, S. (1970). *La vieillesse*. Gallimard.

de Mijolla-Mellor, S. (1992). *Le plaisir de pensée*. Presses Universitaires de France.

Erikson, E. H., Erikson, J. M., & Kivnick, H. Q. (1986). *Vital involvement in old age*. Norton.

Ferenczi, S. (1974). Pour comprendre les psychonévroses du retour d'âge (1921) (J. Dupont & M. Viliker, Trans.). In *Psychanalyse III. Oeuvres complètes 1919-1926* (pp. 150–155). Payot.

Fernandez, L., & Sagne, A. (Eds.). (2013). *Psychologie clinique du vieillissement: 15 études de cas*. In press.

Fossa, P., & Cortés-Rivera, C. (2023). *Affectivity and learning: Why we need an interdisciplinary, a multilevel, and a first-third-person approach?* (pp. 779–783). https://doi.org/10.1007/978-3-031-31709-5_40

Freeman, M. (2011). Narrative foreclosure in later life: Possibilities and limits. In G. Kenyon, E. Bohlmeijer, & W. L. Randall (Eds.), *Storying later life: Issues, investigations, and interventions in narrative gerontology* (pp. 3–19). Oxford University Press.

Freud, A. (with Internet Archive). (1967). *The ego and the mechanisms of defense*. International Universities Press. http://archive.org/details/egomechanismsofd0002freu

Freud, S. (1900). The interpretation of dreams. In J. Strachey (Ed.), *The Standard Edition of the complete psychological works of Sigmund Freud* (Original 1900, Vols. 4–5, pp. 1–627). Vintage.

Freud, S. (1905). On psychotherapy (1904). In J. Strachey (Ed.), *The Standard Edition of the Complete Psychological Works of Sigmund Freud: Vol. VII* (New Edition, pp. 255–268). Vintage.

Freud, S. (1933). New introductory lectures on psycho-analysis. In J. Strachey (Ed.), *The Standard Edition of the complete psychological works of Sigmund Freud* (New Edition, Vol. 22, pp. 1–182). Vintage.

Freud, S. (1957). Five lectures on psycho-analysis. In J. Strachey & A. Freud (Eds.), *The Standard Edition of the complete psychological works of Sigmund Freud: Vol. XI (1910): Five lectures on psycho-analysis, Leonardo da Vinci and other works* (pp. 1–56). The Hogarth Press and the Institute of Psycho-analysis.

Gergen, K. J., & Gergen, M. M. (2010). The new aging: Self construction and social values. In K. W. Schaie (Ed.), *Soci al structures and aging*. Springer. http://www.swarthmore.edu/sites/default/files/assets/documents/kenneth-gergen/The_New_Aging.pdf

Gergen, M. M., & Gergen, K. J. (2001). Positive aging: New images for a new age. *Ageing International, 27*(1), 3–23. https://doi.org/10.1007/s12126-001-1013-6

Gfeller, F., & Grossen, M. (2025). Moving house in older age: Challenges and resources for the sense of self-continuity. In T. Zittoun & F. Gfeller (Eds.), *Ageing, learning and development. Sociocultural and psychoanalytical perspectives on growing older*. Springer.

Gillespie, A. (2007). Time, self and the other. In L. M. Simão & J. Valsiner (Eds.), *Otherness in question. Labyrinths of the self* (pp. 163–186). Information Age Publishing.

Glaveanu, V. P. (Ed.). (2020). *The Palgrave Encyclopedia of the possible*. Springer International Publishing. https://doi.org/10.1007/978-3-319-98390-5

Green, A. (1995). *La causalité psychique*. Odile Jacob.

Green, A. (1999). *The fabric of affect in the psychoanalytic discourse*. Routledge.
Green, A. (2000). *Le temps éclaté*. Editions de Minuit.
Green, A. (2005). *Key ideas for a contemporary psychoanalysis misrecognition and recognition of the unconscious* (1st ed.). Routledge.
Grossen, M., Zittoun, T., & Baucal, A. (2020). Learning and developing over the life-course: A sociocultural approach. *Learning, Culture and Social Interaction*, 100478. https://doi.org/10.1016/j.lcsi.2020.100478
Gubrium, J. F. (2011). Narrative events and biographical construction in old age. In G. Kenyon, E. Bohlmeijer, & W. L. Randall (Eds.), *Storying later life: Issues, investigations, and interventions in narrative gerontology* (pp. 39–50). Oxford University Press.
Gutton, P. (2016). Travail d'adolescence, travail du vieillir. In M.-F. Fuchs (Ed.), *Comment l'esprit vient aux vieux. Penser et vivre un vieillissement durable* (pp. 25–42). érès.
Gutton, P., & Maïdi, H. (Eds.). (2020). *Adolescents et vieux. Deux âges de la liberté?* Editions In press.
Hall, G. S. (1922). *Senescence, the last half of life* (University of California Libraries). D. Appleton and Company. http://archive.org/details/senescencelastha00halliala
Havighurst, R. J. (1952). Social and psychological needs of the aging. *The Annals of the American Academy of Political and Social Science, 279*, 11–17.
Havighurst, R. J. (1961). Successful aging. *The Gerontologist, 1*(1), 8–13. https://doi.org/10.1093/geront/1.1.8
Havighurst, R. J. (1968). Personality and patterns of aging. *The Gerontologist, 8*(1_Part_2), 20–23. https://doi.org/10.1093/geront/8.1_Part_2.20
Henry, W. E. (1998). Engagement and disengagement. Toward a theory of adult development. In (Mortimer Powell) M Powell Lawton & T. A. Salthouse (Eds.), *Essential papers on the psychology of aging* (pp. 56–67). New York University Press.
Hugentobler, V. (with Avramito, M., & Ischer, M.). (2024). *Vieillir et habiter autrement*. Editions HESTL.
Josephs, I. E. (1998). Constructing one's self in the city of the silent: Dialogue, symbols, and the role of 'as-if' in self-development. *Human Development, 41*(3), 180–195.
Kaës, R. (2010). L'appareil psychique groupal, construction transitionnelle. *Psychismes, 3*, 185–217.
Kaës, R. (Ed.) (with Fustier, P., Enriquez, E., Roussillon, R., & Vidal, J.-P.). (2012). *L'institution et les institutions—Études psychanalytiques*. Dunod.
Kemp, C. L., Ball, M. M., & Perkins, M. M. (2013). Convoys of care: Theorizing intersections of formal and informal care. *Journal of Aging Studies, 27*(1), 15–29. https://doi.org/10.1016/j.jaging.2012.10.002
Klein, M. (1975). *Envy and gratitude*. Hogarth Press and the Institute of Psycho-Analysis.
Lawton, M. P. (1977). An ecological theory of aging applied to elderly housing. *JAE, 31*(1), 8–10. https://doi.org/10.2307/1424527
Lawton, M. P. (1985). The elderly in context: Perspectives from environmental psychology and gerontology. *Environment and Behavior, 17*(4), 501–519. https://doi.org/10.1177/0013916585174005
Lieblich, A. (2014a). Narrating your life after 65 (or: To tell or not to tell, that is the question). *New Directions for Child and Adolescent Development, 2014*(145), 71–83. https://doi.org/10.1002/cad.20068
Lieblich, A. (2014b). *Narratives of positive aging: Seaside stories*. Oxford University Press.
Marková, I. (2003). *Dialogicality and social representations: The dynamics of mind*. Cambridge University Press.
Marková, I. (2016). *The dialogical mind: Common sense and ethics*. Cambridge University Press.
Milligan, C., & Wiles, J. (2010). Landscapes of care. *Progress in Human Geography, 34*(6), 736–754. https://doi.org/10.1177/0309132510364556

Moore, K. D. (2014). An ecological framework of place: Situating environmental gerontology within a life course perspective. *The International Journal of Aging and Human Development, 79*(3), 183–209. https://doi.org/10.2190/AG.79.3.a

Moro, M. R. (2001). *Parents en exil: Psychopathologie et migrations* (2e éd.). Presses Universitaires de France.

Muller Mirza, N. (2024). Argumentation and reasoning in people older than 65. A sociocultural and dialogical analysis of focus groups on senior volunteering. In F. Arcidiacono & J. Convertini (Eds.), *The psychology of argumentation and reasoning* (pp. 211–237). Nova Science.

Muller Mirza, N. (2025). Developmental processes and meaning-making in volunteering activity. In T. Zittoun & F. Gfeller (Eds.), *Ageing, learning and development. Sociocultural and psychoanalytical perspectives on growing older*. Springer.

Muller Mirza, N., & Dos Santos Mamed, M. D. S. (Eds.). (2021). *Dialogical approaches and tensions in learning and development: At the frontiers of the mind*. Springer International. https://doi.org/10.1007/978-3-030-84226-0

Nathan, T. (2001). *L'influence qui guérit*. Odile Jacob.

Nelson, K. (2007). *Young minds in social worlds. Experience, meaning, and memory*. Harvard University Press.

Nelson, T. D. (2005). Ageism: Prejudice against our feared future self. *Journal of Social Issues, 61*(2), 207–221. https://doi.org/10.1111/j.1540-4560.2005.00402.x

Neugarten, B. L. (1972). Personality and the aging process. *The Gerontologist, 12*(1_Part_1), 9–15. https://doi.org/10.1093/geront/12.1_Part_1.9

Neuman, Y. (2009). On the alpha-function, chaotic cats, and unconscious memory. *New Ideas in Psychology, 27*(3), 305–311. https://doi.org/10.1016/j.newideapsych.2008.06.002

Noël, J.-L. (2012). Accompagner le projet de vie en service de soins de longue durée, EHPAD, maison de retraite. In B. Verdon (Ed.), *Cliniques du sujet âgé: Pratiques psychologiques* (pp. 235–259). Armand Colin.

Oswald, F. (2024). Rethinking the place of place for aging: Enduring and new challenges for environmental gerontology. *Innovation in Aging, 8*(Suppl_1), 394. https://doi.org/10.1093/geroni/igae098.1281

Pontalis, J.-B. (2001). *Ce temps qui ne passe pas, suivi de « Le compartiment de chemin de fer »* (Original 1997). Gallimard.

Puget, J. (Ed.). (1989). *Violence d'Etat et psychanalyse*. Dunod.

Quinodoz, D. (2009). Growing old: A psychoanalyst's point of view. *International Journal of Psychoanalysis, 90*(4), 773–793. https://doi.org/10.1111/j.1745-8315.2009.00166.x

Quinodoz, D. (2013). Does an elderly psychoanalyst have a role to fill? In G. Junkers (Ed.), *The empty couch: The taboo of ageing and retirement in psychoanalysis*. (Dual Edition, pp. 7–16). Routledge.

Racin, C. (2025). The dynamics of dependency in old age: Psychoanalytic perspectives. In T. Zittoun & F. Gfeller (Eds.), *Ageing, learning and development. Sociocultural and psychoanalytical perspectives on growing older*. Springer.

Repetti, M., & Fassa, F. (2024). *Vieillir en Suisse. Du privé au politique*. Savoir Suisse.

Roncancio-Moreno, M., Ocampo-Cepeda, R. P., & Cleves-Valencia, J. J. (2023). Towards a semiotic cultural clinical psychology: Contributions for the discussion. *Human Arenas*. https://doi.org/10.1007/s42087-023-00372-4

Säljö, R. (2022). Development, ageing and hybrid minds: Growth and decline, and ecologies of human functioning in a sociocultural perspective. *Learning, Culture and Social Interaction, 37*, 100465. https://doi.org/10.1016/j.lcsi.2020.100465

Säljö, R. (2025). Cognitive adaptation, hybrid minds and ageing: Epistemic practices in cumulative cultures. In T. Zittoun & F. Gfeller (Eds.), *Ageing, learning and development. Sociocultural and psychoanalytical perspectives on growing older*. Springer.

Salvatore, S., & Zittoun, T. (Eds.). (2011). *Cultural psychology and psychoanalysis: Pathways to synthesis*. Information Age Publishing.

Sarton, M. (1993). *Endgame: A journal of the seventy-ninth year*. Women's Press.

Schwarz, B. (2012). Environmental gerontology: What now? *Journal of Housing for the Elderly, 26*(1–3), 4–19. https://doi.org/10.1080/02763893.2012.673374
Segal, H. (1958). Fear of death—Notes on the analysis of an old man. In G. Junkers (Ed.), *Is It Too Late?: Key Papers on Psychoanalysis and Ageing* (Original 1958, pp. 65–73). Taylor & Francis Group. http://ebookcentral.proquest.com/lib/cam/detail.action?docID=764969
Shotter, J., & Billig, M. (1998). A Bakhtinian psychology: From out of the heads of individuals and into the dialogue between them. In M. Mayerfeld Bell & M. Gardiner (Eds.), *Bakhtin and the human sciences: No last words* (pp. 13–29). Sage.
Stenner, P., McFarquhar, T., & Bowling, A. (2011). Older people and 'active ageing': Subjective aspects of ageing actively. *Journal of Health Psychology, 16*(3), 467–477. https://doi.org/10.1177/1359105310384298
Talpin, J.-M. (2005). L'âgé en institution, ses droits et l'inconscient. *Gérontologie et société, 115*(4), 135–149.
Talpin, J.-M. (2017a). Deux principes dans l'élaboration psychique institutionnelle des changements: Pensée binaire et pensée qualitative. *Cliniques, 14*(2), 92–106.
Talpin, J.-M. (2017b). *Psychologie clinique du vieillissement normal et pathologique* (2e éd). A. Colin.
Talpin, J.-M. (2020). Chapitre 8. Les institutions gériatriques: Entre désinscription, projet de vie et mort. In *Le travail psychanalytique en institution* (pp. 169–191). Dunod. https://doi.org/10.3917/dunod.pinel.2020.01.0169
Thomas, A. K. (Ed.). (2020). *The Cambridge handbook of cognitive aging: A life course perspective*. Cambridge University Press.
Valsiner, J. (2011). Constructing the vanishing present between the future and the past—Construyendo el desvanecimiento del presente entre el futuro y el pasado. *Infancia y Aprendizaje, 34*(2), 141–150. https://doi.org/10.1174/021037011795377601
Valsiner, J. (2017). Methodology in the new key: The methodology cycle. In *From methodology to methods in human psychology* (pp. 21–30). https://doi.org/10.1007/978-3-319-61064-1_8
Valsiner, J. (2019). *Ornamented lives*. Information Age Publishing.
Valsiner, J. (2021). *General human psychology*. Springer Nature Switzerland AG.
Verdon, B. (2014). Se déprendre de dépendre ? Vieillir parmi la violence des idéaux. *Cliniques (Toulouse, France), 7*(1), 178–192. https://doi.org/10.3917/clini.007.0178
Verdon, B. (2016). *Le vieillissement psychique* (2e éd.). Presses Universitaires de France.
Verdon, B. (2025). Taking care of oneself as an alederly person while being interested in the future of the younger generation: Incompatible concerns? In T. Zittoun & F. Gfeller (Eds.), *Ageing, learning and development. Sociocultural and psychoanalytical perspectives on growing older*. Springer.
Verhaeghen, P. (2011). Cognitive processes and ageing. In I. Stuart-Hamilton (Ed.), *An introduction to gerontology* (pp. 159–193). Cambridge University Press.
Videnović, M., & Baucal, A. (2025). Discourses we are ageing by: The role of personal responsibility and societal obstacles in successful ageing. *European Journal of Psychology of Education, 40*(3), 86. https://doi.org/10.1007/s10212-025-00983-1
Villa, F. (2010). *La puissance du vieillir*. Presses Universitaires de France.
Villa, F. (2015). Des conditions de possibilité d'une approche interdisciplinaire du vieillir. *Psychologie Clinique, 40*(2), 12–18. https://doi.org/10.1051/psyc/201540012
Visentini, G. (2021). Penser et écrire « par cas » en psychanalyse. L'invention freudienne d'un style de raisonnement. *Analysis, 5*(1), 78–81. https://doi.org/10.1016/j.inan.2021.02.001
Wahl, H.-W., & Weisman, G. D. (2003). Environmental gerontology at the beginning of the new millennium: Reflections on its historical, empirical, and theoretical development. *The Gerontologist, 43*(5), 616–627. https://doi.org/10.1093/geront/43.5.616
Wanka, A. (2018). Disengagement as withdrawal from public space: Rethinking the relation between place attachment, place appropriation, and identity-building among older adults. *The Gerontologist, 58*(1), 130–139. https://doi.org/10.1093/geront/gnx081
Wertsch, J. V. (1998). *Mind as action*. Oxford University Press.

White, J. (2013). Thinking generations. *The British Journal of Sociology, 64*(2), 216–247. https://doi.org/10.1111/1468-4446.12015

Winnicott, D. W. (1942). Child department consultations. In L. Caldwell & H. Taylor Robinson (Eds.), *The collected work of D. W. Winnicott: Vol. 2 1939-1945* (Original 1942, pp. 149–163). Oxford University Press.

Winnicott, D. W. (1945). Thinking and the unconscious. In L. Caldwell & H. Taylor Robinson (Eds.), *The collected work of D. W. Winnicott: Vol. 2 1939-1945* (Original 1945, p. 341). Oxford University Press.

Winnicott, D. W. (1991). *Playing and reality* (Original 1971). Routledge.

Woodward, K. M. (2002). Against wisdom: The social politics of anger and aging. *Cultural Critique, 51*(1), 186–218. https://doi.org/10.1353/cul.2002.0024

World Health Organization. (2002). *Active ageing: A policy framework* (WHO/NMH/NPH/02.8). Article WHO/NMH/NPH/02.8. https://iris.who.int/handle/10665/67215

World Health Organization. (2021). *Decade of healthy ageing: Baseline report - summary*. World Health Organization. https://www.who.int/publications-detail-redirect/9789240023307

World Health Organization. (2024). *Beyond the decade of healthy ageing. Extending benefits across the life course*. https://iris.who.int/bitstream/handle/10665/379585/9789240073531-eng.pdf?sequence=1

Zavershneva, E., & Van der Veer, R. (2018). *Vygotsky's notebooks. A selection*. Springer.

Ziegler, F. (2012). "You have to engage with life, or life will go away": An intersectional life course analysis of older women's social participation in a disadvantaged urban area. *Geoforum, 43*(6), 1296–1305. https://doi.org/10.1016/j.geoforum.2012.03.013

Zittoun, T. (2015). Compatibility between early psychoanalysis and pragmatism. In P. J. Rosenbaum (Ed.), *Making our ideas clear: Pragmatism in psychoanalysis* (pp. 23–42). Information Age Pub.

Zittoun, T. (2019). *Sociocultural psychology on the regional scale: A case study of a hill*. Springer.

Zittoun, T. (2023). *The pleasure of thinking*. Cambridge University Press. https://doi.org/10.1017/9781009039802

Zittoun, T. (2025). On being an oxymoron: A sociocutural psychology of development with older age. In T. Zittoun & F. Gfeller (Eds.), *Ageing, learning and development. Sociocultural and psychoanalytical perspectives on growing older*. Springer.

Zittoun, T., & Baucal, A. (2021). The relevance of a sociocultural perspective for understanding learning and development in older age. *Learning, Culture and Social Interaction, 28*, 100453. https://doi.org/10.1016/j.lcsi.2020.100453

Zittoun, T., & Gillespie, A. (2016). *Imagination in human and cultural development*. Routledge.

Zittoun, T., Valsiner, J., Vedeler, D., Salgado, J., Gonçalves, M., & Ferring, D. (2013). *Human development in the lifecourse. Melodies of living*. Cambridge University Press.

Chapter 2
Cognitive Adaptation, Hybrid Minds and Ageing: Epistemic Practices in Cumulative Cultures

Roger Säljö

2.1 Introduction

Humans have an incredible talent for learning, in some sense we are doomed to learn. Unlike other species, even those close to us in an evolutionary sense, we do not adapt to a given environment; instead, we transform the world we inhabit. As the Australian philosopher of evolution Kim Sterelny (2014, p. 1) points out, "living chimps and gorillas", our next of kin in a biological sense, are "broadly similar in habitat and ecology to their ancestors of five million years ago." Put differently, chimps "live in a world as they find it rather than a world as they make it" (ibid. p. 174). This stability in habitats, social organization and behaviours of non-human primates stands in stark contrast to the radical transformations that can be observed in the hominin evolutionary trajectory during the same period. Here we find the emergence of an increasingly complex social organization and sophisticated modes of collaboration (nowadays even on a global scale), language and abstract thinking, writing and imagery, and an amazing variation of technologies and cultural artifacts deployed in almost everything we do. We also see a remarkable ability to adapt to almost any kind of climate and habitat, from the arctic to the desert, from living in small migrating hunter-gatherer societies to coping with the complexities of life in mega-cities with many millions of inhabitants and an incredibly diversified social and technological infrastructure. This flexibility is apparent in our capacity to develop lifestyles that accommodate to such variations, and it cannot be found in any other species.

In terms of adapting to the world as we make it, to paraphrase Sterelny, we find institutions such as schools, hospitals, theatres, bureaucracies, banks, libraries,

R. Säljö (✉)
Department of Education, Communication and Learning, University of Gothenburg, Gothenburg, Sweden
e-mail: roger.saljo@ped.gu.se

T. Zittoun, F. Gfeller (eds.), *Ageing, Learning and Development*, Lifelong Learning Book Series 36, https://doi.org/10.1007/978-3-032-11057-2_2

shopping malls, sports arenas, airports and a host of other of similar settings of immense complexity in terms of the collaborative, cognitive and physical skills they require for their functioning. Furthermore, many of these institutions continuously innovate and adopt novel practices, and, as a consequence, we need to learn, unlearn and relearn how to be students, patients, clients, customers, workers, tourists, professionals, pensioners and how to assume a number of other roles, including that of being citizens in increasingly knowledge intensive and abstract societies.

The background of this article is an interest in a) how societies evolve and transform themselves by building up a "cultural memory" (Donald, 2018), i. e., a pool or reservoir of know-how with solutions to problems encountered over long stretches of time, and b) how the socio-material, institutional and intellectual organization of this cultural memory co-determines how we as individuals and collectives learn and develop through the lifespan. This is a matter of exploring how our cognitive, manual and social skills, and modes of sharing know-how, are coordinated with how knowledge and know-how are organized and communicated at a particular point in history.

Addressing this set of issues, it is necessary to make a few stops in the long history of evolutionary transformations. The background against which I raise these questions, however, is in relatively recent times and concerns the consequences of the dramatic expansion of our cultural memory, from early industrialism and onwards, but especially in the post-War period. My ambition is to explore some of the implications this has had, and continues to have, for the role of learning, development and education in the lives of people living in the twenty-first century as we attempt to accommodate to continuous and rapidly changing circumstances in our everyday lives. In Sweden, as an example of an industrial/post-industrial European society, where education (mandatory and voluntary) has expanded dramatically during this post-War period, more than every third working hour is spent in educational institutions, if we count the time students, teachers and other staff work there (and exclude pre-school, which is a mix of care, play and education) (Nilsson, 2006). If we add to this, the time that is spent learning in in-service training and other similar activities in private and public institutions during the lifespan, we have witnessed the emergence of an Education society, where the social and individual benefits and consequences of learning go way beyond preparing for working life and a narrow focus on economic returns (Becker, 1992).

At present, there is, also a more pragmatic, but equally significant, background to raising questions about age, ageing, and why we continuously have to learn, unlearn and relearn when accommodating to new cultural practices. One obvious factor is demography and the dramatically increasing average life-expectancy in most parts of the world. At present, the average life-expectancy at birth is well over 80 years in many countries, even approaching 85 years in some regions of Europe and other parts of the world (EUROSTAT, 2024). This contrasts with the situation at the beginning of the twentieth century. In many countries life-expectancy almost doubled during this century, from around or even below 40 years of age and up to or above 80 (INED, 2020; STATISTA, 2023). This is a remarkable demographic transformation of many societies, which *per se* is an illustration of our collective capacities for learning and for converting our insights into improvements in health and healthcare, housing, hygiene and nutrition, access to education, safer workplaces and many other factors that lie behind this increase in life-expectancy. If we combine longevity with the current pace of societal transformation, we have a new scenario in the twenty-first century for addressing learning and development and to reflect on how such processes relate to ontogeny and age and ageing.

2.2 The Hominin Lineage and the Cumulation of Know-How

Most organisms, even single cell organisms and amoebae (Kippenberger et al., 2023; Schaap, 2021), adapt to the environment by changing their behaviours in response to their interaction with the world. We may see this as signs of learning or development that seem to shape all living things. But what is a characteristic feature of modern humans—*Homo Sapiens*—as a species (and of our predecessors in the hominin lineage all the way from *Homo Habilis* emerging around 2.4 million years ago and up to now, but I will leave that aside) is our talent for cumulating know-how and skills across generations. Each new generation builds on the insights of earlier generations. The developmentalist Michael Tomasello and his colleagues describe these patterns of continuous reproduction and innovation of cultural practices by arguing that one "generation does things in a certain way, and the next generation then does them in that same way—except that perhaps they add some modification or improvement." The latter generation "then learns the modified or improved version" of a skill or practice, which, in turn, will be the platform for the next generation, which may add further modifications and so on (Tennie et al., 2009, p. 2405). Even though signs of such cumulative processes may be observed in animals, and in our days perhaps even in machines (Whiten et al., 2021), a "gap, an ostensibly unbridgeable gap, exists between the cognitive capabilities and achievements of humanity and those of other animals." (Laland, 2017, p. 2).

The richness and complexity of the contemporary cultural memory of many societies reflect such cumulative processes which have been going on for many thousands of generations. This cumulation of knowledge during the era of modern humans—*Homo* Sapiens, the only representative of the hominin line still around—is a product of a sociocultural evolution, which is driven by our capacity to design and refine our environment, while taking into account the "accelerating cycles of evolutionary feedback" (Laland, 2017, p. 3) we receive from our inventions and solutions to challenges encountered. Thus, we not only learn, rather the feedback we receive serves to propel further learning potentially transforming our environments and, in turn, our cognitive and physical habits. The mechanisms underlying this sociocultural evolution are very different from those that characterize biological evolution (Hill, 1997; Laland, 2017; Pagel, 2012). The two forms of evolution are contingent on each other, but the timescales and evolutionary mechanisms are very different.

In passing, often such developmental trajectories or spirals imply that later generations have vague, if any, insights into how 'things' were done previously. The evolution of sociomaterial activities such as writing, counting, cooking, farming, navigating, measuring, producing artifacts, and the many symbolic and technical innovations which have been made over millennia, often are not visible in our current mastery. Very few contemporary users of inventions such as, for instance, the script(s), number systems and other symbols appearing on their computer keyboards or the apps in their mobile phones, have vague, if any, idea of how these intellectual and physical technologies emerged, and how they have been transformed during history. The material and intellectual tools we use are often "black-boxed" as Latour (1999) puts it, the insights and inventions of earlier generations are not visible. It takes museums, archaeologists, historians of various kinds and other expertise to white-box how 'things' were done in the past.

2.2.1 Development and Learning Under the Umbrella of Darwin

The history of psychology, especially developmental psychology but also other branches of the discipline, has been characterized by the dominance of the platform for understanding development which originated in Charles Darwin's thinking and in his theory of evolution. Darwin provided the conceptual framework and, in addition, defined the research agenda, for the modern version of an empirically oriented research in developmental psychology that took off in the late nineteenth and early twentieth centuries. Thus, the idea that "development can be understood as the progressive adaptation of the child to the environment", can "be traced directly to Darwin", and, furthermore, his theory "located man firmly in nature and raised questions about continuities and discontinuities between man and animals" (Butterworth & Harris, 1998, p. 6–7). The concept of adaptation to a given environment, and the idea of natural selection operating on species and their capacities to reproduce, served as powerful underpinnings of this conception of development. This perspective, in turn, invited research that searched for the origin and functions of the human mind/brain in our evolutionary trajectory in a biological sense. To guide such inquiry, Darwin emphasized that "there is no fundamental difference between man and the higher mammals in their mental faculties" (Darwin, 1889, p. 66), i.e. the difference is not "in kind, although immensely in degree" (p. 147).

This platform had obvious consequences for the intellectual agenda of research on development, learning and human "growth", as Dewey (1963) puts it in a more integrative spirit. One of these is that development came to be understood as tied to physical maturation. The progressive changes in humans in physical characteristics from birth to maturity provided the model to which other features of development should be accommodated. This assumption is reflected in influential theoretical perspectives during the nineteenth and early twentieth century. In the 1860s, the prominent, and controversial, German zoologist/philosopher Ernst Haeckel (1834–1919) famously argued that ontogeny recapitulates phylogeny, a principle referred to as the biogenetic law, which claims that the development of an embryo reflects the evolutionary history of the organism (cf. Richardson & Keuck, 2002). As Koops (2015, p. 634) points out, Haeckel's ideas "strongly inspired the study of child development", and they "gave child development the status of a firm phylogenetically grounded structure" to be analysed by scholars searching for parallels between phylogeny and ontogeny. This "biologizing" of childhood, steeped in Darwinian ideas of adaptation, featured, more or less explicitly, among many of the developmentalists who later came to define the field (cf. Morss, 1990). For instance, and as Koops points out, Piaget in his book on "Biology and knowledge" (1971) specified his ambitions by adding the subtitle "An essay on the relations between organic regulations and cognitive processes."

Another corollary of this Darwinian heritage is that development came to be seen as something that takes place in the early stages of an individual's life, at least this is where the most significant phases are visible. Once maturity has been reached, individuals will be equipped with the intellectual/cognitive toolkit they have to rely on in adulthood. Again, this can be seen as an interpretation of development that fits a stable environment, where innovations are rare and where the demands for flexibility in behaviours and cognitive repertoires of living organisms are limited to what is required in a given biotope or environment.

The metaphor underlying this conception of human life—development, maturity/stability, decline/decay—has had a profound impact on research but also as a cultural construction more generally. As Grossen et al. (2022, p. 33) point out, research has often followed a stereotypical understanding which holds that "children and young adults learn and develop, adults work (and at time learn through work), and older adults… retire." Learning, development and participation in education have been seen as investments for adulthood, and, increasingly, for working life, i. e. the 'productive period' of people's lives following the same metaphorical construction. This reflects a functionalist interpretation of ontogeny, where the early period is projected as preparation for adult life, which is then followed by adulthood where family life and work are the norm, and then retirement as a period of passivity, dependence and need of support/care. In this functionalist mindset (cf. Orsini, 2024), ideas of lifelong and lifewide learning were slow to appear and first seen as exotic and of little relevance for social policy. The idea that learning, formal as well as informal, is a human occupation with its own intrinsic values and contributions across the lifespan in increasingly complex societies was launched in an uphill battle (Knowles, 1973).

2.2.2 Ageing and the Struggle Away from Bio-age Parallelism

In the post-War period, and especially during the 1960s and 1970s, there are several attempts to break out of this Darwinian interpretation of development through different lines of research. Some of these attempts grapple with the problems of how rapidly changing and increasingly diversified societal conditions interact with ontogenetic patterns of development. One influential line of inquiry in this context focused on lifespan development (Baltes, 1978; Baltes & Goulet, 1970). This tradition formulated an interesting research agenda, which later would restructure our understandings of the intricate relationships between learning, development, societal change and the role of age and ageing.

One of the early observations in this research demonstrated the dilemmas involved in linking development to physical age in a straightforward manner. Such dilemmas became visible in the outcomes of research, and especially in the disparities between results obtained when studying lifespan development using different methodologies. For instance, analyses of cross-sectional data (comparing cohorts of different ages at a given point in time) were found to produce results that differed from those generated in longitudinal studies (i.e. studies following the same individuals/cohorts during their lifespan). Baltes (1968, p. 146) found that in research in the cognitive area, "cross-sectional studies of intelligence produce the well-known aging curves which suggest that between the ages of 20 and 30 there is a plateau or a gradual decline in intellectual functioning", while "longitudinal studies suggest an increase in intellectual functioning" rather high up in age. Among the various factors that produce these differences, Baltes points to "the generation effects", i.e. the fact that a cohort growing up during one decade, let us say in the 1940s, has a very different cultural background in comparison to a cohort growing up in the 1960s, even when the samples are taken from populations living in the same areas or countries. Changes in schooling (accessibility, attendance and quality of instruction), media access, health, affluence, child-rearing practices and many other factors characterizing these decades make these cohorts different, and this will inevitably threaten the validity when making comparisons based on cross-sectional data, where plateaus and early decline of cognitive functions repeatedly had been observed.

For some time, longitudinal research designs were seen as the solution to this problem. The assumption was that following the same individuals as the unit of analysis through their lifespan would provide a more valid account of human development. But as soon was found out, and as Baltes concludes, "the age effect of a longitudinal study is [also] generation specific", and, in this sense, "the external validity of age effects" observed "in longitudinal studies is seriously restricted" (loc. cit.) as well. What is interesting here is that in rapidly developing societies of the twentieth century, the life-conditions of cohorts, even when they are only one or two decades apart, changed in many respects, and these variations have consequences throughout life. In the vocabulary of this line of research, societal change, technological development and improvements in schooling, nutrition and healthcare, to mention some of the factors that vary across decades, become confounding variables no matter how research is designed. There is no such entity as a societally disconnected individual or intellect which is not shaped by the social and communicative experiences of her/his time, and this becomes a major theoretical and methodological problem when studying learning and development through the lifespan in dynamically evolving societies.

However, this line of research made an important contribution at the conceptual level by effectively questioning the assumptions of close and unidirectional connections between age and development which can be formulated in terms of causal or pseudo-causal effects. When this research had matured, Baltes et al. (1998, p. 1029) argued that "the basic premise of life-span developmental psychology is that ontogeny extends across the entire life course and that life-long adaptive processes are involved", and, consequently, it is "necessary to reformulate the traditional concept of development." Moreover, "life-span developmental scholars, if they focus on processes of mind and behavior" rather than on age, "proceed from the assumption that these processes and mechanisms express manifestations of developmental continuity and change across the entire life span" (p. 1030). In this sense, and as Lerner (2008) concludes, the idea of a "developmental science" emerged, a line of research premised on an increasingly "age-irrelevant concept of development" (Baer, 1970, p. 238).

However, the ambition of describing lifespan development in terms of trait-like characteristics individuals possess or stages they go through remained. One of the suggestions, pursued by many scholars, has been that qualities such as "wisdom" could be used to better characterize lifespan development (Baltes & Smith, 2008). But the assumption that there are such general characterizations that are possible to apply in a uniform manner to lifespan development in and across complex societies with highly differentiated social conditions and lifestyles seems somewhat abstract.

An interesting observation in this context is that this recognition of the complexities of analysing development in adulthood in contemporary societies has its counterpart also in research in the early childhood area. During the latter half of the twentieth century, several research traditions, often dialoguing with the claims of universalists, pursued empirical research that paved the way for a more contextual and socially sensitive interpretation of development and of how to interpret indicators of development used in research. Not even during the early years of a person's life, when growing up in complex societies, will the developmental trajectories be uniform as documented by scholars such as Perret-Clermont (2004; Zittoun & Perret-Clermont, 2009), Donaldson (1978), Grossen (1988, 2001), Cole et al. (1971) and others (cf. Zittoun & Iannacone, 2014). Some theorizing involving contextual conditions, and how they co-determine cognitive development and growth, will be necessary even during the early periods of children's lives. New approaches to childcare, increasing participation in preschool and access to new activities, such as those involving digital communication and play, are factors that contribute to changes in developmental trajectories at an early age.

2.3 The Hybridity of Human Know-How

One of the corollaries of the view of learning and development embedded in the Darwinian evolutionary framework is that human cognition is seen as localized in the minds, or even brains, of individuals. Thus, and following the Darwinian spirit quoted above, our "mental faculties" are held to differ "in degree" rather than "in kind" when compared with other species. However, in the evolutionary perspective briefly outlined here, this idea of an isolated mind as a container of know-how and cognitive activity becomes less attractive, even untenable, as a unit of analysis for understanding human capacities and their development during ontogeny. Sociocultural evolution implies that human action—cognitive as well as physical—is contingent on the use of what Vygotsky (1930, 1978) refers to as "cultural tools" which have emerged in society over time, and which in themselves are important constituents of our cultural memory. Use of cultural tools implies that people liaise with cultural resources of increasing specificity in social and cognitive action, and this "modifies the entire course and structure of mental functions" and produces "new instrumental act(s)", as Vygotsky (1930) puts it. Concrete examples of such changes of "instrumental acts" are all around us. For instance, remembering as a cognitive act is performed very differently if you have technologies for documentation of events (paper-and-pencil, recorders, cameras, digital tools) than if you do not have such resources available. Counting using mental arithmetic, paper-and-pencil or a digital calculator also takes place through different "instrumental acts." Cognitive activities such as multiplying four-digit numbers with two decimals are quite demanding for most people in the case of mental arithmetic, while they appear trivial when using a digital calculator (cf. Säljö et al., 2006). The strain on our attention span or short-term memory, for instance, disappears completely when using a calculator. By outsourcing many intellectual (and physical) functions to tools with which collaborate when engaging in tasks such as writing, remembering, searching for information and in many other kinds of activities, our know-how and cognitive capacities are no longer restricted by what has been given to us by nature, as it were, i.e. they are not localized in the mind/brain. Rather, thinking, reasoning and physical action emerge at the intersection between our minds, other people and the uses of increasingly specified cultural tools. Put differently, when thinking our mind is not just turned inwards, it is also turned outwards towards other people, and the range of "cognitive amplifiers" (Nickerson, 2005) that are available and that we are able to integrate into our practices. When writing on a computer, our capacity for spelling correctly or finding synonyms are not limited by our intra-cranial cognitive powers. We interact with external tools and the outcomes of such extra-cranial excursions feed into the flow of our activities. Following this line of reasoning, our minds are better conceived as "hybrids" (Donald, 2018) or, alternatively, as "extended" (Clark & Chalmers, 1998), equipped with the capacity to liaise with cultural tools of immense diversity when we engage in cognitive and communicative activities.

The increasing hybridity of our minds, thus, is a consequence of sociocultural evolution and the expansion of the cultural memory. A hybrid mind does not develop by adapting to a given and stable environment. Instead, adaptation takes place by exposure to, and appropriation of, resources—physical and intellectual—available when interacting with an increasingly differentiated cultural memory. This implies that humans do not just learn as individuals, we also engage in in what in the literature is referred to as "social" and "cultural learning." As Henrich (2017, p. 3) points out, the "secret of our success" is that we are a "cultural species" i.e. we pick up tools for thinking, communicating and performing physical activities from communities we have access to and where we are engaged. These modes of learning imply observing, copying and imitating successful behaviours and solutions to problems of our community, and refining them by adapting them to our own situated needs. We learn from others by receiving feedback and tapping into their experiences through social interaction. What we learn often has the character of "cognitive gadgets", as Heyes (2018) points out, i.e. resources for analysing and manipulating the world which have emerged over time, and which have been refined through testing and eventually packaged into conceptual frameworks and procedures for problem-solving. Such cultural learning at the collective level results in new "instrumental acts" among individuals. And, the products of cultural learning, we encounter through interaction with others, i.e. through social learning. We learn from each other in myriads of communicative activities where we observe and collaborate with others and are introduced to the tools they rely on. An important element of social learning is also that we can ask questions when we encounter situations where we do not understand. Instruction, indirect and direct, is ubiquitous.

In complex societies, knowledge reproduction between generations itself becomes a prominent and increasingly time-consuming activity. We see the emergence of schools and universities, and institutions for adult learning, vocational training and a range of other institutionally organized contexts for communicating know-how. Each cohort spends more time in education than earlier ones. In the wake of the expansion of the cultural memory new professions emerge. These professions, in turn, tend to become increasingly specialized through an accelerating division of labour characterizing many areas such as healthcare, engineering, education and production. Much of this kind of learning, which involves interacting with the most specialized forms of know-how in society, takes place during the adult period and is often embedded in extended periods of institutionally organized training at the workplace or in educational settings.

2.3.1 *The Role of Learning and the Nature of Development in Complex Societies*

Using the concept of a hybrid mind as an analytical tool, and considering the expansion of our cultural memory, ontogenetic development must be understood as embedded in the societal practices and communities which the individual participates in, as argued by Zittoun and Baucal (2021). And this is one of the problems that research on lifespan development ran into when comparing cognitive development of different cohorts in dynamically evolving societies during the twentieth century. At a general level, when the cultural memory expands, and when what we have to learn goes beyond what we can pick up in daily practices, learners have to develop generic skills that they rely on when learning and thinking more generally. Put differently, in complex societies the need for being familiar with productive and rather diverse epistemic practices increases. The concept of epistemic practices implies that we not only learn, but we also learn procedures and strategies for finding, manipulating and transforming information and knowledge to fit our situated needs. We learn to "take meaning" (Olson, 1994) from what has been documented, and we accommodate to specific principles for converting these insights into social action in ways that are relevant. Metaphorically, epistemic practices are resources for gap-closing between situated needs and the know-how and information available through our cultural memory.

A central feature of epistemic practices is that they represent some kind of meta-knowledge or meta-skills of how to engage in various tasks, and where to turn if we need support. However, this designation of such know-how about how to access and navigate in our cultural memory as meta-knowledge risks mystifying such cognitive processes, as if they are of a totally different kind. This is not necessarily a productive conceptualization. Instead, what we may be tempted to refer to as meta-knowledge is better understood as know-how that emerges in a complex society when encountering tasks which present challenges and when a response is not immediately available but rather requires overview and consideration of alternatives. When turning to outside resources, and when integrating them into the flow of our activities, the epistemic practices we are familiar with will guide us in specific directions. We turn to written instructions or handbooks or to YouTube or some other online video-sharing website, where solutions to problems may be found. Similarly, as students, familiarity with epistemic practices helps us realize what it implies to study and learn from a book of 200 pages, which clearly cannot be memorized. Through training in academic literacy, we have learned what to focus on and what to leave in the background, we search for what is the core or essence of what is presented. Appropriating such epistemic practices in complex societies generally implies that we encounter hurdles or thresholds when we do not understand how to use a cultural tool (a software, a physical instrument or conceptual resource) and such thresholds have to be overcome. We often rely on instruction and guidance to adjust the cognitive habits of a hybrid mind to new challenges, new technologies and new kinds of know-how. After a period of practice, we have adjusted to the new cultural tool and it clear to us how it is to be used.

Literacy is a good, perhaps the best, illustration of a set of sophisticated epistemic practices which takes a long time to master, and which plays an increasingly important role in people's lives as societies evolve. The sociogenesis of the integration of texts into our daily practices, thus, illustrates how we adapt our cognitive habits to cope with a new technology and its affordances. When the uses of texts spread across societies during the nineteenth and twentieth centuries through printed media such as newspapers, books, pamphlets and other resources used in public communication in document societies, literacy skills spread. What we may think of as "print-literacy" involves epistemic practices that were responses to sociocultural and sociomaterial changes which took place in a relatively short time following industrialism, the spread of democracy, urbanization and other social transformations (Graff, 1981). Initially literacy skills were rather specific and relevant for a limited set of activities, such as in religious practices or legal transactions. As texts became more complex, and the contexts in which such resources were relevant increased, the expectations of what it meant to read and write changed in nature. For instance, early protestant literacy of the eighteenth and nineteenth centuries, involving the ability to read a limited set of familiar religious texts, was no longer sufficient when the genres of texts which people were exposed to became more varied. Eventually, mastery of written communication and the ability to document became elements of many parts of working life, through uses of handbooks, written instructions and other documentary practices characterizing the latter half of the twentieth century (Resnick & Resnick, 1977).

In the sociogenetic perspective outlined here, one of the most significant elements of recent developments is digitalization. During the past 50 years or so, and especially since the introduction of the Internet in the mid-1990s, our access to the cultural memory has changed with implications for our everyday lives and our knowledge needs. Activities such as buying groceries online, ordering food in a hamburger restaurant with a digital interface at the entrance, organizing travel on the website of a travel agent or a bus company, engaging in social media and many other daily practices require familiarity with complex, multilevel interfaces, where actions have to be taken according to a specific logic. These developments, and the transformations of our everyday lives (including our professional activities) that they imply, give us access to new experiences in an increasingly abstract world of digitally mediated activities. At the same time, the epistemic practices in digital contexts become more varied and demanding in comparison to what characterized traditional print literacy.

The epistemic practices we use for accessing, evaluating and manipulating information in digital settings build on those that characterize print literacy, but they also introduce novel elements that have to do with handling the wealth of information that we can access, and coping with problems of overview, trustworthiness. relevance and other factors. A critical element of epistemic strategies in digital environments is that they require an increasing ability to contextualize and recontextualize information and know-how in ways that are relevant for the purposes at hand (Linell, 1998). The knowledge, information and claims we have access to in such environments derive from a multitude of settings that may be very different from the ones we have first-hand experiences of. This, in turn, contributes to the abstract nature of many current practices, where information and know-how are accessed and acted on through digital means.

The transformations of our cultural memory that follow digitalization are multilayered and rather profound, and many people today, to a large extent, live digital lives. In such circumstances, new interactional situations are introduced, and traditional situations are restructured. This is consequential for communicative ecologies in all kinds of activities when we oscillate between digitized information, talk and problem-solving. Calling a help desk to receive help with your computer or home network, requires skills of explaining what happens in your digital gadget so that it can be diagnosed and resolved by a professional agent (Eklund et al., 2011).

In terms of learning, development and our capacities to adopt the many roles in which we have to act in contemporary circumstances, the risks of current media developments have been demonstrated in research. During the past two decades we have seen a new literature on what is referred to as the "digital divide" (Zhao et al., 2023), "digital exclusion" (Anrijs et al., 2023) and even the emergence of a "digital underclass" in what is considered as welfare societies (Helsper & Reisdorf, 2017). Reading this literature, it is obvious that living in many societies today, and not having access to Internet resources, is very complicated, even expensive and limiting in important respects. Several studies point to the limitations involved in not reaching friends and relatives, problems with paying bills, accessing advice from authorities, health agencies and contacting other institutions on whom we are dependent, if we are not accustomed to digital modes of communication (Ross Winthereik et al., 2024).

What we see in this transformation of societies is the emergence of groups who are marginalized by technological innovations, which, in addition, seem to transform themselves at a high pace. These consequences of digitization are not unlike those we have seen in the area of literacy skills, where the problems and significance of variations in literacy skills have been discussed at national and international levels, for instance in the wake of international comparative studies such as PIAAC[1] for adults (OECD, 2024) and PISA[2] (OECD, 2023) for 15-year-old students. What is interesting though, and relevant to my argumentation, is that the explanations of the conditions of marginalized groups are to be found both in their access to material resources (computers, connectivity), and in the knowledge and skills that are needed to be included, often referred to as digital literacy skills (cf. Iacobaeus et al., 2020, for an extensive discussion). Thus, innovations in access to information, knowledge, communicative opportunities and social capital introduce thresholds that risk leaving segments of society behind in important respects including in terms of their training and cognitive readiness (Internetstiftelsen, 2021). And currently we are beginning to see the consequences of a new set of powerful cognitive amplifiers in the products launched in the context of the evolution of AI. With such resources we can dialogue with our cultural memory in ways which have not been possible earlier; we can ask complicated questions and receive substantive summaries of our current knowledge about almost any topic. But, in a sociogenetic perspective and considering the cumulative nature of technological advances, the ability to use such resources builds on proficiency in previous generations of digital skills.

[1] OECD Programme for the International Assessment of Adult Competencies (PIAAC).

[2] OECD Programme for International Student Assessment (PISA).

2.4 Ageing and Cognition: From Biological Determinism to Issues of Cultural Adaptation to Evolving Epistemic Practices

This chapter began with reflections on how issues of the development of human cognitive and communicative abilities through the lifespan, and our capacities to learn, have been conceived in research. In developmental research, the assumptions of parallel trajectories between biological and cognitive/intellectual development/functioning have been dominant. Childhood is a period of development, and adulthood is characterized by plateaus and later decline in abilities. In much research, the phases of decline in capacities set in already in the early or mid-20s of a person's life. This mode of thinking has had a strong impact also in everyday interpretations of the role of age when discussing capacities for learning and development. However, this picture, in important respects, is an artifact of research methods and of the instruments that have been applied in empirical investigations. The approaches taken have built on the assumption that the human mind/brain and its capacities are localized in, and determined by, intra-cranial processes. Conceptually, the alternative to this mainstream view is to consider learning and development as matters that concern how people are able to make use of and appropriate the cultural tools of their society for solving tasks and participating in social practices. Thus, the unit of analysis in our understanding is no longer the isolated mind, but, rather, a mind that is hybrid in nature and that develops in response to changes in the sociomaterial, communicative and cognitive infrastructures of society. In a sociogenetic perspective, we think, reason and argue with material and cognitive resources that have evolved over thousands of generations and with which we collaborate.

In the current societal conditions in complex societies, learning will be a lifelong and lifewide occupation. Indeed, more than ever we are doomed to learn in most spheres of life, we are challenged in terms of our know-how almost every day. Adulthood and maturity can no longer be understood as periods of stable routines for which we are already fully prepared at an early age. Currently, and as an illustration, digital technologies, and their consequences in terms of globalization, media changes and highly abstract modes of performing transactions of various kinds, continuously present us with novel epistemic practices. In addition, these technologies are restless, they seem never to stop transforming our social, communicative and cognitive activities. Challenges of this nature can only be met by learning, in informal as well as in institutionally organized settings. In rapidly changing societies "age-specific" effects still are real, as Baltes noted in this analysis of lifespan development in the mid-tweniteth-century (cf. above). In our time, the "digital divide" between those born, let us say, two decades apart during the late twentieth and early twenty-first century have produced different socializing experiences through the introduction of tools such as the Internet, the mobile phone and constant connectivity. The epistemic skills relevant for handling such tools are not given by nature. Rather, their emergence depends on access to communities in which such resources play a role for successful participation, and, in this sense, they are highly sensitive to social learning, i.e., learning with and from social interaction in informal and formal settings.

Chronological age *per se* as a physical variable is unlikely to be a significant factor in this situation. Even relatively senior citizens will be exposed to the consequences of these transformations during their lifetime. For instance, people who are now in their 50s or 60s, most likely will experience changes in their communicative ecologies that will have an impact on their lifestyles. In addition, the role of learning in people's lives is no longer restricted to working life but is equally consequential for everyday citizenship, access to many social activities and communities, and even health (Folkhälsomyndigheten, 2015). Adapting to transitions in life in complex societies, for instance when moving to a new country, into a care facility (Zittoun et al., 2021) or separating (Richards, 2018), involves challenges that are common in complex societies and that have to be overcome by learning.

At a general level, there is no reason to assume that age will have a uniform and negative impact on our capacities for getting used to and appropriating the epistemic practices that characterize digitized societies. Senior groups will have an understanding of the wider societal issues in which digital resources play a role, and this will serve as platforms for developing epistemic practices that are in tune with societal change and that make it possible to participate in a social life that to an increasing extent itself is becoming digital. It seems more likely that it is continuous access to and participation in digital and other collective practices in different spheres of life that will play a critical role in integrating groups that risk being marginalized when social and technological transformations continue to restructure our lives.

References

Anrijs, S., Mariën, I., De Marez, L., & Ponnet, K. (2023). Excluded from essential internet services: Examining associations between digital exclusion, socio-economic resources and internet resources. *Technology in Society, 73*, 102211. https://doi.org/10.1016/j.techsoc.2023.102211

Baer, D. M. (1970). An age-irrelevant concept of development. *Merrill-Palmer Quarterly of Behavior and Development, 16*(3), 238–245. http://www.jstor.org.ezproxy.ub.gu.se/stable/23082475

Baltes, P. B. (1968). Longitudinal and cross-sectional sequences in the study of age and generation effects. *Human Development, 11*(3), 145–171. http://www.jstor.org.ezproxy.ub.gu.se/stable/26761719

Baltes, P. B. (Ed.). (1978). *Life-span development and behavior* (Vol. 1). Academic Press.

Baltes, P. B., & Goulet, L. R. (1970). Status and issues of a life-span developmental psychology. In L. R. Goulet & P. B. Baltes (Eds.), *Life-span developmental psychology* (pp. 3–21). Academic Press. https://doi.org/10.1016/B978-0-12-293850-4.50007-8

Baltes, P. B., Lindenberger, U., & Staudinger, U. (1998). Life-span theory in developmental psychology. In R. M. Lerner (Ed.), *Handbook of child psychology. Vol. 1: Theoretical models of human development* (pp. 1029–1143). Wiley.

Baltes, P. B., & Smith, J. (2008). The fascination of wisdom: Its nature, ontogeny, and function. *Perspectives on Psychological Science, 3*(1), 56–64. https://doi.org/10.1111/j.1745-6916.2008.00062.x

Becker, G. S. (1992). Human capital and the economy. *Proceedings of the American Philosophical Society, 136*(1), 85–92. http://www.jstor.org/stable/986801

Butterworth, G., & Harris, M. (1998). *Principles of developmental psychology*. Psychology Group.

Clark, A., & Chalmers, D. (1998). The extended mind. *Analysis, 58*(1), 7–19. http://www.jstor.org.ezproxy.ub.gu.se/stable/3328150

Cole, M., Gay, J., Glick, J., & Sharp, D. W. (Eds.). (1971). *The cultural context of learning and thinking*. Basic Books.

Darwin, C. (1889). *The descent of man*. Appleton.

Dewey, J. (1963). *Experience and education*. Collier Macmillan. (Original published 1938).

Donald, M. (2018). The evolutionary origins of human cultural memory. In B. Wagoner (Ed.), *Handbook of culture and memory* (pp. 19–40). Oxford University Press.

Donaldson, M. (1978). *Childern's minds*. Fontana.

Eklund, A.-C., Mäkitalo, Å., & Säljö, R. (2011). Noticing the past to manage the future: On the organization of shared knowing in IT-support practices. In S. Ludvigsen, A. Lund, I. Rasmussen, & R. Säljö (Eds.), *Learning across sites. New tools, infrastructures and practices* (pp. 122–137). Routledge.

EUROSTAT. (2024). *EU life expectancy estimated at 81.5 years in 2023*. Retrieved May 16, 2024, from https://ec.europa.eu/eurostat/fr/web/products-eurostat-news/w/ddn-20240503-2

Folkhälsomyndigheten. (2015). *Utbildningsnivå och hälsa–hur hänger de ihop? Socioekonomiska skillnader i hälsa ur ett utbildningsperspektiv* (Level of education and health—How do they relate? Socioeconomic differences in health from the an educational perspective). Folhälsomyndigheten.

Graff, H. J. (Ed.). (1981). *Literacy and social development in the West*. Cambridge University Press.

Grossen, M. (1988). *L'intersubjectivitë en situation de test [Intersubjectivity in test situations]*. Editions Delval.

Grossen, M. (2001). Origin sociale et performances cognitives; contribution psycho-sociologique à une redéfinition de la problematique [Social origin and cognitive performance: Psycho-sociological contributions to a redefinition of the problem]. In M. Grossen & M. Nicolet (Eds.), *Interagir et connaitre [Interacting and knowing]* (pp. 249–264). L'Harmattan.

Grossen, M., Zittoun, T., & Baucal, A. (2022). Learning and developing over the life-course: A sociocultural approach. *Learning, Culture and Social Interaction, 37*, 100478. https://doi.org/10.1016/j.lcsi.2020.100478

Helsper, E., & Reisdorf, B. C. (2017). The emergence of a "digital underclass" in Great Britain and Sweden: Changing reasons for digital exclusion. *New Media & Society, 19*(8), 1253–1270.

Henrich, J. (2017). *The secret of our success. How culture is driving human evolution, domesticating our species and making us smarter*. Princeton University Press.

Heyes, C. (2018). *Cognitive gadgets. The cultural evolution of thinking*. The Belknap Press.

Hill, J. (1997). Biology and socioculture in human evolution. *Journal of Social and Evolutionary Systems, 20*(2), 157–170. https://doi.org/10.1016/S1061-7361(97)90005-9

Iacobaeus, H., Francisco, M. Nordqvist, C., Sefyrin, J., Skill, K., & Wihlborg, E. (2020). *Digitalt utanförskap. En forskningsöversikt* [Digital exclusion. A research review]. DINO rapport 2019:3.

INED. (2020). *L'espérance de vie en France*. https://www.ined.fr/en/everything_about_population/graphs-maps/interpreted-graphs/life-expectancy-france/

Internetstiftelsen. (2021). *Digitalt utanförskap slår mot samhällets svagare grupper* [Digital exclusion hits the weaker groups in society]. https://internetstiftelsen.se/nyheter/digitalt-utanforskap-slar-mot-samhallets-svaga-grupper/

Kippenberger, S., Pipa, G., Steinhorst, K., Zöller, N., Kleemann, J., Özistanbullu, D., Kaufmann, R., & Scheller, B. (2023). Learning in the single-cell organism Physarum polycephalum: Effect of propofol. *International Journal of Molecular Science, 24*(7). https://doi.org/10.3390/ijms24076287

Knowles, M. (1973). *The adult learner: A neglected species*. Gulf Publishing.

Koops, W. (2015). No developmental psychology without recapitulation theory. *European Journal of Developmental Psychology, 12*(6), 630–639. https://doi.org/10.1080/17405629.2015.1078234
Laland, K. N. (2017). *Darwin's unfinished symphony. How culture made the human mind.* Princeton University Press.
Latour, B. (1999). *Pandora's hope. An essay on the reality of science studies.* Harvard University Press.
Lerner, R. M. (2008). The contributions of Paul B. Baltes to the transformation of the field of child development: From developmental psychology to developmental science. *Research in Human Development, 5*(2), 69–79. https://doi.org/10.1080/15427600802034744
Linell, P. (1998). *Approaching dialogue. Talk, interaction and contexts in dialogical perspectives.* John Benjamins Publishing.
Morss, J. R. (1990). *The biologising of childhood. Developmental psychology and the Darwinian myth.* Routledge.
Nickerson, R. S. (2005). Technology and cognition amplification. In R. J. Sternberg & D. D. Preiss (Eds.), *Intelligence and technology. The impact of tools on the nature and development of human abilities* (pp. 3–27). Erlbaum.
Nilsson, A. (2006). Utbildningsvetenskap i ett ekonomiskt och socialt sammanhang [Educational science in an economic and social context]. In B. Sandin & R. Säljö (Eds.), *Utbildningsvetenskap - ett kunskapsområde under formering [Educational science – a knowledge area under formation]* (pp. 253–273). Carlssons.
OECD. (2023). *PISA 2022 Results: The state of learning and equity in education* (Vol. 1). OECD Publishing. https://doi.org/10.1787/53f23881-en.
OECD. (2024). *Do adults have the skills they need to thrive in a changing world? Survey of adult skills 2023*. OECD Publishing. https://doi.org/10.1787/b263dc5d-en.
Olson, D. R. (1994). *The world on paper. The conceptual and cognitive implications of writing and reading*. Cambridge University Press.
Orsini, A. (2024). Functionalism. In A. Orsini (Ed.), *Sociological theory: From Comte to Postcolonialism* (pp. 281–360). Springer. https://doi.org/10.1007/978-3-031-52539-1_9
Pagel, M. (2012). *Wired for culture. The natural history of human cooperation*. Penguin.
Perret-Clermont, A.-N. (2004). The thinking spaces of the young. In A.-N. Perret-Clermont, C. Pontecorvo, L. B. Resnick, T. Zittoun, & B. Burge (Eds.), *Joining society: Social interaction and learning in adolescence and youth* (pp. 3–10). Cambridge University Press.
Piaget, J. (1971). *Biology and knowledge: An essay on the relations between organic regulations and cognitive processes*. Chicago University Press.
Resnick, D. P., & Resnick, L. B. (1977). The nature of literacy: An historical exploration. *Harvard Educational Review, 47*(3), 370–385.
Richards, M. (2018). Learning from divorce. In C. Clulow (Ed.), *Rethinking marriage. Public and private perspectives* (pp. 27–38). Routledge. (Original published 1993).
Richardson, M. K., & Keuck, G. (2002). Haeckel's ABC of evolution and development. *Biological Reviews, 77*(4), 495–528. https://doi.org/10.1017/S1464793102005948
Ross Winthereik, B., Aanestad, M., & Mäkitalo, Å. (2024). *Digital inclusion*. Djøf Forlag.
Schaap, P. (2021). From environmental sensing to developmental control: cognitive evolution in dictyostelid social amoebas. *Philosophical Transactions of the Royal Society B: Biological Sciences, 376*(1820), 20190756. https://doi.org/10.1098/rstb.2019.0756
STATISTA. (2023). *Life expectancy (from birth) in the United States, from 1860 to 2020*. https://www.statista.com/statistics/1040079/life-expectancy-united-states-all-time/
Sterelny, K. (2014). *The evolved apprentice: How evolution made humans unique*. The MIT Press.
Säljö, R., Eklund, A.-C., & Mäkitalo, Å. (2006). Reasoning with mental tools and physical artefacts in everyday problem solving. In L. Verschaffel, F. Dochy, M. Boekaerts, & S. Vosniadou (Eds.), *Instructional psychology: Past, present and future trends* (pp. 73–90). Pergamon.

Tennie, C., Call, J., & Tomasello, M. (2009). Ratcheting up the ratchet: On the evolution of cumulative culture. *Philosophical Transactions of the Royal Society of London. Series B, Biological sciences, 364*(1528), 2405–2415. https://doi.org/10.1098/rstb.2009.0052

Vygotsky, L. S. (1978). *Mind in society: The development of higher psychological processes.* Harvard University Press.

Vygotsky, L. S. (1930). *The instrumental method in psychology.* https://www.marxists.org/archive/vygotsky/works/1930/instrumental.htm

Whiten, A., Biro, D., Bredeche, N., Garland, E. C., & Kirby, S. (2021). The emergence of collective knowledge and cumulative culture in animals, humans and machines. *Philosophical Transactions of the Royal Society B: Biological Sciences, 377*, 20200306. https://doi.org/10.1098/rstb.2020.0306

Zhao, Y., Zhang, T., Dasgupta, R. K., & Xia, R. (2023). Narrowing the age-based digital divide: Developing digital capability through social activities. *Information Systems Journal, 33*(2), 268–298.

Zittoun, T., & Baucal, A. (2021). The relevance of a sociocultural perspective for understanding learning and development in older age. *Learning, Culture and Social Interaction, 28*, 100453. https://doi.org/10.1016/j.lcsi.2020.100453

Zittoun, T., Grossen, M., & Tarrago Salamin, F. (2021). Creating new spheres of experience in the transition to a nursing home. *Learning, Culture and Social Interaction, 28*, 100458. https://doi.org/10.1016/j.lcsi.2020.100458

Zittoun, T., & Iannacone, A. (Eds.). (2014). *Activities of thinking in social spaces.* Nova Publishers.

Zittoun, T., & Perret-Clermont, A.-N. (2009). Four social psychological lenses for developmental psychology. *European Journal of Psychology of Education, 24*(3), 387–403.

Chapter 3
Taking Care of Oneself as an Elderly Person While Being Interested in the Future of the Younger Generation: Incompatible Concerns?

Benoît Verdon

I cannot imagine a life without work as truly enjoyable;
for me, living through imagination and working are one and the same; nothing else amuses me.
It would be the recipe for happiness, were it not for the dreadful thought that productivity relies entirely on a random disposition;
what can one undertake during a day or a period when ideas refuse to come and words refuse to align?
This possibility continues to make me tremble.
That's why, while submitting myself to fate, as befits an honest man,
I still silently pray: above all, no prolonged illness, no physical misery that paralyzes my creative faculties.
Letter from Sigmund Freud to Pastor Oskar Pfister dated March 6, 1910.

Nous sommes accablé.e.s, misérables. Notre fragilité se mue en arme de guerre.
Nous sommes des tyrans flaccides, involontaires, les pires. Nous ne sommes plus bon.ne.s à rien.
Pire, seulement à causer de la peine. On se croyait des êtres d'empathie, d'altérité. Des sangsues en fait.
Qui pourrait croire que nous avons quelque chose à transmettre ?
Nous, nous y croyons encore, nous débordons d'affection, d'amitié, de sentiments, plus que jamais.[1]
Jane Sautière, *Tout ce qui nous était à venir (All that was to come to us)*, 2024

[1] *"We are overwhelmed, miserable. Our fragility turns into a weapon of war. We are flaccid, involuntary tyrants, the worst. We are no longer good for anything. Worse, only good for causing pain. We thought of ourselves as beings of empathy, of alterity. We are leeches, in fact. Who could believe that we have something to convey? Yet, we still believe in it, we overflow with affection, friendship, feelings, more than ever."*

B. Verdon (✉)
Laboratoire PCPP, Institut de Psychologie, Université Paris Cité, Paris, France
e-mail: benoit.verdon@u-paris.fr

T. Zittoun, F. Gfeller (eds.), *Ageing, Learning and Development*, Lifelong Learning Book Series 36, https://doi.org/10.1007/978-3-032-11057-2_3

Too often, to avoid dealing with complex questions that nevertheless require nuance, we stick to dichotomous representations: the elderly, too preoccupied with their fragilities, have no interest in the affairs of the young; the elderly, immersed in their idealized past, understand nothing of today's world; the only way to age well is to remain cognitively intact, connected to digital technologies, physically fit. While such observations may sometimes be made here and there, they fail to accurately account for the diverse and always singular experience of aging. For on one hand, aging inevitably confronts us with diminished vigor, decreased endurance, and loss. But aging does not in itself diminish the desire to cast a curious eye on the world, to want to hold a place in it among others, even to continue to play a fruitful role, to want to learn something from it. However, this dynamic is not automatic: the individual is indeed enriched by their history and experience, cultivating their curiosity and sometimes their eagerness to consume, undertake, and experiment, but their physical, cognitive, and psychological resources are confronted with precarity and finitude. And the realization of desires, the desire to continue as before, sometimes as if nothing had changed, are tested, and sometimes undermined.

Some older adults envision their future under the illusory, yet sometimes exclusive ideal of performative aging, where it would be possible to avoid the ravages of time altogether. Others, on the contrary, renounce all pleasure and withdraw, or even disengage from social relationships, struggle to take care of themselves, claiming more or less explicitly that there is nothing good left to live for and that they are as good as dead already. Still, others, despite experiencing increasing incapacity, strive to stand tall among their fellow citizens in full strength and youthfulness, and to participate, from their unique position, between renunciation and commitment, in the life of the city. However, it is exhausting to feel out of step, on the margins, not like others, on the sidelines.

Let's revisit this magnificent testimony of Virginia Woolf confronted with the experience of illness. She evokes "how astonishing, when the lights of health go down, the undiscovered countries that are then disclosed, what wastes and deserts of the soul a slight attack of influenza brings to view, [...] what ancient and obdurate oaks are uprooted in us by the act of sickness, how we go down into the pit of death and feel the waters of annihilation close above our heads" (1926, p.7). She continues: "Directly the bed is called for, or, sunk deep among pillows in one chair, we raise our feet even an inch above the ground on another, we cease to be soldiers in the army of the upright; we become deserters. They march to battle. We float with the sticks on the stream; helter-skelter with the dead leaves on the lawn, irresponsible and disinterested and able, perhaps for the first time for years, to look around, to look up—to look, for example, at the sky" (*ibid.*, p.15).

The state of fragile health, whether acute or chronic, linked to aging or resulting from pathologies, thus does not only appear confined to idleness and the undoubtedly downward slope of senescence, when thought of as fundamentally opposed to maturity. What it imposes in terms of limitations can open up new potentialities, support ancient curiosities, sources of pleasure that are still or newly accessible. "Because one is lying down, one looks at the sky," says Woolf. Some, horrified, see this only as a foretaste of the position of the corpse their body will one day be and want instead to remain upright at all costs. Some take pleasure in this unhealthy position, deriving secondary benefits from being the recipients of others' attention and empathy. Others welcome the experience as an opening to oneself, to one's internal reality, and to others, nonetheless hoping to regain better health as soon as possible. The anxious agitation underlying sometimes frenetic behaviors of sports addiction, risk-taking, self-endangerment likely fights against depressive collapse, inner emptiness, the dread of nothingness. And despite the proliferation of experiences and encounters, it may not at all witness an appropriation of aging. Between falling into a bottomless pit and manic exaltation that denies all vulnerability, a wide range of resources and fragilities can be mobilized, articulating the desire to always learn and continuously develop, and the ambivalent recognition of limitations.

It is therefore important that psychological research focuses on clinical populations experiencing states of psychological or physical suffering that hinder opportunities for development and fulfillment. Yet it is equally important that such research also attend to those who, time and again, manage to mobilize their capacity for self-investment and investment in others—despite age and the inherent difficulties associated with aging. Freud was mistaken when, in a short text on psychotherapy written in 1904, he expressed marked pessimism regarding the appropriateness of undertaking psychoanalysis with individuals over the age of 50, citing in particular a supposed lack of plasticity in psychic processes (he referred then to the "viscosity of the libido" to signify the difficulty of shifting investments and the risk of becoming fixed in rigid modes of functioning). He was 48 years old when he wrote those lines, and in hindsight, he himself proved to be a perfect counterexample to the idea of rigidity in older age—considering his ongoing creative activity, the continuous reworking of his writings, the sheer number of footnotes he added over time, and his insatiable curiosity for intellectual debate, acquisition of new knowledge, and passionate concern for the world's affairs, which he watched darken until his death in 1939.

The research I conduct or supervise, as well as the studies carried out by colleagues with whom I collaborate, is always guided by the aim of discerning more precisely the psychic resources that can be mobilized in the face of the inevitable progression of age and the accompanying vulnerabilities of the body, cognition, and one's place in the society in which one grows, matures, and ages. We listen to our patients in our offices, in their homes, or in their hospital rooms, but we also remain attentive to public voices—the positions and expressions that our elders still and always seek to articulate. At a time when older people often complain of being neither acknowledged nor heard, it is crucial that research and reflection be directed toward these voices, which also tell us something essential about what it means to grow old, to be old in a world in turmoil, in which one strives to find meaning and a sense of security.

The elderly men and women I will discuss in this text are not representative of their fellow citizens, and my argument is by no means intended to be easily generalizable. They are particularly committed to the scientific, cultural, and political causes they advocate for. They have experienced or are experiencing a level of renown that has undoubtedly influenced their consistent and steadfast engagement.

Their inner motivations are sometimes difficult to grasp, as I have not been able to conduct interviews with each of them that would allow for an articulation of their life stories and current realities, or to discern figures who may have played a role in shaping their identifications and ideals. However, it is evident how external conditions, expectations, and even pressures have determined, shaped, and sustained their way of being in the world, likely leading to a situation where they may feel they have little choice but to continue in this manner. Caught between noble concerns about the future of humanity, the demand to remain faithful to a narrative marked by ideals—though not necessarily devoid of complexity—that they have constructed, and that others have constructed with and about them, and the high regard in which they are held, the intricate balance between narcissistic investment and object investment is further reinforced. This balance is known to play a vital role in navigating the tumultuous passage of aging and old age.

A reflection on aging that takes such data into account does justice to the richness and diversity of the figures of old age—figures that are too often reduced either to pathological stereotypes or, conversely, to performative ideals focused solely on self-maintenance through physical activity. Alongside my clinical and research work in the hospital setting—where I paid close attention to the knowledge gained about the modes of psychic functioning involved in the experience of physical or mental illness—my research and reflective approaches also sought answers by drawing on diverse sources, such as the diaries of major writers, in which a voice is expressed that is rarely heard elsewhere or in other forms (Verdon, 2012, 2017). My reflections and research have thus aimed to better understand what enables women and men of advanced age to function well on a psychological level.

In this respect, I align myself with the French psychoanalyst François Villa, who provocatively asserts that death is not the consequence of aging, but rather occurs "when we are no longer able to age in order to keep on living" (2010, p.2). For despite fatigue, life's hardships, and illness, women and men continue to engage with society and to voice words they want their fellow citizens to hear. These individuals—resilient and enduring—share a capacity to stand firm in the face of the adversity and insecurity that accompany old age, illness, or political instability that threatens the freedom to live as one chooses. They demonstrate a clear investment in the social realities of their time, a desire for connection, for the future of younger generations, and for the betterment of the individual and humanity as a whole.

Their public voices can serve not only as material for civic reflection but also as valuable sources for professionals in the field of mental health. I have thus been interested both in their experience of aging and in the way they speak of it—how they bear witness to the challenges they face as well as to the convictions that sustain them, giving meaning to their long lives—convictions that, quite evidently, have not aged a bit.

3.1 A Paradoxical Dynamic

On September 21, 1939, in London, aged 83 and seriously ill, Sigmund Freud grasped the hand of his physician, Max Schur, and told him: "You promised me not to forsake me when my time comes. Now it's nothing but torture and makes no sense any more" (Schur, 1972, p. 529). Up until this limit, Freud had worked incessantly; shortly before, he continued to receive patients. Until the end, he remained concerned with understanding and learning more, with expressing his thoughts and analyses in his writings, with seeing his works translated, disseminated, and discussed. He despaired and became irritated when his strength failed him, when the pain was such that it prevented him from thinking and concentrating, from receiving colleagues and friends with ease and pleasure (Verdon, 2015). « Life at my age is not easy, but spring is beautiful and so is love » he wrote a few years earlier to the American novelist and poet Hilda Doolittle (1956, p.180). At the time, although very aware of his old age and illness, Freud still wished to live on: « The second half of this term I spent in suffering owing to the bad effects of another slight operation which was intended to relieve my habitual ailings. But after all it was not a tragic affair, only the inevitable expression of old age and the degeneration of tissues dependent on it. So I do not complain. I know I am overdue and whatever I still have is an unexpected gift » (*ibid.*, p.176). Freud remained curious and concerned about world affairs until the end, deeply troubled by the Nazi onslaught ravaging his country, particularly tormented by the future of his four sisters for whom he could not obtain permission to leave Austria. While his engagement through thought and writing remained enduring, he was sometimes overcome by discouragement. He confided, for example, to Arnold Zweig: "I would really not like to delay any longer, because everything around me is becoming darker, more threatening, and the awareness of my own distress is becoming more pressing. [...] The fear of losing through aging important parts of my still intact personality is a factor that hastens my wish" (Freud & Zweig, 1927–1939, p.180).

What is happening here is essential to grasp. For it says something about the density of this potential and unheard-of human creativity that seizes paradoxes and puts them to work. It coexists, better yet, it articulates, knits together, constructs a dynamic where strength and weakness, desire to move forward and desire to stop everything intertwine their respective logics, sometimes difficult to reconcile. And yet reality will prove to be this: being invited to admit to not mastering everything, to not being all-powerful, nor immortal, perhaps diminished, even handicapped, without however tipping into the conviction that life is no longer worth living. It is indeed a matter of acknowledging the psychic dynamic mobilized by this inherent tension between the potential for robustness that may remain, and the increasing fragility inherent in aging. How do the need for rest, diminished endurance, feelings of vulnerability, or even physical incapacities coexist with the deliberate decision to remain active in a world that the older adult claims as still and always theirs, in which they wish to be recognized, and in which they aspire to leave something of themselves? What does the desire to remain combative entail, and what does it mean to not always be able to fulfill it?

Such a dynamic does not wait for aging or old age to manifest itself. Every age experiences this tension between wanting to do, wanting to learn, wanting to interact, and doubting one's ability to do so, renouncing certain unattainable ideals, yet still remaining in contact with internal and external sources of pleasure. But with advancing age, the radicality of death imposes itself as a traveling companion with a more or less imminent deadline. And to this uncompromising radicality, other radicalities respond. Thus, two pitfalls in the psychic treatment of this tension are quite easily discernible:

- On one hand, there's the risk of depressive decompensation, resignation, disengagement, narcissistic withdrawal into conservative positions, succumbing to regression and complaints, being confined to a position of needing help and being no longer capable of anything. Associated with this are the consequent representations of loss of autonomy, free will, even of one's home, rights, and the risk of abuse, exploitation, etc. In short, aging as failure, collapse, shipwreck...
- Conversely, there's the refusal, even denial, of aging and its changes, which may be accompanied by a radically different litany: the exclusive concern for maintenance and performance, the rejection of slowness, stagnation, and fatigue, the idealized exaltation of youth (as an illusory self-mirroring), of full form, of late style and late creativity (Billé & Martz, 2010).

It interests me, therefore, from my position as a clinical psychologist and psychoanalyst, to consider the conviction of learning and development as potentially always possible by putting it in tension with what aging and old age inevitably entail. For it is not without reason that we speak of growing, maturing, and then aging, even if the demarcation lines between these realities are sometimes blurry, changing, dependent on both objective criteria and subjective considerations. Certainly, we can always potentially learn, educate ourselves, deepen and diversify our skills, find pleasure, and have new experiences and encounters. But aging still involves being modified by being altered, and ultimately not being able to do much about it. And while it's important not to confine the experience of aging to loss, it's just as important not to deny its actual reality: the multiplication of frustrations and separations, the announcement of the impending end inevitably engender a more or less conscious reaction of avoidance, even dread, a sense of injustice, or even of tearing away (Verdon, 2013). And it's not self-evident to recognize oneself in others and to recognize them, to want to learn from them and develop with them, because some of these others are young while I am aging, some are thriving while I am declining, some potentially have many years of life ahead while I am heading towards the final years of my life.

What psychoanalysis has illuminated about psychic functioning is particularly valuable for understanding this complex dynamic. Its ability to render the psychic conflict between unconscious and conscious elements intelligible—between temporalities, agencies, desires, and ideals that are different, contrasting, and sometimes contradictory—provides a heuristic perspective on what animates, and at times undermines, the psyche. Indeed, the time of external reality does not align with that of psychic life (what is past is never truly past); event-based reality does not equate to psychic reality (the source of anxiety cannot be reduced to what we are consciously aware of); and we are imbued, enriched, and burdened by this dynamic.

The coexistence of the pleasure principle and the reality principle generates tensions, at times painful, that the psychic apparatus strives to manage as effectively as possible by mobilizing defenses to contain anxiety, seek pleasure in relationships, and find meaning in life. The balance between self-focus and attention to others is fragile, constantly challenged by internal demands (such as ideals or vulnerabilities) and external constraints. Among the latter are aging with illness and the prospect of death. The latter annihilates all potential for being, acting, and undertaking. The former tests, and sometimes threatens, the capacities for autonomy, decision-making, action, the fulfillment of desires, and resilience. It then becomes crucial to discern how the subject manages—or fails—to mitigate the conflict inherent in the coexistence of vulnerability, which hinders possibilities for fulfillment, and ideals, which drive one forward, aspiring to pleasure and securing minimal self-esteem.

However, loss, lack, and renunciation are not exclusive to old age. These terms resonate with numerous experiences, starting from early childhood, that alternately mobilize a drive to move forward—requiring the shedding of certain aspirations to find oneself anew—or a lethal disillusionment, marked by feelings of worthlessness and insignificance, both to others and oneself. The aging individual must again confront the risk of no longer being able to please those whose recognition they seek, as well as the potential loss of strength and endurance to fight for their ideals. How do they strive to continue pursuing the objects that give their life meaning without becoming depleted? How do they negotiate renunciations without succumbing to disillusionment? How does the desire to live coexist with the inescapable thought of impending death? Speaking of the "mortal-immortal Self," psychoanalyst André Green suggests that "the Self is thus this very duplicity, its split structure being part of its most intimate functioning—masked in normality, revealed in illness. Recognition of material reality—whose importance should not, incidentally, be underestimated—and its misrecognition by psychic (unconscious) reality, such is the dialectic that accounts for how the wish for immortality only takes on meaning through its coexistence with the awareness of death" (1983, p. 265).

3.2 Learning and Development

It is potentially always possible to learn. However, one must be internally and externally capable of doing so. On one hand, it's necessary to remain interested, motivated, and to have cognitive functions that are sufficiently efficient and mobilizable. On the other hand, it's necessary to have access to potential objects of investment. Learning, investing in various objects of knowledge, finding pleasure in it, all participate in processes that psychoanalysis has discerned, with potential sublimatory dynamics that draw from libido, redirect and transform satisfactions towards socially valued, even noble goals. So, we can wish for people to remain free from what motivates them, so as not to engage in superficial learning, to conform to others, to try to remain within the acceptable normative markers of a given society, to meet expectations in terms of prevention or compensation for physiological declines. Thus, the process of learning should not be limited to adaptive or normative educational concerns; nor should these concerns be underpinned by the idea that older adults are necessarily surpassed by contemporary digital, technological, or societal phenomena and that there is no salvation outside of knowledge and understanding of these sweeping movements. The process of learning, the desire to do so, and the resulting experience must remain meaningful for the individual, be a source of pleasure, without tipping into challenge, self-realization, and the risk of failure, where the conduct consists of testing oneself in difficulty or pain to conform to others and convince oneself and others that one is still in the game, that one does not give up anything, that one is up-to-date, and that one hopes, on this condition, to remain inserted, included. These concerns have sometimes been directed towards success and social conformity, sometimes tinged with neoliberal ideology that emphasizes the principle of meritocracy and individual responsibility alone to explain inequalities, thus encouraging the adoption of individual strategies to resolve them.

Experiencing a lesser ease in mobilizing cognitive and intellectual capacities can be very upsetting, even when it only reflects variations within the normal range considering age and socio-cultural level. On one hand, it's due to the specter of brain pathologies with demential expression, loss of autonomy, and the terrible anxiety of no longer being able to trust oneself. But also because intellectual abilities fundamentally contribute to self-esteem from early school years: succeeding or failing, surpassing others or falling behind are experiences whose possible repercussions are not always fully understood. We too often forget that older adults were once young men and women, and before that, children and adolescents, and that they experienced setbacks and successes. They may have overcome some failures, but probably not all; wars and financial difficulties prevented many from continuing their education and pursuing a career commensurate with their expectations, if not their abilities. All of this plays a role, whether quietly or loudly, in the attention individuals pay to their difficulties, whether common or accentuated. The re-experiencing of a situation involving interaction with others, in a learning environment that requires vigilance, memorization, and understanding, can be stimulating or painful.

There is indeed great interest in developing spaces and experiences that are both adapted to aging and elderly individuals, without being discriminatory, thus avoiding the risk of creating ghettos that undermine inclusion projects. Therefore, one can only rejoice in seeing the creation of training and counseling spaces, universities for the elderly—remarkable devices for sharing knowledge—, cultural activities, workshops providing information and advice to support cognitive mobilization, adaptation to changes in the body in daily life activities, fall prevention, knowledge of assistance and care devices, etc. (see also Muller Mirza, this volume). These various initiatives that promote the creation and support of social ties are absolutely to be promoted as long as they ensure respect for the singularity of each individual, and grasp the movements of ambivalence that potentially traverse people: the desire to learn and the fear of not succeeding, the conviction of not being capable, or on the contrary, the excitement in performative challenges. Filling oneself with knowledge, engaging in multiple activities, claiming to always and forever develop oneself are sometimes underpinned by the fear of dying if one slows down, gives up, or stops... Here again, balance is to be ensured by taking into account the difficulties inherent in aging and the conviction that engaging in activities can meet needs and desires and support self-investment and that of others.

I believe that movements such as Old'Up or the CNaV in France, and undoubtedly many others elsewhere, testify to this. They advocate for aging while confronting serious questions, difficulties, hardships, and even pitfalls, while remaining mobilized as actors in society, proposing solutions, and distancing themselves from proactive or deficit stereotypes. Founded in 2008, the Old'Up association,[2] "led by elders, for and with them", aims to be a "learning space for life represented by aging" in order "to give meaning and utility to the extension of life". It serves as a place for exchange and conviviality, research and debate, to support citizen action, intergenerational dialogue, more accurate representations of aging, etc. Created more recently, in 2021, the CNaV[3] (self-proclaimed National Council of Old Age) is a citizen movement that also fully embraces the self-determination of "older persons". It seeks to promote "an inclusive, egalitarian, fraternal, and respectful look at the freedom and identity of each individual, in continuity with their unique history and major life choices". There is no denial of the potential vulnerability associated with aging, but rather a refusal to be exclusively designated by those who especially do not want to be associated with it, and to be relegated to a position of assisted individuals without freedom or independent thought beyond complaint and gratitude. Engaging in collective reflection to "develop alternative ideas and submit them to a multidisciplinary and plural perspective" fully participates in the unifying spirit of the movement.

The initiatives of Old'Up and the CNaV steer clear of the fetishistic idea of a choice that would necessarily be successful, a "successful aging", as if it were an exercise for which one had learned the rules and codes to be applied in an educated and universally valid manner. Above all, the strong idea is that self-realization cannot do without others, who support, whom one supports, whom one loves, whom one loves less, those who are similar, those who are different.

---

[2] https://www.oldup.fr/

[3] https://www.cnav-demain.fr/. The admirable wit lies in the playful and knowing twist of the acronym CNaV (National Council of Old Age), which humorously echoes the acronym of CNAV (National Old-Age Insurance Fund), the French social security organization responsible for managing basic and/or supplementary pensions.

3.3 Learning and Identification

Because learning and development involve others. From early childhood to the complex constructions of adolescence, each person is invited/compelled to change while remaining the same. They strive to build themselves and their own path while wanting and not wanting to resemble their parents and family members, as well as other identificatory models, whether close or distant, real, famous, or imaginary, that offer themselves as reference points (Cahn, 2002; Jeammet, 1994). The stakes are high: it is about building one's own identity amidst others. This identity consists partly of common elements, similar to other individuals but without merging with them, and partly of elements that distinguish and individualize, without becoming too distant or alien. There is a nameless complexity in weaving together elements from various sources over the years, assimilated in a uniquely personal and more or less harmonious manner. The individual endeavors to be like others, to find their place alongside others, within a group, a family, a community, while also distinguishing themselves. This process involves back-and-forth movements, identifications and counter-identifications, varying degrees of freedom dictated by societal norms, gender and age, social status and culture, family constraints, generations, and so on. Not to mention, of course, an unconscious psychic dynamic where self-construction in relation to others is not solely determined by the subject's goodwill and decision, but also by internal processes and motivations that elude them: sometimes one constructs oneself to please others, sometimes to be nothing like them, without always being able to decide or discern the factors at play. Ultimately, individuals often try to claim the free will of their approach and express satisfaction with having become who they are, having achieved ambitions. Or, conversely, they attribute what they have become, which they may not always be proud of, to external coercive influences.

There are indeed individuals, sometimes at an advanced age, who realize that the life they have built, the life they have led, remains unsteady, unsatisfying, perpetually filled with constraints and frustrations. They may have wished to lead a different life, pursue a different career, have a different affective life. Some have the terrible impression of having missed out on their life and deep desires that remained buried under the weight of family expectations, social norms, and pressing concerns, however legitimate they may have been. Maturity and the perspective of the end of life sometimes mobilize unexpected resources to upheave priorities. The individual refuses to continue along a path that has been laid out since forever, and instead aspires to take a step aside, to continue learning, to develop internal potentialities (artistic, emotional, sexual) that have lain fallow, withered, stifled under the weight of constraints and inhibitions, sidelined by other priorities whose meaning now loses its obviousness and radicality.

But let's not lose sight of the dynamic and sometimes conflicting dimension of this subtle weaving of complex temporalities (André, 2010). Psychoanalysis has extensively explored the intertwining of narcissistic cathexes and object cathexes (Freud, 1914; Green, 1983). On the one hand, one tries to make sense of the significant withdrawal and restrictive behaviors in certain patients who, presenting various psychopathological organizations, refuse contact and touch. They retreat into themselves and no longer leave their homes, adopt fragmented, restrictive, ascetic eating, affective, and sexual behaviors, to prevent anyone from entering their living space or their body. On the other hand, one attempts to understand behaviors characterized by greed, adhesiveness, and hyper-dependence on others or substances, where the urgency lies in filling a void. The person cannot let any temporal or spatial space intrude into contact with the object of satisfaction; she must move from one object to another because she finds in herself no narcissistic resource reliable enough to remain somewhat alone without feeling abandoned and insecure.

Learning, therefore, implies the ability to maintain a sufficiently good distance with the other, a space that is both flexible and firm, conducive to a dynamic exchange: without ignoring each other or merging; by accepting that something of the other enters oneself without violating or overpowering; by appropriating this knowledge, making it something that becomes one's own; by recognizing what the other brings, thus acknowledging the other's difference, alterity, and value. However, some elderly individuals, for example, feel overwhelmed by contemporary phenomena and have the painful impression of being worthless and left on the sidelines of a society that no longer recognizes them or accords them any place or esteem. This is despite the fact that they potentially have much to testify about their own history and the broader history of which they have been witnesses. Their way of life, sometimes out of sync with today's priorities and trends, is valuable for society to consider, and, above all, it is inherently respectable. Indeed, some elderly individuals, on the contrary, claim to have nothing to learn from modernity, nor from the youth, their experiences, and aspirations, believing that everything was better in their own youth. Consequently, they may be less open to understanding how others live, speak, and dress. However, they also have much to learn from the youth, from their lives, concerns, worries, and values.

Indeed, the ability to identify with others is invaluable for investing the other within oneself, supporting the possibility of their recognition as someone other than oneself and, at the same time, as oneself—the young person one once was, the elderly person one will become. Some young and old individuals can show genuine complicity, as if they, beyond the counter-identifications that may occur, sense, respect, and acknowledge the unique gravity of the changes experienced by others. The other is recognized for their potential capacity to open up a space of experience; they reveal something that was not seen before, was seen differently, or was no longer seen. And this movement can also be associated with the ability to identify with what the other experiences apart from me, with someone other than me—an identification with what motivates them, with what causes them anxiety: the concern of the other resonates with mine and becomes mine as well.

Indeed, the depressive problematic can sometimes be mobilized—though not always tolerable—as it is fundamentally inherent to the investment of the object recognized as other. When someone claims to be self-sufficient and operates in isolation, the investment of the object is heavily conditioned by narcissistic defenses (idealization, investing in the other as a mirror of oneself) aimed at warding off any idea of lack. Conversely, when someone invests in the object in an adhesive manner, the depressive problematic is undoubtedly underlying but counter-invested by addictive behaviors that also combat any idea of lack. But if I recognize the other's otherness and independence, if I acknowledge their right to be interested in and attracted to objects other than myself, then I am seized by the fear of losing them, that they might leave or die; but also by the fear that they might suffer because their fate becomes mine, without control or confusion. To avoid conflating the positive dimension of depressive capacity with the negative dimension of pathological depression, psychoanalyst Pierre Fédida (2001) proposed the term "depressivity" to describe this precious psychic capacity to endure conflict, navigate trials, acknowledge one's limits, and mourn what can no longer be possessed or controlled. Such a capacity provides protection, balance, and regulation in life, even if it is accompanied by temporary sadness. Depressivity enables one to acknowledge the reality of the impact of disenchantments and losses without collapsing into the breakdown of psychic equilibrium, the withdrawal from sources of pleasure, or the self-devaluation often exacerbated by isolation, ostracism, and ageism. And then we discern how difficult it is to develop oneself amidst others who are both similar and different. This certainly involves a conscious goodwill to be interested in what the other has to say, but also unconscious dynamics imbued with the desire to be like the other, to please them, to acquire their qualities, or even to take their place. And here we find again the intertwining of narcissistic and object cathexes mentioned earlier.

3.4 Expanding the Possibilities

Learning is not just about staying connected to technological advancements and having an Instagram or TikTok account. It's not just about doing cognitive performance exercises (e.g., Aerobics of the Mind) *via* phone applications that blur the lines between brain mass, IQ level, cognitive performance, and self-esteem, or continuing to read and listen to the media to keep up with current events or take an interest in contemporary literature and art. The risk then would be to promote the new simply because it's new, pleasure in novelty, the ephemeral because it's replaceable. The risk then is to organize oneself into an as if personality by promoting an adaptive approach that conforms to external expectations at the expense of personal aspirations, or to want to stay young to remain alive. While the result may be successful and accomplished, the process nevertheless leads to a distortion of one's own desire, if not of psychic organization, which tries to find a balance, however precarious, in conformity to expectations, norms, and trends. The simulacrum allows some people to hold on, to maintain appearances, and to superficially display satisfactory adaptation. But others struggle to find lasting satisfaction in this arrangement and experience states of discomfort that they find difficult to discern the source of, so convinced are they of the validity of the incessantly performative priorities that organize their lives (Verdon & Rexand-Galais, 2021). They aspire to still be part of the workforce even though they no longer work, to get involved in activities to always be in the mix, even though they get lost in them more than they inhabit them. We can see how this active dynamic counter-invests representations of unbearable and anxiety-inducing passivity: learning, self-realization, development, continuous growth are underpinned there by performative dimensions where the focus is on not losing; it's about knowing, acting, mastering, controlling, remaining effective and useful, legitimate and lovable. We change, but not because we are prey to senescence and involution; we change because we continue to acquire; indeed, we are modified but not altered. Such a dynamic can be very stimulating and trophic; it propels us forward and gives meaning to the continuity of life. But it runs the risk of violently colliding with the blows dealt by life's accidents if little room is left for the possibility of contemplating and internalizing lack, loss, inevitably linked, sooner or later, to the passage of aging and old age.

It is therefore very important to discern what drives the commitment, learning, and involvement of aging individuals. Through these actions, they testify to their refusal to resign themselves to the caricatured image of the elderly person inevitably secluded, content with little, or unenthusiastic because they are so withdrawn into their past and former references. This echoes the firm assertion of the novelist and Nobel laureate François Mauriac: upon reading a portrait of himself painted by a young colleague highlighting that "week after week, one feels the pulse of the old writer decrease, one senses the ultra-aging of his bones, one suffers the progressive blindness of his eyes", he retorted forcefully, "just because I have one foot in the grave doesn't mean you can trample on the other!" (Barré, 2010, p. 459). However, the same Mauriac, in his *"Nouveaux Mémoires intérieurs" ["New Inner Memoirs"]*, expresses another inner position that inhabits him: "Preparing for death means untying, one by one, the ties that bind us, breaking as many moorings as we can, so that when the wind suddenly rises, it will carry us away without our resistance. *Detachment that takes place within us and does not betray itself outwardly.* Our outer life is not affected by it" (1965, p. 76; emphasis is mine). The paradox is remarkable: the psychic work of relinquishing control, recognizing losses and fragility, is not necessarily measured by disinvestments in daily life activities. These activities can remain places of engagement and social fertility, they can have a precious narcissistic value and nevertheless accompany the possibility of an inner consent, never complete, never easy, to be only what one is and not to become more one day.

I am particularly interested in better understanding the potential to expand possibilities despite the diminishing of one's strength, to maintain an engagement as an actor in society as an ongoing experience of self-continuation, development, or even learning while confronting the increasing, if not already established, vulnerability. Being an actor in society does not necessarily mean being a consumer, exclusively an amateur of entertainment. Not all aging adults are polluting boomers who disregard the consequences of their actions on the state in which they leave the planet for future generations. Identifying with others and their future is also a form of engagement; it involves allowing others and their concerns to find a place within oneself and therefore continuing, for example, a long-standing fight from which one could have legitimately retired. It then becomes a matter of listening to the pulse of the world, taking an interest in and caring about it, allowing oneself to be influenced by others, their attitudes, their innocence, their combativeness, and to testify and transmit, to pass the torch, in the interest of those who remain. And the dialectic is inevitably dynamic: we learn to act, to transmit, we welcome and testify to continue to contribute to the construction of the world. The French author Jane Sautière powerfully addresses this significant issue: "It is not the inevitability of the end that frightens us. It is being subtracted from the absolute 'we' that is the collective movement of the streets. We are erased from this matrix, we no longer know how to make our presence in the world visible, a deficit of existence. We will no longer go to the woods, the laurels are cut down. To consider: no longer having ecstasy, no longer having ecstasy with the collective body? Our winter begins" (2024, p.38).

The concern for the future of society, cultures, and the world as a whole is a source of engagement for many aging or elderly adults. Political engagement, artistic engagement, and intellectual engagement, for example, are experiences of development and learning facilitated by identification with and interest in the younger generation. They resonate with the convictions that have sometimes driven the elderly since their own youth, which may have given meaning to life, self-construction, and cathexis of others (Chiarelli, 2016), issues that are particularly crucial at the end of life.

"I am happy to still be able, however brief the hours that remain, to continue reflecting on it."

Let's revisit the immense success of the small book *"Indignez-vous!" ["Time for Outrage!"]* by the nonagenarian Stéphane Hessel, published in 2010 in the aptly named collection « Ceux qui marchent contre le vent » ["Those who Walk against the Wind"] by Éditions Indigène.[4] The title, content, and approach undoubtedly resonated with audiences far beyond just the aging and elderly demographic.[5] The former Buchenwald deportee, the former diplomat who contributed to the drafting of the Universal Declaration of Human Rights, shows an unwavering commitment to political, economic, social, media, and cultural affairs of his society and time. He was scandalized, for example, by educational reforms "too far removed from the ideal of the republican school, too much in the service of a money-driven society, and no longer fostering enough creative and critical thinking". These reforms went against "the effective possibility for all French children to benefit from the most advanced education" (2010, pp.10–11) and were being forcibly imposed on teachers (some of whom rebelled and were sanctioned by their administration). Hessel is incisive, critical, committed, and uncompromising. His conviction is of great intensity and entirely focused on the future, especially that of the young and their living conditions in contemporary societies. However, he inaugurates, or perhaps he effectively inaugurates, his text by embracing his advanced age: "93 years old. *It's a bit like the very last stage. The end is not far off.* What a chance to take advantage of it to recall what served as the foundation for my political commitment: the years of

[4] The English version was published by Charles Glass Books, London, 2011.

[5] In 1 year, the book was translated into 34 languages and sold 4 million copies.

resistance and the program developed sixty-six years ago by the National Council of the Resistance! [...] We need these principles and values more than ever today. It is up to all of us to ensure that our society remains one of which we can be proud" (*ibid.*, p.9; emphasis is mine). He, the nonagenarian, requests permission to speak in schools to urge young people to discern the sources of injustice in their time and oppose them. He, the nonagenarian, steadfastly maintains that "the worst attitude is indifference, saying 'I can't do anything about it, I'll manage'" (*ibid.*, p.14). He, the nonagenarian who knows his days are numbered, expresses his unchanging concern for infringements on ethics, the development of all peoples, access to healthcare for poor citizens, women's rights, and the future of the planet where future generations will live.

The elderly figure is undeniably grounded and engaged. In the preface added to the second edition of his work *"Danse avec le siècle" ["Dance with the Century"]*, which was published a few months later, Hessel writes: "I finished this 'dance' fourteen years ago, fully convinced that my already eighty-year-old life would end with the century. Now I am reaching the end of a new stage, as fertile in commitments as those that preceded it. [...] I am happy to still be able to reflect on it, no matter how brief the hours that remain to me" (1997, p.7–8). In this book, which traces his life journey linked to the events of his time, Hessel does not deny that he has experienced "much contested candor and lost illusions, observed horrors and bitter assessments" (ibid., p.12), but that he has kept hope and "always preferred the future to nostalgia and reminiscences. But, at my age, one is a witness to one's time" (*ibid.*, p.11). The last chapter, titled "Crépuscule ou aube?" ("Twilight or Dawn?"), is thus inaugurated: "Remember: I began these memoirs in the fall of 1994. I bring them to a close in the fall of 1996. I, myself, have aged" (*ibid.*, p.302). The sensitivity to the passing of time is undeniable, but the rest of the text nonetheless unfolds a sharp analysis of the world's situation, not centered on personal concerns, despite the impending twilight.

"With the strength that remains to me"

Let's also think about Claude Alphandéry. A French Resistance fighter during World War II, a senior civil servant, and an economist sensitive to wealth distribution inequalities, he was committed for a long time to fighting exclusion and promoting job creation. At the age of 68, he was appointed President of the National Council for Economic Integration through Employment. Later, at the age of 88, he founded the Laboratory for Social and Solidarity Economy, a think tank dedicated to this specific issue at the national and European levels.

In early March 2024, 3 weeks before his death at the age of 101, he sent a short text to the French weekly newspaper *Le Nouvel Observateur*. In it, he addressed all citizens, saying: "*While hospitalized and feeling my strength decline*, I come to ask you to commit to doing everything, wherever you are, *with the means you have*, to prevent a new dark night for humanity. It is the former resistance fighter speaking to you. [...] Everywhere, the rise to power of authoritarian and populist regimes is a vital threat to the rule of law, to public freedoms, to peace, and leads us towards a new tragic night against which I fought so hard. *My very last appeal, with the strength that remains to me*, is to urge you to do everything possible to ensure that what has motivated my life, the fight against fascism, against barbarism, and for human rights, is once again mobilized in a great humanistic alliance of life forces. *Act as if you cannot fail*".[6] The centenarian man is resourceful! Even as he is greatly weakened and knows he is dying, his energy is mobilized for the future of a planet he will soon leave. The fate of those who remain, not only his loved ones and those he holds dear, but every person of goodwill, matters to the exhausted yet tenacious elder. His concern for those who remain is an indication of this identification steeped in otherness, illustrating the capacity to pursue something of oneself in others and to fight to ensure the continued flourishing of their lives. Not to mention that, concurrently, paradoxically, in the intensity of the final days of this certainly ending singular life, the question of self-continuity and coherence remains central. Narcissistic cathexes fuels object relations and vice versa. The one who will inevitably lay down arms before the grim reaper shares with the survivors a conviction that has long sustained him: to act as if failure were not an option...

Hugues Sibille, current president of the Laboratory for Social and Solidarity Economy, paid tribute to him by saying: "We had come to believe he was immortal! His rallying cry 'live and resist' was so powerful, he was so present at the Lab until our General Assembly in January where he spoke magnificently, that we refused to entertain the idea of his death. [...] I accompanied him to the end, and to the end he wanted to fight against the major risks of our societies *of which he had a keen awareness*. [...] A great resistor, *he leaves us his combativeness, his hope in dark times, his desire to act, to undertake, to fight* as if we could not fail. [...] Despite his old age, Claude was *always in tune with his time*, and continued until the end to anticipate and imagine positive changes for our society. [...] And after living through a century, and while worrying about the world and the direction it was taking, he remained fundamentally optimistic, and retained a deep belief in humanity's capacity for progress".[7] It wasn't to live a little longer that Alphandéry fought, it was so that others could live in dignified and secure conditions; and that undoubtedly kept him alive until the end.

Already at the beginning of 2024, Alphandéry had joined the international call initiated by the philosopher and sociologist Edgar Morin, 102 years old, and the philosopher Patrick Viveret, only 76 years old (a youngster!), for a "creative resistance of humanity for peace, justice, and freedom"[8] while terrible wars rage in so many parts of the world. Their call promotes an urgent awareness of the need to restore dialogue and curb any act of barbarism. Once again, these elderly people express their conviction of a "creative resistance and hope in the alliance of forces of life, justice, and freedom" to mobilize for tomorrow, a tomorrow which, to varying degrees, is primarily the reality of younger generations.

---

[6] https://www.nouvelobs.com/idees/20240326.OBS86257/claude-alphandery-son-appel-bouleversant-contre-le-retour-de-la-barbarie.html The emphasis is mine.

[7] https://www.lelabo-ess.org/hommage-a-claude-alphandery-1922-2024-ancien-resistant-fondateur-du-labo-de-l-ess-et-eternel-engage The emphasis is mine.

[8] https://www.archipel-confluences.org/WikiAdC/?AppelPaix1

In 2016, Edgar Morin himself had issued a call at the closing of the Utopia Movement University. He reiterated that beyond cultures and generations, *"our individualities in their singularity are part of the human community"* and that "the vital problems and perils brought about by globalization now bind *all human beings in a community of destiny*".[9] No rigid distinction between generations, no conflict between boomers and Gen Z with incompatible values and irreconcilable desires, no division between those who learn and develop and those who decline and wither away. The concerns are common, and the diverse forces are called upon to ally.

"Our anger against injustice remains undiminished"

On May 27, 2020, the National Council of the New Resistance, founded by French citizens of all ages, young and old, already issued a call to alert about the dismantling of post-war achievements, social protection, labor rights, public services, wealth redistribution, and job security. Their text proclaims from the outset: "'To resist is to create. To create is to resist', as great resistance fighters told us in 2004 in their Appeal to the younger generations. This call resonates within us".[10]

The "Appeal to the Younger Generations" they refer to is a call from the Resistance to the younger generations dated March 8, 2004, on the occasion of the 60th anniversary of the National Council of the Resistance's Program: "Our anger against injustice is still intact"[11] signed by 13 former resistance members, including the youngest, Georges Séguy, who was born in 1927 and was 77 years old, and the eldest, Germaine Tillion, who was born in 1907 and was 97 years old. Twenty years separate them, one generation. Yet, they are often categorized as "old", "seniors"; the group sometimes exclusively imagined as exhausted, fragile, inclined to withdraw and enjoy a calm, if not entertaining, and finally carefree life—freed from professional constraints—, or even as withdrawn into their past, unaware of modern worldly affairs. Given the average age of the signatories of this solemn appeal, one might readily imagine that they are weakened by the inevitable effects of passing time, that their bodies bear the weight of years and perhaps the burden of illness and disabilities. They are sometimes also imagined as exhausted, weary, and desiring to withdraw from the overflow of solicitations, troubles, and even anxieties that disturb the final years of their long lives. And why not? The need for rest, the legitimate desire to protect oneself and stay away from battles, or even physical, mental, and cognitive limitations that sometimes undermine any possibility of expressing a desire to move forward, formulate projects, and satisfy any desire, all contribute, as we have seen, to the challenging, sometimes painful reality of the experience of old age. The renowned French journalist François Giroud, aged 86 and confined to bed due to health issues, once wrote on a day when discouragement overcame her usual resilience: "I think I will stop reading the newspapers; the picture is too bleak from end to end when one feels powerless. Tonight, my leg hurts a lot. As Henri Michaux

---

[9] https://mouvementutopia.org/site/wp-content/uploads/2016/09/Edgar-Morin-Appel-Centre.pdf The emphasis is mine.

[10] https://www.cnnr.fr/la-declaration/

[11] https://blogs.mediapart.fr/solon63/blog/080223/appel-des-resistants-aux-jeunes-generations-du-8-mars-2004

wrote: “When you have a needle in your eye, what does the future of the British Navy matter to you?”” (2003, p.349).

And yet, these elderly ladies and gentlemen proclaim: “We call on the younger generations to keep alive and transmit the legacy of the Resistance and its timeless ideals of economic, social, and cultural democracy. [...] We call on children, youth, parents, elders, grandparents, educators, and public authorities to engage in a true peaceful uprising against all mass media outlets *that offer our youth nothing but mass consumption, contempt for the weakest and for culture, widespread amnesia, and cutthroat competition among all.* [...] More than ever, to those who will shape the century ahead, we want to say with our affection: ‘To create is to resist. To resist is to create.’”[12]

No denial of aging here, nor retreat into protected territories: these women and men marked by age, who are no longer at their peak in terms of health and endurance, nevertheless continue to exist for others, to pass on a meaningful torch, which undoubtedly fuels their desire to live on. Yet, it is also important not to sugarcoat the untranquility, worry, even disenchantment and disillusionment that such passionate commitments on the frontlines of the battle, noble as it may be, entail. For the reasons behind the commitment are serious, dark; the knowledge of past events and their ongoing relevance confronts us with grave, weighty representations, ones we would rather do without.[13] The passing of the torch signifies the inability to fully continue a heartfelt struggle, partly waged for decades and also motivated by concern for the future of today’s youth. And while the emotional *“anger against injustice remains intact”*, the intellectual and physical means to hope to win the battle, knowing it is long and recurrent, are not destined to last in order to perhaps one day prevail.

This struggle can easily be compared to that of movements such as European Grandparents for Climate, whose motto is: “We are seriously worried about the world we are leaving to future generations. We understand that solving the effects of our man-made climate crisis needs an international and multilevel effort, and we realize that social and intergenerational climate justice are crucial aspects in this transition process. The urgency of the situations calls for strong civil engagement”.[14]

---

[12] The emphasis is mine. It’s worth noting that another call will be issued on the eve of the 2012 presidential elections in France: https://www.lemonde.fr/idees/article/2011/05/14/l-appel-d-anciens-resistants-aux-jeunes-generations_1522251_3232.html The resignation is not on the agenda.

[13] It’s very interesting to note that the campaign for participation in the 2024 European elections initiated by the European Parliament features grandparents and grandchildren from across Europe, capturing authentic and unscripted moments between the different generations. What’s more, it combines the life stories of these elderly individuals who survived war and oppression with their explicit appeal to their grandchildren, evoking the necessary defense of freedom and democracy through participation in the elections: « I’m glad the way you are, and I love you for it. You should never take democracy for granted. You should always support it and protect it. You have to fight for it, you always have to be vigilant and fight for it. *If I could leave you with one message before I go*: Live democracy. Listen to one another. Take good care of democracy, when I’m not here anymore...” (Use_your_vote_European_Elections_2024_Grandparents_to_Grandchildren).

[14] https://grandparentsforclimate.eu/

Or the "Danish Grandparents" Campaign for Refugee Children, which strongly declares: "Our goal is to fight for the humane, considerate and fair treatment of asylum seekers and refugee families, especially refugee children. We speak with an authority borne of age, experience and long perspective".[15]

"Suffering when one ages, it's tougher"

In an interview she gave to the cultural and political journal *Les Inrockuptibles*, French writer Annie Ernaux discusses the eventful year 2022 that has just passed for her: the publication of the novel *"Le jeune homme" ["the young man"],* the release of the film *"Les années super 8" ["The Super 8 Years"]* and being awarded the Nobel Prize in Literature "for the courage and clinical acuity with which she uncovers the roots, estrangements and collective restraints of personal memory".[16] She testifies there how, at the age of 82, she remains highly capable of sharp, informed, uncompromising judgment, very attuned to the world in which she lives, eager to understand it and find her place within it. Already, in her speech given at the Nobel Prize ceremony, she could express how she had written and continued to write from her singular experience, aiming to address social injustice, to erase what her own, her family's, her lineage of peasants, workers, and ordinary people had endured in terms of domination, contempt, and poverty. "I conceived of writing as nothing less than the possibility of transfiguring reality", she strongly asserted. The reality of poverty, but also that of predefined social, professional, marital, and familial roles based on one's gender or lack thereof.

Writing is a struggle, to express the ruptures, the wounds, the shame: "Avenging my people and avenging my sex would, from that time on, be one and the same thing". Hence, a writing fueled "by strength and anger" that hides nothing of the violence of things seen and experienced. Annie Ernaux listens, integrates, and learns; she aims to "capture sensations: those which memory has buried, those which the world around us keeps on giving, everywhere and all the time" because "only writing can bring into being and perhaps pass on to the consciousness and memories of others". She thus advocates the idea that the "I" of a story told can become, "in the same way if the 'I' of the book becomes transparent, in a sense, and the 'I' of the reader comes to occupy it. If this 'I', to put it another way, becomes transpersonal, that the singular reaches the universal". To write is an act "to change in private life, help to shatter the loneliness of experiences endured and repressed, and enable beings to reimagine themselves". Through her writing, Annie Ernaux engages and rebels; she writes for women, fights, from her position, for women.

And she doesn't hesitate to voice her opinion publicly, denouncing any class and gender domination, advocating for individual and collective emancipation. She mentions the stances she feels compelled to support in the face of ideas, events and conflicts. At 82 years old, she bears witness to a sharp and relevant critical perspective on today's political situation in France, Europe, and elsewhere in the world.

---

[15] https://www.bedsteforaeldreforasyl.dk/filer/Danish%20Grandparents%20Campaign%20for%20Refugee%20Children.pdf

[16] © The Nobel Foundation 2022.

Thus denouncing that "an ideology of withdrawal and closure is on the rise, […] founded on the exclusion of foreigners and immigrants, the abandonment of the economically weak, the surveillance of women's bodies", Annie Ernaux advocates: "*it requires a duty of extreme vigilance, for me and all those for whom the value of a human being is always and everywhere the same*. […] Silence is not appropriate in certain moments of history". Thus, she shares the pride of her Nobel Prize "with those who, in one way or another, hope for greater freedom, equality and dignity for all humans, regardless of their sex or gender, the color of their skin, and their culture; and with those who think of future generations, of safeguarding an Earth where a profit-hungry few make life increasingly unliveable for all populations". The fighting spirit is undeniable, as is the attention paid to others for themselves but also for oneself, because Ernaux does not deny anything of what she owes to the encounters that provide access "to other worlds and other ways of being",[17] places to learn, always and again, even if it means being shaken, placed back on the front lines of battles as strength declines.

It's very important to note that in the interview she gave to the newspaper *Les Inrockuptibles*, after talking about her successes, achievements, and testifying to a creativity that is always mobilizable and fruitful, she also confides: "Until 2017, I had the opportunity to live a love story with a man who was younger than me. But I was afraid of being too in love. *Suffering when one ages, it's tougher*. We see the problems that arise, and between the immediate pleasure and the problems that will come, we hesitate, we think much more. *I no longer wanted the upheaval that passion brings*. But the feeling doesn't age, I would be very capable of loving someone. [...] I wish for myself to be able to be tranquil and to write" (2022, p.53; emphasis is mine).

How can one not think back to what Freud says to his friend Hilda Doolittle after receiving from her a gift, a plant, a white datura? The gesture, which intertwines past and present, deeply touches him, perhaps too much: "In front of my window in the inner room stands a proud, sweet-smelling plant. Only twice have I seen it in bloom in a garden, at the Lago di Garda and in the Val Lugano. *It reminds me of those bygone days when I was still able to move around and visit the sunshine and beauty of southern nature myself.* […] *It is hardly advisable to give and octogenarian something beautiful. There is too much sadness in with the enjoyment*" (Doolittle, *op. cit.*, p.178; emphasis is mine).

"This moment of childlike trust, which still helps me today"

Let's now take the example of the academician Jacqueline de Romilly, who remained very demanding and intellectually engaged until the end of her life. Retiring from the Collège de France at the age of 70, she mobilized, for example, to ensure that Greek and Latin remained present in contemporary culture. She co-founded with colleagues the Association de la Sauvegarde des Enseignements Littéraires *(Association for the Safeguarding of Literary Education)*, "a training ground for combat and initiative, intervention, and even pressure" to maintain links

[17] © The Nobel Foundation 2022. The emphasis is mine.

between civilizations, if not between generations. Despite severe impairment of her visual abilities, and thanks to the support of her colleagues and friends, she remained deeply involved in writing and publishing scholarly essays as well as more personal content such as short stories.

In one of her very last texts, *"Les révélations de la mémoire" ["The Revelations of Memory"]*, she expresses her surprise at being strongly struck, at the age of 96, by a childhood memory she hadn't thought about in a long time: "Everything came to me as if, so many years later, I suddenly found myself in that big bed and that empty room, where I would soon fall asleep. I see everything so clearly". Left alone one evening in a hotel room during a trip with her mother and a couple of her mother's friends who are dining and staying up, she struggles to find the tranquility necessary for sleep. The sheets are cold and rough, the blankets heavy, and the feeling of solitude is oppressive, even frightening. But the contact with the fur collar of her mother's coat that she had left on the bed in case the little girl got cold brings her unexpected comfort: "With an instinctive gesture, like seeking refuge in a familiar place rediscovered at last, I buried my face in that fur collar and curled up in it, knowing I could find shelter against everything" (2009, p.43).

The scent of her mother, the softness of the fur, provide her with a soothing, tender, and reassuring regressive pleasure: "the fur was, for a moment, my mother. And I naturally felt an intense and indefinable relief: I felt that I was falling asleep, pacified, as if a real embrace had come to calm my anxiety. With my face buried in the fur, I felt saved from any threat. [...] It was the scent of my mother, very much alive, the one I found, when I kissed her, in the hollow of her neck; it was also her that I found in her scarves, with which I loved to play. It evoked our constant bonds of tenderness". The great Hellenist, academician, renowned for her demanding and always mobilizable intellectual fertility, can thus evoke the soothing value of such a refreshed representation: "And here it was enough, even at the end of my life, to suddenly revive this moment of childlike trust, which still helps me today. I still sometimes huddle against the tapestry cushions she embroidered in petit point. It was yesterday: I was a frightened little girl in a large unfamiliar room, but the help I received then still shines on my present and on those sometimes difficult days of old age" (2009, p.45). Thus are articulated the concern for others, the concern for the future of a youth that might be cut off from its Greek and Latin roots and whose quality of education and openness to ancient culture must be preserved, and the concern for oneself, closest to the need for comfort as one's vitality gradually fades away.

3.5 Conclusion

Although different, these various experiences speak to the fascinating and challenging paradox of old age. Longevity is indicative of strength and resilience, of solid experience and a sharp, both embodied and overarching, perspective on the world and oneself. But it inevitably comes with fragility and less ease.

None of the women, none of the men I have mentioned resign themselves. They assert their belonging to the world, still, always; they think, write, act and interact with others, young and old alike. But very aware of their acquired vulnerability and their finitude, they jointly express that their journey will soon come to an end. It matters to them not to abandon the fight but to pass on the torch, both to preserve something that has been meaningful to them and in the interest of younger generations.

Furthermore, some admit that they aspire not to be too burdened and that comfort is important when facing each day, each minute of each day, with the precariousness of their bodies and the impending death. Knowing that one has been able to place a last stone in the building of the world, that one has been able to develop until the last minute while being part of this world, and that something of oneself continues in others is certainly not without importance for finding some comfort and perhaps solace, and bidding farewell.

This singular, exceptional experience in many respects, yet one in which many anonymous citizens who support it and are encouraged by it recognize themselves, prevents us from overly separating life before old age from life marked by old age. For life asserts itself here in its dense continuum, where each person's history intertwines with their present-day reality. Are these men and women still involved and committed because of what they have lived through? Are they wise, aware of grave matters, because a maturity linked to age is solely at play? Reality always reminds us of the diversity of modalities of psychic functioning and life stories, here shaped by World War II but also by the liberation of morals, struggles for equal rights, the flourishing of media phenomena, the anniversaries of events related to the war, and the need to safeguard memory in the face of revisionist movements. No one can control the complex network of influencing factors, the multiple causalities whose dynamics intersect in always unique paths. Similarly, unless one risks oversimplifying and diluting the concept, old age cannot be confined to a singular wisdom characterized by "a lack of certain kinds of feelings—the passions, for instance, including anger, (...) coolness of reason and evenness of judgement, self-control, (...) serenity, calm and detachment from the world" (Woodward, 2002, p. 187, 193, 207). Woodward, moreover, echoes conceptions that advocate for "new belligerency, (...) alliance of wisdom with anger" (ibid., p. 195, 197), an interesting representation of wisdom as the capacity to confront the gravity of a situation, to mobilize oneself to the extent of one's abilities without seeking to be distracted by it, and without being overwhelmed by anxiety to the point of paralysis or retreating into solely self-focused concerns. In short, a conception very close to the depressivity mentioned earlier.

For what interests us here is the fact that this example of aging that relies on the endlessly reborn dawn, which remains engaged despite precariousness and unrest, strongly illustrates a fertility that testifies to remarkable psychological resources. Narcissistic cathexes and object cathexes intersect their reciprocal dynamics for a personal fulfillment that remains fully connected to others, a fulfillment that in no way denies the violence of the world and the reality of finitude but continually strives to contain and transform them. The projects of continually striving to change and improve a world one will soon leave undoubtedly participate in this dynamic, forever "invented by the ego in its attempt to assuage the inconsolable wound that is its finiteness" (Triandafillidis, 2010, p. 443), challenging death rather than denying it by initiating endeavors one hopes others will carry forward—a way of shielding them from the potentiality of death, disappearance, or failure.

We are far from the depleting and abusive considerations of Sándor Ferenczi, who argues that "elderly people become narcissistic again—like children—lose much of their family and social interests, and a large part of their capacity for sublimation is lacking [...]. The old person experiences a cessation of libidinal production which results in a decrease in overall quantity [...]. The symptoms of old age are like the rock that emerges when a golf course, cut off from the sea, dries up and is no longer fed by any river" (1921, p.150–151). Fortunately, from this time onwards, many works by psychoanalysts have come to qualify and criticize this unfounded representation in its generalization, just as they have come to question the obviousness of aging that must necessarily be successful, and necessarily successful if one demands of oneself and others to remain intact and performant. What do our societies say when they uphold such contrasting representations, aging oscillating between the Charybdis of an assured shipwreck and the Scylla of exclusive self-determination? Marked with either positive or negative valence, the narcissistic question reveals itself to be central, in proportion to the scandal of our impending death. Therefore, the recognition of limits, the renunciation of the satisfaction of all desires, and the questioning of performative ideals marked by perfection and excellence appear highly valuable for facing the ordeal of aging, provided that a balance is found with what remains of drive, curiosity, and interest in oneself and others.

Each one attempts to find a balance that is unique to them in this irreducible paradox. And we are witnesses to these elderly individuals who dare to assert with conviction their determined mobilization, sometimes even when their health is compromised, to remain active participants in the world they claim as still and always theirs. And it is important to acknowledge that the issues and processes at play are not only complex and intertwined, but also contradictory and potentially conflictual. The flexibility and solidity of narcissistic foundations, object cathexes, identificatory processes, and potentials for change are thus particularly put to the test in dealing with this inner tug-of-war, embracing it, and loosening it so that it does not hinder us from living.

But let us not forget the step aside, or perhaps rather the re-centering, that psychoanalysis offers in relation to the existential question mobilized by the fact of finitude. Freud formulates it thus: « To the ego, therefore, living means the same as being loved" (1923, p.58). To live, to be, to exist is irreducibly linked to the question of the meaning of life and the pleasure of living; thus, living inevitably engages the question of love. To exist, for whom? For the love of whom? Without self-awareness, without awareness of others, living is a challenging trial. This is what the young novelist and journalist Paul Nizan, aged only 26, senses with rare lucidity: "Death disgusts me if it is less the negation of everything that is to come than a still human condition like illness, cold, physical pain. True death is what it is, what life is not, what is *the state of a man when he thinks nothing, when he does not think himself, when he does not think others thinking him*" (1931, p.125; the emphasis is mine). And undoubtedly, one can add, in light of the testimonies collected here and there and reported above, "when he does not think others". For we have seen how intensely the concern for the other who remains while one is preparing to move on is articulated, and the question of what, for whom one exists, for the love of what, for the love of whom...

What do Hessel and Alphandéry tell us when they mention: *"It's a bit like the very last stage. The end is not far off"* and *"feeling my strength decline"*? What do Ernaux and Romilly tell us when they mention: *"I no longer wanted the upheaval that passion brings"* and *"the help I received then still shines on my present and on those sometimes difficult days of old age"*? They appeal to our respect for their vulnerability, to our love, to our memory so that they are not forgotten too quickly. But their messages collectively call on us to engage in remembrance far beyond their own selves, so that we do not forget the collective adventure of humanity, woven by successive generations, sometimes burdened with heavy legacies, memories marked by horror, and bursts of hope. And there, the program is ambitious, serious, and essential, for there is surely material to learn from and to develop...

References

André, J. (2010). *Les Désordres du temps [The Disorders of Time]*. Presses Universitaires de France.

Barré, J. L. (2010). *François Mauriac. Biographie intime [Intimate Biography] 1940-1970*. Fayard.

Billé, M., & Martz, D. (2010). *La tyrannie du Bienvieillir. Vieillir et rester jeune [The Tyranny of Agingwell. Aging and Staying Young]*. Le bord de l'eau.

Cahn, R. (2002). Les identifications à l'adolescence [Identifications during Adolescence]. In *Monographies de Psychanalyse [Psychoanalysis Monographs]. Identifications* (pp. 111–125). Presses universitaires de France. https://doi.org/10.3917/puf.danon.2002.01.0111

Chiarelli, C. (2016). Le temps de l'adolescence et l'engagement politique [Adolescence and political engagement]. In A. Muxel (Ed.), *Temps et politique: Les recompositions de l'identité [Time and Politics: The Recompositions of Identity]* (pp. 165–180). Presses de Sciences Po.

Doolittle, H. (1956). *Tribute to Freud. With unpublished letters by Freud to the author*. Pantheon Books.

Ernaux, A. (2022). Vers la mémoire. Interview. (Towards Memory. Interview). *Les Inrockuptibles, 16*, 50–53.

Fédida, P. (2001). *Des bienfaits de la dépression. Éloge de la psychothérapie [The Benefits of Depression. A Praise of Psychotherapy]*. Odile Jacob.

Ferenczi, S. (1921). Pour comprendre les psychonévroses du retour d'âge [To understand the Psychoneuroses of the Midlife Transition]. In *Œuvres complètes. Psychanalyse III [Complete Works. Psychoanalysis III] (1919-1926)*. Payot, 1974.

Freud, S. (1904). *On psychotherapy. The Standard Edition of the Complete Psychological Works* (Vol. VII, pp. 255–268). Vintage, 2001a.

Freud, S. (1914). On Narcissism: An introduction. *The Standard Edition of the Complete Psychological Works* (Vol. XIV, pp. 67–102). Vintage, 2001b.

Freud, S. (1923). The ego and the id. *The Standard Edition of the Complete Psychological Works* (Vol. XIX, pp. 3–66). Vintage, 2001c.

Freud, S., & Zweig, A. (1927–1939). *Correspondance [Correspondence]*. Gallimard, 1973.

Giroud, F. (2003). *Demain, déjà. Journal 2000-2003 [Tomorrow, already. Journal 2000-2003]*. Fayard.

Green, A. (1983). *Narcissisme de vie, narcissisme de mort [Life Narcissism, Death Narcissism]*. Les Éditions de Minuit.

Hessel, S. (1997). *Danse avec le siècle [Dance with the Century]* (2nd ed.). Seuil, 2011.

Hessel, S. (2010). *Indignez-vous ! [Be outraged!]*. Éditions Indigènes.

Jeammet, P. (1994). Adolescence et processus de changement [Adolescence and the process of change]. In D. Widlöcher (Ed.), *Traité de Psychopathologie [Treatise on Psychopathology]* (pp. 686–726). Presses Universitaires de France.

Mauriac, F. (1965). *Nouveaux mémoires intérieurs [New Inner Memoirs]*. Flammarion.

Nizan, P. (1931). *Aden Arabie*. La découverte, 2002.

Romilly (de) J. (2009). *Les Révélations de la mémoire [The Revelations of Memory]*. Éditions de Fallois.

Sautière, J. (2024). *Tout ce qui nous était à venir [Everything that was yet to Come]*. Gallimard.

Schur, M. (1972). *Freud: Living and dying*. International Universities Press.

Triandafillidis, A. (2010). Immortality strategies. *Adolescence, 28*(2), 449–460. https://doi.org/10.3917/ado.hs01.0047

Verdon, B. (2012). Jusqu'à la fin, le sein. Subversion dans le consentement au vieillissement [The Breast until the End: A Subversive Approach to Aging]. In F. Marty & V. Estellon (dir.), *Cliniques de l'extrême [Clinics of the Extreme]* (pp.195–212). Armand Colin.

Verdon, B. (2013). *Le vieillissement psychique [Psychical Aging]* (3rd updated edition). Puf. Que-sais-je ? 2022. https://doi.org/10.3917/puf.verdo.2013.01

Verdon, B. (2015). Le chemin vers l'inévitable. Freud, la vieillesse, la maladie, la mort [The Path towards the Inevitable: Freud, Old Age, Illness, Death]. In R. Perron & M. Missonnier (Eds.), *Sigmund Freud* (pp. 74–80). Cahiers de l'Herne.

Verdon, B. (2017). Retenir le temps qui passe. Tourments et entêtements dans l'œuvre tardive d'Eugène Ionesco [Grasping Time as It Slips Away: Torments and Stubbornness in the Late Works of Eugène Ionesco]. *Cliniques, 14*, 137–148. https://doi.org/10.3917/clini.014.0136

Verdon, B., & Rexand-Galais, F. (2021). À propos de « super vieillissement ». Idéalisation, hypomanie, renoncement [About "super-aging": Idealization, Hypomania, Renouncement]. *Gérontologie et Société, 43*(166), 201–214. https://doi.org/10.3917/gs1.166.0201

Villa, F. (2010). *La puissance du vieillir [The Force of Aging]*. Puf. https://doi.org/10.3917/puf.vill.2010.01

Woodward, K. M. (2002). Against wisdom: The social politics of anger and aging. *Cultural Critique, 51*, 186–218. https://doi.org/10.1353/cul.2002.0024

Woolf, V. (1926). *On being ill*. Renard Press, 2022.

Chapter 4
On Being an Oxymoron: A Sociocultural Psychology of Development with Older Age

Tania Zittoun

4.1 The "Foreign Country" of Older Age

The longer life expectancy people have acquired in many countries over the world is a recent phenomenon. In Switzerland, for instance, since the creation of retirement age at 65 in 1948, when the average life expectancy was of a few months after 65, until today, it has expanded over 20 years, up to 82.2 for men and 85.8 for women in 2023.[1] These numbers have to be understood together with the fact that there is an important increase of centenarians (Office fédéral de la statistique, 2021; Uittenhove et al., 2024). In other words, since less than a century, people have been lucky enough to start a period of their lives, after their mid-60s, that may last 20, 30, and for the luckiest ones, more than 40 years. This ageing population has finally triggered a great interest among politicians because of its financial and social implications. Psychology and social sciences have still much to learn about people's experiences during this long and new period of their lives—a new experience that Mary Sarton, herself aged 79, describes in the following terms: "There's no doubt that old age is a journey into a foreign country, so that one is being astonished by what is not possible. Or by what is different from anything that has gone before" (Sarton, 1993, p. 72).

In this paper, I wish to explore this "foreign country" that is ageing from the perspective of sociocultural developmental psychology. I first present some

[1] https://www.bfs.admin.ch/bfs/fr/home/statistiques/population/naissances-deces/esperance-vie.html/

T. Zittoun (✉)
Institute of Psychology and Education, Université de Neuchâtel, Neuchâtel, Switzerland
e-mail: tania.zittoun@unine.ch

T. Zittoun, F. Gfeller (eds.), *Ageing, Learning and Development*, Lifelong Learning Book Series 36, https://doi.org/10.1007/978-3-032-11057-2_4

important contributions in gerontology and psychology of ageing, before proposing a sociocultural psychology of development with age. Its specificity is to focus on the singularity of each developmental course, and on dynamics of sense-making. Here, I suggest that ageing may be associated with the emergence of modalities of sense making specific, or at least more visible, in older age. After a short methodological section, I support this argument with the cases of three older persons. I finally highlight the implications for developmental psychology of ageing.

4.2 Social and Psychological Approaches to Development with Age

In developmental psychology, ageing has been considered as a specific period of the lifespan for almost 50 years (Baltes & Mayer, 1999; Erikson et al., 1986). Nevertheless, if the first 15 years of life—from birth to adolescence—have been analysed in the most minute emotional, relational and cognitive changes, the psychological development that may occur during the last 20 or 40 years of the lifecourse is still largely unknown. Recently there has been a rapid increase of studies of ageing in gerontology and in psychology.

On the one hand, gerontology has developed a whole strand of ecological approaches, which consider that trajectories of ageing have to be understood together with the social and material environments in which the person lives (Bigonnesse & Chaudhury, 2020; Hoh et al., 2021; Lawton, 1985; Peace et al., 2007). Environments make pressing demands for an ageing person, who may experience body frailty or a relative loss of capacities; conversely, environments may also provide various facilitating affordances, which enable people, with the use of adequate resources, to carry on the activities that are important and relevant to them (Söderström et al., 2025). Studies have thus examined the lived environments (types of housing, institutional arrangements) (Lawton, 1992) as well as more relational support, notably through the studies of the "landscape of care" (Milligan & Wiles, 2010), showing that these caring environments could also be transformed along the person's trajectories (Kemp et al., 2013). These approaches have shed light on the fact that how persons age is not only dependent on their own body or mind, but that it is linked to complex interactions between them and their environment; to play with a well-known African saying, it needs a village to make an older person. However, in these approaches, the experience of the ageing persons themselves, and the fact that they have to adjust and learn to live in changing environments, is little considered.

On the other hand, since seminal debates on whether aging brings people to start new activities or rather to disengage (Cumming & Henry, 1961; Erikson et al., 1986; Havighurst et al., 1998), dominant studies in psychology, mostly conducted in the laboratory, focused on cognitive ageing, which examines the change, if not the decline, of various specific psychological functions, related among others to reasoning, remembering, or personality (Anderson & Craik, 2017; Ferring, 2018; Findsen & Formosa, 2011; Mather, 2010; Schaie, 2021; Verhaeghen, 2011). If these have enormously progressed, notably showing the unexpected flexibility and variability of cognitive capacities of older persons, they also raise the usual problem of ecological validity, and the absence of consideration for the embodied, relational and situated aspects of learning and development. Still, interestingly, one line of cognitive studies shows the importance of affects: cognition and memory performances are significantly better when the topics thought about are emotionally significant, or make sense, to older persons (Carstensen, 2019; Hess, 2022; Mather & Carstensen, 2005).

This would not really come as a surprise for a third line of approaches that focus more on meaning-making, studying older persons through their narration, with a more hermeneutic stance. Studies in cultural and narrative gerontology show that people engage in activities that make sense to them, which they may or may not want to verbalise, and may, but not always, connect to an overall search for consistency (Butler, 1963; Gubrium, 2011; Kenyon et al., 2011; Lieblich, 2014a, 2014b; Muller Mirza, 2025; Serrat et al., 2021). The importance of sense-making is also quite clear to psychoanalytical approaches, which have put to the fore how much older person may still be open to, or even yearning for change and development, especially about issues that matter and are of vital importance to them. Given that they assume that such interests are supported by desire, they also could show that thinking in older age is not only about the past, but is also oriented towards the future (Assoun, 2021; Bergeret-Amselek, 2016; Quinodoz, 2009; Verdon, 2012, 2025; Villa, 2010).

4.3 A Sociocultural Investigation of Development with Age

Acknowledging these findings—the importance of the social, material and symbolic environment in which people live, their potential for development, and the importance of sense-making and affects in the life of each unique older person—we started to sketch a sociocultural perspective of development in older age. From such a perspective, the sociocultural environment is not only what surrounds the person, but it provides the very means by which the person experiences the world (Boesch, 2007; Bruner, 2003; Cole, 1996; Valsiner, 2021; Vygotsky, 1986). Along their trajectories, it is through activities in dialogue with others and with the world, internalisation of social discourses, symbolic means, and cultural guidance, that people learn to act, move, think, make sense of their experience, and express themselves (Säljö, 2025). They may do so in a diversity of settings and domains; over time, they develop a configuration of spheres of experiences—a constellation of preferred activities, with the specific knowledge people have acquired, engaging their bodies and identity, and affective tonalities. These configurations of spheres of experience, some concrete, other more symbolic, constitute people's singular personal cultures, ways of acting and thinking, developed along unique trajectories. These configuration of spheres of experience function through an overall dynamic equilibrium, which corresponds to what Erikson called the need for continuity and consistency (Erikson, 1968). Thus, at every age, when people experience ruptures—a new situation requiring the establishment of one or more new spheres of experiences, or the disappearance of some, or their transformation—they tend to engage in learning and development processes characterising transitions (Zittoun, 2006, 2009). And thus, alone and with others, people participate in the making and the transformation of their social environment (Zittoun, 2012, 2022; Zittoun et al., 2013; Zittoun & Gillespie, 2016).

These principles are quite general and also apply to older persons. Hence, the use of new supporting tools, or the move to a nursing home, may engage transitions as occasions for learning and development in older age (Engeström et al., 2015; Zittoun et al., 2021). Yet from this perspective, there are also specificities in the development of older persons and in their modalities of sense-making. First, by having lived longer, they simply have been mostly exposed to more situations, and as they have experienced more ruptures, they had more occasions to learn or develop. Second, they also have had the unique opportunity of having seen the social and cultural world change itself, which gives them a reflective distance on their environment that younger people may not have (Grossen et al., 2020; Zittoun & Baucal, 2021). Hence, from these simple elements, one may suppose that older persons had more opportunities to learn from their long-lasting experience.

But what is it that is learned, what is specific to older age, if anything? Studies have long searched for some specific wisdom acquired with age, a type of balanced examination of circumstances; yet studies have shown that such type of reasoning is not specific to age (Ardelt & Oh, 2016; Baltes, 2004; Staudinger, 2008; Wink & Staudinger, 2016). Our sociocultural theoretical framework invites us to focus not primarily on cognitive or activities performances, but on sense-making, a process which is culturally mediated, and deeply dialogical—as one makes sense of experience in dialogue with others, and social discourses (Grossen, 2021; Marková, 2003, 2016). In addition, it also emphasises that sense-making is not disincarnated; it is connected to specific situated activities, which require skills, ways of doing, feeling, and being perceived by others, and perceiving by them (Zittoun, 2012, 2022). On this basis, we made the hypothesis that, if there are modalities of learning and development which are specific to older persons, then these should appear through people's variations of modalities of sense-making also uniquely achieved with age (Zittoun, 2019; Zittoun et al., 2013).

My reading of the literature and repeated interviews and conversations with older persons made me aware of something quite obvious—especially to psychoanalysts—yet often forgotten in practice: there are as many ways of ageing as there are many ways of living one's life. This brought me to accept, yet to modulate, many of the propositions found in the classical literature on the psychology of ageing. Hence if some older persons enjoy being active, that is, maintaining their activities or starting new ones, others may be less so (Fernandez-Ballesteros, 2008; Havighurst et al., 1998; Stenner et al., 2011); some people like to narrate their life trajectory and put them in perspective, while others prefer to focus on their daily lives and are less inclined to do so (Lieblich, 2014b). Consequently, any attempt to qualify the development of older persons needs to account both for change, and for such diversity; it needs to be a psychology of dynamics, not of states and results; and it has to focus on a diversity of processes, rather than on normative ways of acting or thinking.

A focus on sense-making thus invites us to consider diverse developmental dynamics taking place with age. First, as suggested in the literature, it is quite likely that some older persons may be wanting to focus on what matters to them. Yet focusing on sense-making may take many temporal orientations: it may involve activities oriented toward the past, such as reminiscing (Butler, 1963) or narrating one's life story, with the intention of grasping better or transmitting one's experience; it can be focused on the present to be enjoyed (Lieblich, 2014b); or it can be oriented toward the future, as when older persons get committed to political causes (Caissie, 2011; Hviid, 2022); and it can involve a way of getting more detached from daily concerns, such as in more spiritual or contemplative experiences (Laceulle, 2013; Quinodoz, 2009). Second, my hypothesis is that, if a person has developed interests and engagements over their lives, these are likely to remain present—as is the case for people committed to voluntary work (Muller Mirza, 2025), and in some case, become more prominent with time; these can simply be continued as these are, or require some reorganisation of daily activities and spheres of experiences; in any case, these may be recognisable as "thematic engagements" (Zittoun & Cabra, 2024). And third, across any of these other modalities of sense-making, some people may develop, over time, a style of handling issues, a general preferred type of positioning or interpreting their lives—a form of "dynamic pattern" (Zittoun, 2019). Of course, each person may manifest any of these modalities, in any form of combination, in link to the necessary changes and learning required by the many facets of ageing. This is what I now propose to further examine.

4.4 Methodology

We undertook a regional case study to understand the trajectories of ageing of older persons in their environment (Zittoun, 2026).[2] We limited the region to a Swiss Canton; in Switzerland, indeed, Cantons have autonomy to apply locally the national educational, social or public health policies, under the leadership of the cantonal and communal governments. A region is thus defined both by its geographical and its political boundaries. Geographically, this region, which we call the Vineyard region, is bordered on the one side by a lake, with wine-covered slopes gentling leading to its shore, and on the other side, by a chain of mountains separating the region from the neighbouring country. In this territory, there are two urban centres, and three rural valleys expanding between long, forest-covered mountain

[2] HomÂge, led by Tania Zittoun, with the collaboration of Fabienne Gfeller, Michèle Grossen, and others, supported by the Swiss National Fund.

chains. Due to these topographic specificities, the Vineyard region offers contrasting living environments for its ageing population—yet all are characterised by slopes.

On a political level, the Vineyard region is going through an important transformation of its social and housing policy regarding the older population. Hence, over the 5 years of our qualitative longitudinal research project, we could observe various and mutually related processes of change. At a sociogenetic level, we could follow the development and implementation of a new cantonal "medico-social plan" aimed at supporting people's aging in place (Gfeller et al., 2021, 2022); we also documented the creation and the first months of the life of a new building of flats with referents, the Beaulieu house, and followed some of its tenants before, during after moving in (Gfeller, in preparation; Gfeller & Grossen, 2025; Gfeller & Zittoun, 2023). At a more microgenetic scale, we did ethnographic observations of daily encounters with and between older persons in and outside of institutions (56 h of paper-pen observations), some of whom we then interviewed, and followed over a couple of months (N=10 for about 25 h of recorded interviews) (Zittoun et al., 2024). And to approach ontogenesis, we undertook a repeated interviews with a small group of older persons over 2½ years on which I will focus below. In addition, our dialogical perspective brought us to create a series of encounters aiming at stakeholders and research participants, including a theatrical forum around a theatre play which presented to the audience some of the dialogical tensions we observed in the region[3] (Zittoun, in preparation-b). Most of these data was collected through desk analysis, observation, participant observations, focus groups, and semi-structured, biographical or more open repeated interviews over 4 years, giving thus access to a wide range of qualitative data.

We thus constituted a sub-sample of seven persons with contrasting sociocultural status and housing modes in the Vineyard region. We had already met these persons as part of a parallel participatory project aiming to avoid social isolation in the region (Söderström et al., 2025).[4] In this former project, two researchers, Isabelle Kloepper and Aurora Ruggeri, had met a series of older persons living in three contrasting sub-regions.[5] These older persons accepted to join the present project and the same researchers continued to visit a selected subgroup of seven participants (among which one couple). The researchers went to visit them over 2 years and ½, every 3 months, that is, about 10 times, in their house or around, for repeated informal interviews lasting between 2 and 3 h; during the pandemic, some of the participants were also given a phone call between these meetings. The home-visits and

[3] Staging Age I & II, led by Tania Zittoun and Fabienne Gfeller, with the collaboration of the theatre author and director Nicolas Yazgi, and Michèle Grossen, supported by AGORA at the Swiss National Fund and co-produced by the theatre abc.

[4] ReliÂge, lead by Ola Söderström and Tania Zittoun, with the collaboration of Fabienne Gfeller, Isabelle Kloepper and Aurora Ruggeri, supported by the Health service of the Canton Neuchâtel.

[5] In the suburbs of the larger city in the region, in a very isolated village high in the hills, and in a large village in a valley.

walk-along interviews done with these persons were recorded; these recordings are currently under computer-assisted transcription, and manual analysis.

The analysis is carried out with the help of atlas-ti and uses both theoretically deduced categories and data-induced ones. It aims at retracing the social and material arrangements in which these persons live; the obstacles they meet and the social, material and symbolic resources they find; people's main domains of activity, including those that represent significant engagements, whether they take place in proximal or distal spheres of experiences; and across this material, dominant themes, reflexive moves, or ways of expressing oneself. In addition, I attempt to identify changes of these components over time (both in everyday life arrangements, and in ways of making sense of events).

The names of the participants as well as some details about their lives have been modified to preserve their privacy.

4.5 Case Studies

In what follows, I present the cases of a woman living alone, Agathe, and of a married couple, Emma and Marc. The choice is both theoretical—these cases are rich, and they share some features while being contrasting on others—and due to current state of the analytical work at the time of writing this chapter.[6] For each of these cases, I first present their life-story and current activities, networks and engagements, and then propose an analysis of emerging developmental dynamics.

4.5.1 Agathe

Agathe is, at the time of the visits, in her early 80s. She lives alone, in a small flat on the fourth floor of a building without elevator, in a working-class suburb of a city, not far from the lake. She is in relatively good health, only has a low and quickly diminishing eyesight. She was born in the mountains in the next canton in a large family; she moved to the region first to work in a factory in a valley, then in a tea-room in town, in a bakery in her current neighbourhood where she met her husband, and later, in a series of small shops and then supermarkets to demonstrate products. Eventually, she opened her own clothes shop, which she managed until her retirement. She and her husband had three children; she separated from him when their children were teenagers; he died since. She then had another partner with whom they shared retirement projects, and who also died. Now, she has fairly regular visits from her children who live in other Swiss cantons and from her grandchildren. She

[6] For a more complete analysis see (Zittoun, 2026).

mainly meets older women from the neighbourhood, and a younger divorced bus driver for whom she does some sewing and knitting work.

In terms of her daily activities, she takes care of her cooking, eats well and regularly, and likes to enjoy a glass of the regional aperitive on her balcony before dinner. The balcony is her preferred place in the flat for its view on the lake, reason for which she also would prefer not to move to another type of housing. As younger retiree, she did some charity work for a large organisation where she met many people and groups with which she maintained activities for years. Now, she still goes regularly for walks in the region, on the lake side, alone or with other older women—sometimes to do what she calls her "good deed". She took a seasonal card for boat trips, and before the covid, had also a train card in order to travel in the country for daily excursions (she renounced driving years back). She still knits, which she can do even with her diminished sight. She listens to TV and radio quiz—she says she always "liked numbers and the like".

She has pleasure talking about her life to the researchers, although she does not mention much her more painful past, from which she prefers to part—she thus threw away the pictures of her husband and avoids mentioning her daughter-in-law with whom she had arguments. On the other hand, she is oriented toward the future: she is giving some of her clothes in the eventuality of having to move to a more adapted housing, she still explores possibilities of finding a partner for a camping-car trip she wishes to do. Hence, on the whole, she is aware of her age—she often says "I am an old one"—while being active and quite energetic. She reports that when she talks to older friends who are desperate (for instance after losing their husband), she tells them that they are not alone; "One as to continue alone, with those who remain"; and "One has to stay busy, one has to stay busy". She also says that she enjoys her time and does not expect to meet another partner—"I have a good life now, you don't want to put an old geezer on my back!"[7]—with an irony which is between contentment and renouncement—she also says "it's my fate to finish alone", to which she adds: "Better to be alone than in bad company".

In the past years, significant events were connected to trips she undertook to other continents with friends or alone. She knitted woollen socks for children of a mountain hospital abroad and insisted on delivering them herself in her very late 70s. The first time, she went there with a friend; the second time, as the friend was now deceased, she went alone. During the first trip she told her friend: "If I die there, I stay here, they can burn me!". The second time, "I explained the traveling agent where I had my papers, in case something happened to me. But nothing happened to me, I came back!". There, she met a cook in his mid-30s and his family and staid with them; later, they met in Switzerland. She wishes she could go back but admits she is now too old. The only trip she still wishes to do is a 2–3 weeks long camping-car tour; yet she has not found the right partner to do so. She also tells the researchers that she always has underwear and a toothbrush in her handbag, to be

[7] In French: « Moi j'ai une belle vie, maintenant, vous ne voulez pas me mettre un vieux lulu sur le dos ».

ready to go for a trip. These improbable travels, the readiness for surprise, the courage also for a woman from relatively modest circumstances, made the two researchers note that Agathe was quite an adventurer.

Two other events stand out of her narration. First, Agathe explains how, after her separation from her husband, she met a series of difficulties because they didn't formally divorce. She was held responsible for his debts, and later, did not receive the pension she was entitled to. She told us that she directly wrote to Ruth Dreifuss, then state minister in charge of social affairs, a woman known for her defence of social rights and especially active for woman's rights: "I wrote that I didn't write to congratulate her (…) but to ask her to instruct the personnel of the pension offices (in the case of separated persons). (…) It took her three weeks to respond, but in the meantime, I had received a note saying that they had checked the accounts and would wire my pension. She simply responded that she had studied my case, and that on such and such date the pension office fixed it. But if I hadn't done anything!"

Similarly, she more recently decided to suspend her train yearly pass, which she had had for 25 years, because of the covid (a general card which for a few thousands Swiss francs a year, allows to travel freely on the entire transport network in the country, including trains, buses and boats). In such cases, the train company should reimburse the part of the sum corresponding to the remaining months of validity. So she says: "I wrote to the director of the Swiss Railway company, to ask them to put things in order. (…) I made calculations, (…) and I said, I don't ask you to reimburse me the card, but perhaps you could offer my daily travel cards to young people in need, because I don't feel like traveling anymore. They responded that they could not find trace of my 25 past yearly cards; (…) but what they didn't know, is that I had everything, all the yearly cards, and the receipts, it's all classified!" and thus, proving she had been loyal to this card for so many years, she obtained a compensation.

4.5.2 *"One Has to Defend Oneself"*

To understand this surprising combination of courage, boldness, and unusual capacity to defend her rights characterising Agathe's stories, we can examine how she presents herself notably though some childhood memories she shares with the researchers. First, one can relate her skills—knitting, accounting—to a childhood memory:

> I am old, now... But when we started school, it was better to know how to knit, in order not to stay behind… I had three older sisters, I had put in my mind… when my mother wanted to teach me, I said, 'No, I don't go to school to learn knitting, I want to learn to read, to write, I don't want to knit.' (…) Then suddenly 8 days before the school started, my mother often told me that story, I asked my mother, 'don't you want to teach me so that I am not the last one?'

In this anecdote, Agathe presents herself as someone who knew early how to argue for what she wanted, and in that case, to learn to read and write—not the knitting activity much more expected for women; she defines herself against the others. Interestingly, this memory crystallises both her later engagements: using her mind to calculate, write and think, and knitting. It is combining these skills that she could both keep tracks of her expenses so as to fight for her financial rights, and open a shop on her own. Knitting itself is the activity she has maintained all her life, as a way to help and give others, as with the socks for a mountain hospital.

Second, her capacity to defend her rights also seems to echo another anecdote: "Actually… we were eight children. We were raised quite straight. But we had enough to eat, we were taught to work, we were clean, and I think it also teaches to defend oneself. And later with everything that happens to me…". Hence, "to defend oneself", because nobody else will do that, seems to give her the boldness to write to these important state or company representatives—something which is very uncommon in Switzerland—undertakings which here were successful. This does not prevent Agathe to be very much caring for others, as we have seen: she helps the young bus driver in the memory of his deceased mother, she knits for children from other continents, she takes older women of the neighbourhood for daytrips, or coffee. She also was very generous with the two researchers that visited her regularly.

Agathe has thus had a life story characterised by many moves and bumps: growing up in a modest family, little formal education, moving canton to find work, marrying and separating with two children, going through a large variety of jobs until developing the skills and confidence to open and manage her own shop, living alone yet having the skills and courage to develop and maintain a good-enough social network—Agathe is now an older woman, autonomous and yet not lonely, reflexive on her past and open to the future.

Interestingly, through her narration, we see emerging two domains of interests, both grown out of from initial childhood curiosities—counting, and knitting. Both were maintained along her life trajectories, probably more or less foregrounded or backgrounded, willingly or less so—e.g., when running a household after a husband left—yet coming back to the fore later in her life. In effect, opening a clothes shop seems, in this light, a perfect combination of these two interests, which somehow became engagements (Zittoun, 2023). Indeed, as a retiree, that she still knits for others, and proudly keeps her accounts tidy, indicates how these are invested, both as activities considered for themselves, as well as relational means or resources to meet others and maintain dialogue with them. More transversally, through Agathe's capacity and boldness to address figures of authority to fight for her right, we see manifested her deep conviction that "one has to defend oneself"—a moto, or pattern, that can be found all along her complex life course (Zittoun, 2019). Finally, in a fainter mode, Agathe seems also to have slowly turn to calmer, more meditative activities—a boat tour on the lake, a walk on the lakeside, or simply, sitting on one's balcony to enjoy the beautiful landscape with a glass of aperitive.

4.5.3 Emma and Marc

In their early 90s at the start of the project, Marc and Emma live together in a small villa with a garden in the same popular neighbourhood than Agathe. They are in relatively good health, yet during the 2½ years of the study, Marc's mobility has progressively reduced; he started to walk with sticks, and later had back problems and an infection that brought him to the hospital. With time, he also needed a hearing-aid and sometimes lost the thread of the conversation. Emma's memory also slows down. At home, they installed handles in various places and learned to use the stairs backwards; they have occasional, yet increasing help from neighbours or family, and eventually the visit of a nurse. Nevertheless, they go along their daily activities, which they seem to share harmoniously (cooking, washing up). Along their visits, the two researchers feel progressively closer and touched by this couple. A form of ritual did develop: they were invited for lunch and brought a dessert; Marc prepares anecdotes and tricks to demonstrate, Emma some memories or notebooks to share. Marc and Emma seem very close, completing and at times supporting each other in the dialogue—inviting the other to tell a story, or Emma gently reminding Marc of the line of his narrative.[8] They thus seem to have built a strong complicity and complementarity; they wish to die at home together.

Marc and Eva were also born and raised in the mountains in the next canton. Marc did a technical school and worked in the local industry; Emma studied to become a schoolteacher. They started their working life in the mountains, Marc biking kilometres down to take the train and go to school and work lower in the valley, Emma hiking or skiing to the remote village school in which she worked. When they were a young couple, Marc accepted a teaching position in a vocational school in the Vineyard region. Emma and Marc married to facilitate Emma's residency rights, and the young couple moved to a large town. They borrowed money from their friends and built their little house, where they first lived in very simple conditions, and progressively turned into a more comfortable house. Since they moved, Emma did a few replacements at school, but didn't take a stable job anymore. They had four children and now have grandchildren and great-grand-children that they see weekly and call regularly.

In their daily life, Marc and Emma go weekly to the market in town where they also have coffee with one of their children; they attend the church. They take their car weekly to explore and visit various spots in the regions, mainly in the mountains, where they usually eat a home-made prepared picnic. For instance, to celebrate their wedding anniversary, they did an unusual car trip, with a richer picnic; they tell with enthusiasm the adventures that occurred to them that day, and especially, a scary incident on the snow-covered road. They have friends who are artists and teachers; they stopped visiting museums, which starts to be too difficult for them. Marc and Emma share their interest in gardening; with time, as it became

[8] At the same time, they seem to respect each other's intimacy: she doesn't know all what he has in his workshop, and he had never read some of the notebooks she will be reading aloud.

more difficult for them, they however decided to split the garden with neighbours that had none, and some of the tasks are helped by their son. They actively cultivate vegetable and fruits in their part of their garden, and they eat from it. He comments: "We look a bit like crazy people in the neighbourhood. At our age. I planted two apricot trees last fall. People say, when are they going to have apricots?".[9] They know the name of plants and trees, and use with great ease these technical terms. They both are attentive to their food: they eat Budwig cream in the morning, wholesome cereals and fresh vegetables with meat or beans for lunch, and a soup in the evening. In addition, they both have a great knowledge of animals and especially birds, that they observe daily; they know their names, their songs, and their habits. They speak about the joy of observing the redstarts at the water spot in their garden, of listening to the blackbird, or admiring a rare white-throated dipper ("cincle plongeur") installed by a spring in the neighbourhood. During one of the visits, Marc, made clear that he is "a scientist" and Emma "a literary"; and this seems to summary their main interests… but not exactly so.

Emma seems to have developed a specific line of interests related to writing. She keeps diaries and notebooks. She started to do so as young woman, writing these, with poems, observations, and sketches and added pictures and postcards. She still writes down daily events, notes about what they did, who they met, etc. During the interviews, she can thus refer to events, visits to their children, etc. with the help of this journal as resource for remembering and sharing. She also writes notebooks of interesting words, linguistic expressions and sayings. During the researcher's visits, she thus shares some of her drawing, collection of expression comprising names of animals, etc. Over time, she progressively gives more space to a more personal notebook.[10] At one of the meetings, she says that she wishes to read some part of her diary: "I am going to read this story. My life is made of other things, but there is a passage of my life which I have lived in Village... it must not fall into oblivion. I don't know if my children will read it once, or if my notebooks will be thrown away before, but so, someone would have had listened to it"[11] (3.02.22). During this session, Emma reads for over 2 h from these diaries, about her first teaching position in a small village in the mountains, a position that she could not refuse given her fragile status as foreigner. She describes the dire living and hygienic conditions, the

[9] « On passe un petit peu pour les fous dans le quartier. A notre âge. J'ai planté deux abricotier l'automne passé. Les gens ils disent quand est-ce qu'ils auront les abricots ? » (Marc, 15.04.21).

[10] In response to this movement, one of the researchers offered to scan these notebooks, which pleased Emma very much.

[11] « Alors je vous lis un peu cette histoire. Ma vie est faite d'autres choses comme chez vous, mais il y a un passage de ma vie qui est celui que j'ai vécu à Village qui est.. il faut.. Il faut pas faire passer ça… dans les oubliettes. Je ne sais pas si un jour mes enfants liront ça... ou bien si les cahiers seront débarrassés avant, mais voilà, il y aura quelqu'un qui aura entendu ». (90:14 ¶ 166, Emma, 3.02.22).

state of the children, the characters surroundings, the hardship of the climate (winters at −35 °C), as well as the beauty of the nature. Here is one of the striking anecdotes. When she took her position, she had to replace an old teacher at retirement age. She realised then that she was totally deaf. Thus, the children, from different school age, never had properly learnt to read, and when trying to, where making strange sounds. Her first job was therefore to alphabetise the whole class! All this is described with meticulously chosen words—and Emma insists that she wanted it to be so, in order to capture these unique memories that haunted her for years at night. She seems reassured to hear the researchers tell her how these words transport and touch them.

On his side, Marc appears curious about everything and enjoying sharing his knowledge and life experience. He has a workshop, where he keeps building things—he built "soapboxes"—home-made cars—for his children and grandchildren, he builds things for the house and for himself… He prepares an "exercise" for each researchers' visit: a mind-game, an enigma to solve, or a technical demonstration. Once, he demonstrated how one can "break the wall of sound" with a folded paper; another time, he attached the researchers' hands with a rope with knots and they had to find out how to get out of it. Marc's other great engagement is the mountain. Although both Emma and Marc enjoyed hiking and skiing, Marc in particular, joined the Alpine Club, where he learned high-mountain techniques, and with whom he discovered many of the Swiss mountain refuges. He also took Emma on some high-mountain hikes:

> Once I knew how to use the ropes and ensure someone thanks to the courses of the Alpine Club I took my wife, the two of us we did these things... sometimes I think, we had no mobile phones, we were crossing these glaciers… these two oldies in this nature, that was a bit mad. But we are here, we are here, and we have memories (15.04.21).

Marc continued high-mountain hiking until recently: he proudly speaks about a famously difficult climb done when he was over 70; he mentions a high-mountain hike 7 years ago, and he did country skiing until he was 85. As accomplished mountaineer, Marc seems to fight again his progressive physical losses—he often starts the interviews by saying "I am broken now" or "I am old now". However, he very much enjoys telling anecdotes about past exploits and hikes, often interrupting a boring or more practical conversation to do so. Marc does so with the use of photo albums and hiking maps as resources to discuss places where he has been; he often punctuates this with comments such as "I was a bit mad" or "that's beautiful memories". Marc thus enjoys telling anecdotes and jokes, often using humour to reduce some of the limitation of ageing. For instance, once Emma speaks about the word "oxymoron" written in her notebook; Marc says "I am an oxymoron", and when asked why, he says "Because I am a young old man" ("un jeune vieilliard"); and later he would add: "I am a nyctalopic oxymoron".

4.5.4 Aha and Against Oblivion

Marc and Emma are growing old together, surrounded by a rich and well-functioning network of family and friends, later completed by professional homecare. They are aware of their luck of living in the house they built for themselves and their family. If both had a very active life, this seems to have been progressively transformed. They still go in the neighbourhood and to town, and enjoy their tours by car, discovering places and picnicking. A large part of their daily life is now centred in or around the house and its garden, even though they have to progressively learn to move around with diminishing physical activity, or to readjust their gardening habits. There, they seem to have developed a deep observation of nature and its beauty, which they do in a not only contemplative, but also active and informed way.

In terms of the evolution of interests, Emma's engagement in writing seems to be in continuity with her work as teacher, and perhaps a marginalised one. She developed her own passion as "word collector", which may feed in the couple's rich vocabulary for nature. Her daily journal writing also supports the couple's progressive weaker memory (Säljö, 2022)—she at times corrects her husband's dates confusion with the help of the notes. In addition, she had developed her creativity in these personal and illustrated notebooks, as well her own reflexivity over her impressive youth years. She doesn't remember when she wrote these stories, yet she often came back to it, adding drawings, pictures and postcards to illustrate them. And as mentioned, she took a particular care in choosing the words that would enable the reader to feel and see what she experienced them. She therefore seems to be taken in a double movement of active reminiscence and creative elaboration, and of sharing and transmitting these experiences (Coleman, 2005; Erikson et al., 1986).[12]

There also seem to be a great continuity in Marc's scientific engagements, from his work as engineer to his professional life as teacher in physics, his passion to create and construct small cars with his grand-children, and his pleasure of tricking and surprising the researchers. Indeed, when he sets an enigma, or asks for a calculation, he enjoys particularly the moment of revealing the trick, or solving the enigma, or telling the last line of a joke—the discovery (Stenner, 2017; Zittoun, 2023), or aha moment, a notion he himself introduced.[13] On the other hand, his great passion for mountaineering had to be transformed from a proximal experience to a distal one (Zittoun, 2020)—from experiencing the mountains, to remembering his past adventures, with the use of various resources, and sharing them in stories that usually end

[12] It so happens that it is the researchers that became the audience of these; one can hear a bit of bitterness or sadness in Emma's mention of the fact that her children are not interested—she seems to strongly feel that someone has to know.

[13] Not in the most explicit way, though—here is the story he told: one day a mathematician explained him the Aha moment: a zoologist from Basel hanged bananas in a monkey's cage and placed three wooden boxes in the corners, to verify if the monkey would be able to pile them up to reach the bananas. After disposing the boxes, as he was about to leave the cage, the zoologist passed under the hanging bananas—that's when the monkey jumped on his shoulder (and got the bananas)... Emma had to comment "therefore the Aha".

up with a pun or a joke. Here, there is thus a transformation of the engagement. Through both, and his pleasure of sharing jokes and good words—such as him being an oxymoron—there seem to be a common pattern: Marc's pleasure to discover (the Aha moment).

4.6 Developing in Older Age

Agathe, Marc and Emma by chance all came from the same mountains in the nearby Canton, and moved to the Vineyard region, in a small working-class neighbourhood; yet they dealt with their lives and ageing in contrasting manners. In life-course terms, they seem to stem from the same socioeconomic background, although not strictly to the same cohort (Agathe is 10 years younger than the couple); the case of Marc and Emma in addition beautifully illustrates the importance of interrelated lives (Levy et al., 2005). Yet their developmental trajectories are different. To account for these specificities, I proposed to focus not on some individual characteristics—their personality, their dispositions—yet to focus on their activities and modalities of sense-making: their relationship to time, their interests and engagements, and their transformation over time.

Agathe has, for different reasons—childhood, difficult marriage—learned to deal with things alone; and she seems to be ambivalent about the possibility of sharing intimacy again. She is not so keen on reexploring the past (not with the researchers) and yet is deeply engaged in her daily life, where she feels it is important to be busy and to be with others. She is not keen on religion; and although she likes her view, she does not engage in much contemplation. Her life circumstances have brought her to all kinds of unqualified jobs, yet through all this, she has chosen to imagine and then actively explore the world far beyond the confines of her daily life. She has kept an interest in numbers and in knitting, which both became an engagement; she was once able to open her own shop, and she knitted socks to offer. The dynamic pattern emerging through her life story is that of "standing for one's right", and so she likes to present herself. Yet while doing so, she is also generous and caring for other people around her.

Marc and Emma dealt with most of their adult lives as a couple living in harmony, and they have a rich family life. They both are keen on exploring and sharing their past, albeit in different modalities. Emma, who seems to be a collector of words and memories, is now engaged in a creative process of writing and illustrating her life; more specifically, she wishes to transmit some vital experiences (Brown & Reavey, 2015). Marc has had two main engagements—the mountain and science and technologies. Mountaineering, he was able to both live alone and share with Emma and many others; it is only lately that his body weakened and that he had to renounce to these activities. Yet it transforms his proximal sphere experience in a distal one (Zittoun & Gillespie, 2015): he becomes very keen on telling mountain anecdotes and remembering his exploits. Regarding physics, he has always been a teacher, and he still loves to share his knowledge and enthusiasms for tricks—he appears especially keen on Aha moments—a discovery pattern. Both are religious; and with age, they developed also more contemplative activities, such as bird watching (Tornstam, 1997). Yet this activity is still informed by their respective previous engagements, Emma through her love for words and collections, and Marc full of anecdotes.

Hence, in terms of development in the lifecourse we can first observe that, with time, and as their social lives and their physical capacities change, these three persons had to develop new skills and resources to maintain a satisfying daily life—they change diet, rearrange their houses or the size of their trips, etc. All experience physical losses which worry them—Agathe's view, Marc's mobility—and deal with at times with anger, and at times, with humour, which may be an important resource in ageing (Anaut, 2014). More specifically, if we put our observations in dialogue with our hypothesis about development with age, we can see, first, that these three persons have contrasting positions toward reminiscing (Butler, 1963; Coleman, 2005). Agathe is not so much keen on reminiscing the past, while the two others are, with a strong need to share and transmit; yet all speak about their death, without much fear (Quinodoz, 2009). Regarding the hypothesis proposed here, all have developed and transformed their engagements with time, Agathe as lateral fil rouge, Emma as creative hobby, and Marc as main professional and leisure activity. All have developed through their activities a clear style or a leitmotiv—a cultivation of discovery (Marc), the pride of defending oneself (Agathe), the need to save things from oblivion (Emma). All, in their own ways, also deal with the paradoxes of growing older: Agathe is both proud to be independent from others, and caring for others; Marc feels both young in his mind and old in his body; Emma wishes to retain something alive from a time long gone.

Of course, what is presented here is very limited—people's life cannot be summarised in one or two themes; and also, it is to be read within the limits of the method chosen here—open ended repeated interviews with a small number of older persons, during which they also chose how they present themselves within the relation they develop with the researchers. Yet, still, these observations are consonant with, and expand, what we have observed elsewhere (Zittoun, 2019, 2023, in preparation-a).

The psychology of development in older age is only starting to explore this new continent (Sarton, 1993). In this chapter, along the cases of three persons, I have suggested that each person is unique, yet defined in and through their relationships to others, and has a very own life trajectory. The specificity of the approach proposed here is that it takes in account the sociocultural situatedness of the person over time. It admits that who we become, emerges from the multiple encounters we have with the worlds, and notably, through the activities, material and symbolic activities, we maintain with time, in one or many places, alone or with others—activities to which we feel more or less acknowledged, enjoy pleasure or pain, or recognize ourselves more or less (Zittoun, 2012), and with the social and cultural discourses and expectations that have are guiding our lives and that we more or less internalize or resist to (Valsiner, 1998). Over the lifecourse, these spheres of experience form a complex and constantly evolving configuration; and with age, these spheres of experiences and life domains may slowly be reorganised, change their relative importance, or realigned. People may thus feel tensions and conflicts, between social requirements and personal engagements, between what they wish to do and what they can, or within their experiences of temporality. Interestingly, some persons also find creative way to contain and transform the tensions they are exposed to, as when Marc expresses them as being an oxymoron. Drawing both on different insights in psychology (Hess, 2022; Villa, 2010), I thus suggest that, with less pressure and demands from the social and professional world, with age, these reorganisations may take place along affective attractors—along what makes sense, existential sense, for the person, and/or, where there is pleasure in doing and thinking (Zittoun, 2023).

Altogether, this exploration thus suggests that, with ageing, like the razing evening sun, the reliefs of one's life become more visible: retrospectively, dominant engagements come to the fore, like the crest of mountain chain visible from afar; contemplating these, one may recognize recurrent patterns, expressing deeper undercurrent, almost like the signature of one's life work.

References

Anaut, M. (2014). Créativité, humour et résilience avec l'avancée en âge. In L. Ploton & B. Cyrulnik (Eds.), *Résilience et personnes âgées* (pp. 19–38). Odile Jacob. https://doi.org/10.3917/oj.ploto.2014.01.0019

Anderson, N. D., & Craik, F. I. M. (2017). 50 years of cognitive aging theory. *The Journals of Gerontology: Series B, 72*(1), 1–6. https://doi.org/10.1093/geronb/gbw108

Ardelt, M., & Oh, H. (2016). Theories of wisdom and aging. In V. L. Bengtson & R. A. J. Settersten (Eds.), *Handbook of theories of aging* (3rd ed., pp. 559–619). Springer.

Assoun, P.-L. (2021). Le retour à l'inconscient du vieillissement. Le désir à l'épreuve du temps. In C. Racin, C. Caleca, & P. Gutton (Eds.), *Le vieillissement saisi par le soin* (pp. 41–63). Editions In press.

Baltes, P. B. (2004). *Wisdom as orchestration of mind and virtue*. Max Planck Institute/unpublished manuscript.

Baltes, P. B., & Mayer, K. U. (Eds.). (1999). *The Berlin aging study: Aging from 70 to 100*. Cambridge University Press.

Bergeret-Amselek, C. (2016). Qui sont ces nouveaux analysants de plus de 70 ans? Quel est leur désir? In M.-F. Fuchs (Ed.), *Comment l'esprit vient aux vieux. Penser et vivre un vieillissement durable* (pp. 103–112). érès.

Bigonnesse, C., & Chaudhury, H. (2020). The landscape of "aging in place" in gerontology literature: Emergence, theoretical perspectives, and influencing factors. *Journal of Aging and Environment, 34*(3), 233–251. https://doi.org/10.1080/02763893.2019.1638875

Boesch, E. E. (2007). The sound of the violon. In W. J. Lonner & S. A. Hayes (Eds.), *Discovering cultural psychology* (pp. 177–195). Information Age Publishing.

Brown, S. D., & Reavey, P. (2015). *Vital memory and affect: Living with a difficult past*. Routledge.

Bruner, J. S. (2003). *Making stories: Law, literature, life*. Harvard University Press.

Butler, R. N. (1963). The life review: An interpretation of reminiscence in the aged. *Psychiatry, 26*, 65–76.

Caissie, L. (2011). The raging grannies: Narrative construction of gender and aging. In G. Kenyon, E. Bohlmeijer, & W. L. Randall (Eds.), *Storying later life: Issues, investigations, and interventions in narrative gerontology* (pp. 126–142). Oxford University Press.

Carstensen, L. L. (2019). Integrating cognitive and emotion paradigms to address the paradox of aging. *Cognition & Emotion, 33*(1), 119–125. https://doi.org/10.1080/02699931.2018.1543181

Cole, M. (1996). *Cultural psychology. A once and future discipline*. The Belknap Press of Harvard University Press.

Coleman, P. G. (2005). Reminiscence: Developmental, social and clinical perspectives. In M. L. Johnson, V. L. Bengtson, P. G. Coleman, & T. B. L. Kirkwood (Eds.), *The Cambridge handbook of age and ageing* (pp. 301–309). Cambridge University Press.

Cumming, E., & Henry, W. E. (1961). *Growing old, the process of disengagement*. Basic Books.

Engeström, Y., Kajamaa, A., & Nummijoki, J. (2015). Double stimulation in everyday work: Critical encounters between home care workers and their elderly clients. *Learning, Culture and Social Interaction, 4*, 48–61. https://doi.org/10.1016/j.lcsi.2014.07.005

Erikson, E. H. (1968). *Identity: Youth and crisis*. Faber & Faber.

Erikson, E. H., Erikson, J. M., & Kivnick, H. Q. (1986). *Vital involvement in old age*. Norton.

Fernandez-Ballesteros, R. (2008). *Active aging: The contribution of psychology*. Hogrefe & Huber.

Ferring, D. (2018). Memory in old age. A lifespan perspective. In B. Wagoner (Ed.), *Oxford Handbook of Culture and Memory* (pp. 237–256). Oxford University Press.

Findsen, B., & Formosa, M. (2011). *Lifelong learning in later life: A handbook on older adult learning*. Sense Publishers.

Gfeller, F. (in preparation). *Les appartements avec encadrement: La naissance d'un lieu de vie pour personnes âgées*. Antipodes.

Gfeller, F., & Grossen, M. (2025). Moving house in older age: Challenges and resources for the sense of self-continuity. In T. Zittoun & F. Gfeller (Eds.), *Ageing, learning and development. Sociocultural and psychoanalytical perspectives on growing older*. Springer.

Gfeller, F., Grossen, M., Cabra, M., & Zittoun, T. (2022). Réformes politiques face au vieillissement démographique: Diversité des perspectives dans la mise en œuvre d'une politique socio-sanitaire. *Revue pluridisciplinaire d'Education par et pour les Doctorant-e-s, 1*(1), Article 1. https://doi.org/10.57154/journals/red.2022.e990

Gfeller, F., & Zittoun, T. (2023). A new housing mode in a regional landscape of care: A sociocultural psychological study of a boundary object. *Human Arenas*. https://doi.org/10.1007/s42087-023-00363-5

Gfeller, F., Zittoun, T., Grossen, M., & Cabra, M. (2021). *L'offre de logement pour personnes âgées dans le canton de Neuchâtel. Évolution, état des lieux, tensions*. (Rapport de Recherche HomAge 1) Université de Neuchâtel. https://www.unine.ch/ipe/home/recherche/personnes-agees/homage.html

Grossen, M. (2021). When dialogism crosses the frontiers of psychology. In N. Muller Mirza & M. Dos Santos Mamed (Eds.), *Dialogical approaches and tensions in learning and development: At the frontiers of the mind* (pp. 13–32). Springer International. https://doi.org/10.1007/978-3-030-84226-0_2

Grossen, M., Zittoun, T., & Baucal, A. (2020). Learning and developing over the life-course: A sociocultural approach. *Learning, Culture and Social Interaction*, 100478. https://doi.org/10.1016/j.lcsi.2020.100478

Gubrium, J. F. (2011). Narrative events and biographical construction in old age. In G. Kenyon, E. Bohlmeijer, & W. L. Randall (Eds.), *Storying later life: Issues, investigations, and interventions in narrative gerontology* (pp. 39–50). Oxford University Press.

Havighurst, R. J., Neugarten, B. L., & Tobin, S. S. (1998). Disengagement and patterns of aging. In M. P. Lawton & T. A. Salthouse (Eds.), *Essential papers on the psychology of aging* (pp. 68–85). New York University Press.

Hess, T. M. (2022). Subjective perceptions of cognitive costs. Determinants and impact on motivation and engagement. In G. Sedek, T. M. Hess, & D. R. Touron (Eds.), *Multiple pathways of cognitive aging: Motivational and contextual influences* (pp. 19–39). Oxford University Press.

Hoh, J. W. T., Lu, S., Yin, Y., Feng, Q., Dupre, M. E., & Gu, D. (2021). Environmental gerontology. In D. Gu & M. E. Dupre (Eds.), *Encyclopedia of gerontology and population aging* (pp. 1686–1693). Springer International Publishing. https://doi.org/10.1007/978-3-030-22009-9_1126

Hviid, P. (2022). Aged experience – A cultural developmental investigation. *Learning, Culture and Social Interaction, 37*, 100386. https://doi.org/10.1016/j.lcsi.2020.100386

Kemp, C. L., Ball, M. M., & Perkins, M. M. (2013). Convoys of care: Theorizing intersections of formal and informal care. *Journal of Aging Studies, 27*(1), 15–29. https://doi.org/10.1016/j.jaging.2012.10.002

Kenyon, G., Bohlmeijer, E., & Randall, W. L. (Eds.). (2011). *Storying later life: Issues, investigations, and interventions in narrative gerontology*. Oxford University Press.

Laceulle, H. (2013). Self-realisation and ageing: A spiritual perspective. In J. Baars, J. Dohmen, A. Grenier, & C. Phillipson (Eds.), *Ageing, meaning and social structure: Connecting critical and humanistic gerontology* (pp. 55–79). Policy Press.

Lawton, M. P. (1985). The elderly in context: Perspectives from environmental psychology and gerontology. *Environment and Behavior, 17*(4), 501–519. https://doi.org/10.1177/0013916585174005

Lawton, M. P. (1992). A future agenda for congregate housing research. *Journal of Housing For the Elderly, 9*(1–2), 167–182. https://doi.org/10.1300/J081V09N01_12

Levy, R., Ghisletta, P., Le Goff, J.-M., Spini, D., & Widmer, E. (Eds.). (2005). *Towards an interdisciplinary perspective on the life course*. Elsevier.

Lieblich, A. (2014a). Narrating your life after 65 (or: To tell or not to tell, that is the question). *New Directions for Child and Adolescent Development, 2014*(145), 71–83. https://doi.org/10.1002/cad.20068

Lieblich, A. (2014b). *Narratives of positive aging: Seaside stories*. Oxford University Press.

Marková, I. (2003). *Dialogicality and social representations: The dynamics of mind*. Cambridge University Press.

Marková, I. (2016). *The dialogical mind: Common sense and ethics*. Cambridge University Press.

Mather, M. (2010). Aging and cognition. *Wiley Interdisciplinary Reviews: Cognitive Science, 1*(3), 346–362. https://doi.org/10.1002/wcs.64

Mather, M., & Carstensen, L. L. (2005). Aging and motivated cognition: The positivity effect in attention and memory. *Trends in Cognitive Sciences, 9*(10), 496–502. https://doi.org/10.1016/j.tics.2005.08.005

Milligan, C., & Wiles, J. (2010). Landscapes of care. *Progress in Human Geography, 34*(6), 736–754. https://doi.org/10.1177/0309132510364556

Muller Mirza, N. (2025). Developmental processes and meaning-making in volunteering activity. In T. Zittoun & F. Gfeller (Eds.), *Ageing, learning and development. Sociocultural and psychoanalytical perspectives on growing older*. Springer.

Office fédéral de la statistique. (2021). *La population de la Suisse en 2020*. https://www.bfs.admin.ch/bfs/fr/home/statistiques/population.assetdetail.19964431.html

Peace, S., Wahl, H.-W., Mollenkopf, H., & Oswald, F. (2007). Environment and aging. In J. Bond, S. Peace, F. Dittmann-Kohli, & G. J. Westerhof (Eds.), *Ageing in society: European perspectives on gerontology* (3rd ed., pp. 209–233). Sage.

Quinodoz, D. (2009). Growing old: A psychoanalyst's point of view. *International Journal of Psychoanalysis, 90*(4), 773–793. https://doi.org/10.1111/j.1745-8315.2009.00166.x

Säljö, R. (2022). Development, ageing and hybrid minds: Growth and decline, and ecologies of human functioning in a sociocultural perspective. *Learning, Culture and Social Interaction, 37*, 100465. https://doi.org/10.1016/j.lcsi.2020.100465

Säljö, R. (2025). Cognitive adaptation, hybrid minds and ageing: Epistemic practices in cumulative cultures. In T. Zittoun & F. Gfeller (Eds.), *Ageing, learning anddevelopment. Sociocultural and psychoanalytical perspectives on growing older*. Springer.

Sarton, M. (1993). *Endgame: A journal of the seventy-ninth year*. Women's Press.

Schaie, K. W. (2021). History of adult cognitive aging research. In K. W. Schaie & S. L. Willis (Eds.), *Handbook of the psychology of aging* (9th ed., pp. 3–17). Academic Press. https://doi.org/10.1016/B978-0-12-816094-7.00017-9

Serrat, R., Chacur, K., & Villar, F. (2021). Ageing activisms: A narrative exploration of older adults' experiences of political participation. *Sociological Research Online, 28*. https://doi.org/10.1177/13607804211025310
Söderström, O., Zittoun, T., Gfeller, F., Ruggeri, A., & Kloepper, I. (2025). Designing landscapes of affordances for ageing in place. *Geographica Helvetica, 80*(1), 67–79. https://doi.org/10.5194/gh-80-67-2025
Staudinger, U. M. (2008). A psychology of wisdom: History and recent developments. *Research in Human Development, 5*(2), 107–120. https://doi.org/10.1080/15427600802034835
Stenner, P. (2017). *Liminality and experience. A transdisciplinary approach to the psychosocial*. Palgrave Macmillan.
Stenner, P., McFarquhar, T., & Bowling, A. (2011). Older people and 'active ageing': Subjective aspects of ageing actively. *Journal of Health Psychology, 16*(3), 467–477. https://doi.org/10.1177/1359105310384298
Tornstam, L. (1997). Gerotranscendence: The contemplative dimension of aging. *Journal of Aging Studies, 11*, 143–154. https://doi.org/10.1016/S0890-4065(97)90018-9
Uittenhove, K., Rohner, S. L., Falciola, J., Gomes da Rocha, C., Röcke, C., Cavalli, S., Herrmann, F., Jopp, D. S., & von Gunten, A. (2024). Mental health among centenarians living in Switzerland. *Psychogeriatrics, 24*(4), 887–896. https://doi.org/10.1111/psyg.13137
Valsiner, J. (1998). *The guided mind. A sociogenetic approach to personnality*. Harvard University Press.
Valsiner, J. (2017). From cultural psychology to geropsychology. *GeroPsych, 30*(4), 137–143. https://doi.org/10.1024/1662-9647/a000174
Valsiner, J. (2021). *General human psychology*. Springer Nature Switzerland AG.
Verdon, B. (2012). Changing while remaining the same: Self-representation confronted with aging. *Rorschachiana, 33*(2), 145–168. https://doi.org/10.1027/1192-5604/a000033
Verdon, B. (2025). Taking care of oneself as an alederly person while being interested in the future of the younger generation: Incompatible concerns? In T. Zittoun & F. Gfeller (Eds.), *Ageing, learning and development. Sociocultural and psychoanalytical perspectives on growing older*. Springer.
Verhaeghen, P. (2011). Cognitive processes and ageing. In I. Stuart-Hamilton (Ed.), *An introduction to gerontology* (pp. 159–193). Cambridge University Press.
Villa, F. (2010). *La puissance du vieillir*. Presses Universitaires de France.
Vygotsky, L. S. (1986). *Thought and language* (A. Kozulin, Ed.; Revised). The MIT Press.
Wink, P., & Staudinger, U. M. (2016). Wisdom and psychosocial functioning in later life. *Journal of Personality, 84*(3), 306–318. https://doi.org/10.1111/jopy.12160
Zittoun, T. (2006). *Transitions*. Information Age Publishing.
Zittoun, T. (2009). Dynamics of life-course transitions – a methodological reflection. In J. Valsiner, P. C. M. Molenaar, M. C. D. P. Lyra, & N. Chaudhary (Eds.), *Dynamic process methodology in the social and developmental sciences* (pp. 405–430). Springer.
Zittoun, T. (2012). Lifecourse. In J. Valsiner (Ed.), *Handbook of culture and psychology* (pp. 513–535). Oxford University Press.
Zittoun, T. (2019). *Sociocultural psychology on the regional scale: A case study of a hill*. Springer.
Zittoun, T. (2020). Imagination in people and societies on the move: A sociocultural psychology perspective. *Culture & Psychology, 26*(4), 654–675. https://doi.org/10.1177/1354067X19899062
Zittoun, T. (2022). A sociocultural psychology of the life course to study human development. *Human Development, 66*(4–5), 306–324. https://doi.org/10.1159/000526435
Zittoun, T. (2023). *The pleasure of thinking*. Cambridge University Press. https://doi.org/10.1017/9781009039802
Zittoun, T. (2026). *Developing in older age – an integrative view*. Cambridge University Press.
Zittoun, T. (in preparation-b). Playing with time: Stirring or stitching the multiple temporalities in dialogical case study on ageing. *Culture & Psychology*.

Zittoun, T., & Baucal, A. (2021). The relevance of a sociocultural perspective for understanding learning and development in older age. *Learning, Culture and Social Interaction, 28*, 100453. https://doi.org/10.1016/j.lcsi.2020.100453

Zittoun, T., & Cabra, M. (2024). Thematic engagements: Affects and learning in older age. *Learning, Culture and Social Interaction, 45*, 100806. https://doi.org/10.1016/j.lcsi.2024.100806

Zittoun, T., Cabra, M., Gfeller, F., & Grossen, M. (2024). Développement des personnes « âgées » et transformation des espaces vécus. In A. Iannaccone, E. Cattaruzza, & E. Schwab (Eds.), *Expériences socio-matérielles: Objets, interactions et espaces* (pp. 159–178). Éditions Alphil.

Zittoun, T., & Gillespie, A. (2015). Integrating experiences: Body and mind moving between contexts. In B. Wagoner, N. Chaudhary, & P. Hviid (Eds.), *Integrating experiences: Body and mind moving between contexts* (pp. 3–49). Information Age Publishing.

Zittoun, T., & Gillespie, A. (2016). *Imagination in human and cultural development*. Routledge.

Zittoun, T., Grossen, M., & Tarrago Salamin, F. (2021). Creating new spheres of experience in the transition to a nursing home. *Learning, Culture and Social Interaction, 28*, 100458. https://doi.org/10.1016/j.lcsi.2020.100458

Zittoun, T., Valsiner, J., Vedeler, D., Salgado, J., Gonçalves, M., & Ferring, D. (2013). *Human development in the lifecourse. Melodies of living*. Cambridge University Press.

Chapter 5
Developmental Processes and Meaning-Making in Volunteering Activity

Nathalie Muller Mirza

5.1 Introduction

Retirement represents a significant transition in one's life course. Like any transition, it involves important identity issues. In a society that values productivity and where professional activity is often associated with social identity, "being retired" represents a socially undervalued category that connotes passivity and uselessness, essentially being "in retreat." While this phase of life, both imposed and regulated, may be anticipated by some, it is often a source of concern and, for some people, raises existential questions: *what will I do with the remaining time? In this new period of my life, what is the meaning of the experiences and competencies I developed until today?*

In adult development theories, retirement is seen as a "psychosocial crisis" (Erikson, 1959). The transition from work to retirement coincides with the onset of old age and confronts individuals with multiple losses. As a crisis or rupture of familiar and identity-based reference points, it necessitates the establishment of new ways of acting and thinking, adapting to a changing environment, and can be considered an opportunity for self-redefinition and development. Research has shown that development can be catalyzed when people experience ruptures and find resources to support processes of transition, such as social relationships, past experiences or cultural elements, for example (Zittoun, 2008). Moreover, the current demographic context of aging, where a larger portion of the population can enjoy 15 years of life without major health issues post-retirement, leads to redefining this

N. Muller Mirza (✉)
Faculty of Psychology and Education, University of Geneva, Geneva, Switzerland
e-mail: Nathalie.MullerMirza@unige.ch

T. Zittoun, F. Gfeller (eds.), *Ageing, Learning and Development*, Lifelong Learning Book Series 36, https://doi.org/10.1007/978-3-032-11057-2_5

period as an opportunity for construction of new knowledge, transmission and doing things differently (Tremblay & Lazzari-Dodeler, 2017).

Erikson and subsequent researchers highlight that one way to give meaning to this period is through an attitude of "generativity", that is, contributing to younger and other generations with solicitude by providing one's time, experiences, and knowledge. Volunteering is among the activities of generativity described as enhancing the well-being and development of those who engage in it.

Volunteering has been the subject of research in geriatric psychology over the past few years. Serrat and colleagues (2020) for example define it as a "gold standard for achieving a good old age" due to its capacity to benefit both older people and their communities. This research has led to studies showing the motivational sources and effects of this activity. However, this research is generally conceived in terms of independent variables and little is known about the developmental dynamics it involves for the individuals themselves, and how volunteering activity can be seen as resources in reshaping coherence and continuity for people experiencing a time of transition.

In this contribution, drawing on developmental conceptions as articulated in a sociocultural and dialogical approach in psychology, particularly for individuals after retirement (Grossen et al., 2021; Muller Mirza & dos Santos Mamed, 2021; Zittoun & Baucal, 2021), we analyze interviews conducted within the framework of the VIVRA research (Fassa et al., 2018, 2023). The participants were volunteers in associations. Contrary to other studies on senior volunteering that focus on its effects on various psychological dimensions, we are interested here in the activity itself and what we call "acted competencies"—the cognitive, relational and affective resources mobilized by people in the actualization of a specific and situated task—(Muller Mirza et al., submitted) as deployed by volunteers in the context of their engagement. Given this perspective, the present study aims to investigate how older adults over the age of 65 mobilize and transform their 'acted competencies' within volunteering activities, and how this process contributes to the construction of coherence and meaning in their lives during a psychosocial transition period such as retirement.

This chapter aims to contribute to the body of work questioning the decline often associated with old age (Gergen & Gergen, 2001) and to the study of developmental processes after retirement. It will try to better understand how volunteering may serve as a privileged space for development among individuals over the age of 65, enabling them to creatively and meaningfully mobilize competencies acquired throughout their lives. We assume that volunteering offers a space where older adults can actively mobilize and transform their 'acted competencies,' which in turn supports the construction of coherence and meaning during a period of psychosocial transition.

5.2 VIVRA Research and Volunteering by Older People

The European population aged over 65 represents 19% of the inhabitants, a figure that is mirrored in Switzerland as well. This demographic's proportion of the total population continues to rise. Projections suggest a growth of over 30% by 2050, at which point they will constitute 25.6% of the population (OFS, 2023). This trend, while beginning in wealthy countries, is becoming a global phenomenon (Oris, 2020).

The aging population is accompanied by four major phenomena: an increase in life expectancy (with an average of 83.5 years in Switzerland as of 2022), an extension of the period without major health issues (on average, about 15 years post-retirement are spent in relatively good health), a decline in extreme poverty among seniors, and an increase in the number of individuals who have benefited from compulsory education. Although these advances are evident today, they do not eliminate issues such as the marginalization of individuals facing financial and health vulnerabilities documented in Switzerland as well. Oris (2020) for example shows that while older adults with low educational attainment were once the norm, they have now become a socially marginalized minority. This is particularly true for seniors with limited educational capital, whose life trajectories have been shaped predominantly by manual occupations, often of foreign origin, and who are poorly equipped to seek the social assistance to which they are entitled: "These individuals left behind by societal progress reveal the extent to which models of successful aging are implicitly elitist" (Oris, 2020, p. 34).

Volunteering among young people is a practice that plays a significant role in resumes and is often associated with the development of competencies. Similarly, many individuals after retirement engage in cultural, sports, or care-related associations. In Switzerland, 42% of seniors were engaged in a formal volunteering during the last 6 months (European Values Study, 2018). Research on senior volunteering shows that the benefits of this activity can be seen at the cognitive (skill development, sense of mastery), psychosocial (reduction of symptoms of depression), and health levels (Cook, 2011). However, it appears that these effects are variable and largely dependent on how the activity is recognized and the efforts appreciated (Andersen et al., 2014).

The VIVRA research project (funded by the Leenaards Foundation), bringing together sociologists and psychologists, aimed to better understand the contributions of these engagements among seniors in Switzerland (Fassa et al., 2018). The general questions of this project were: How do individuals over the age of 65 cope with the social and psychological challenges posed by retirement, and how can volunteer engagement affect their quality of life? The project spanned 3 years in collaboration with 14 associations involving senior volunteers in two French-speaking regions of Switzerland. The methodological approach included conducting 23 focus groups with 106 men and women on a voluntary basis, who were invited to document a "life calendar" (that aimed at documenting their activities of volunteering all along their life in articulation with other important events such as professional activities, moves, marriage, the birth of children and grandchildren if any, etc.), and 36 individual interviews. The research questions addressed the reasons of their engagement, the challenges encountered, and the competencies mobilized and developed during their engagement. It also aimed to highlight these competencies to document how seniors contribute to the functioning of society.

5.3 Theoretical Framework

5.3.1 The Transition to Retirement: An Identity Challenge

The transition to retirement is perceived ambivalently. While it is sometimes anticipated and hoped for, increasingly prepared for, and relatively well-experienced today (Caradec, 2008, 2017), the moment of retirement is associated in the literature with identity fragility. The individuals lose their status, and the instrumental and symbolic role associated with it, can no longer refer to their group of colleagues, and thus lose their socio-emotional support (Cumming & Henry, 1961). Beyond the actual financial loss, being retired can also be linked to negative social representations (Repetti, 2018) and the feeling of experiencing a "great rupture", a "social death" (Lalive d'Epinay & Spini, 2007), a loss that is particularly important regarding the competencies or expertise that were often associated with the way to define oneself. Regardless of how it is experienced, this transition can be supported by various forms of support: collective, personal or identity-based, relational, familial, or friendly (Caradec, 2008).

Some authors define it as a "psychosocial transition"(Gfeller & Zittoun, 2023) since it involves significant transformations in the relational and material environment and in activities and commitments. From this perspective, transitions can be occasions for development, at the conditions people can find and mobilize appropriate resources and create a new equilibrium (Sapin et al., 2007; Zittoun, 2023). It involves the articulation of three interdependent processes of change: identity processes, knowledge construction processes, and the meaning-making attached to experiences and emotions (Zittoun, 2008). Under certain conditions, these processes are conducive to reflective self-examination and developmental processes.

5.3.2 Retirement as a Developmental Crisis in the Life Course

The study of aging has long been dominated by research focusing on cognitive and health aspects, primarily concerned with decline and loss (Tournier, 2022). However, since the 1950s, some psychologists have contributed to a theory of adult development post-retirement. Alongside the works of Levinson and Havighurst, Erik H. Erikson's research demonstrates that each stage of life presents its challenges: changes and development occur throughout the lifespan, and the adult's relationship to themselves, others, and the world continuously evolves. Individuals must face internal and external conflicts "to gradually control their environment effectively, exhibit a sense of personal unity, and be able to understand themselves and the world accurately" (1959, p. 93). Erikson developed the concept of a psychosocial crisis, which he defines as having a dual potential: while the crisis is a source of tension and fragility, it can also, provided the individual finds meaning in it, be an opportunity to emerge from the difficulty with a reinforced sense of personal unity (Erikson et al., 1986). Erikson identifies eight "psychic dispositions" to be nurtured to navigate the crises characterizing each developmental stage: trust, autonomy, initiative, achievement, identity, intimacy, generativity, and integrity.

Let us focus on the notion of generativity, defined by Erikson in his theory of psychosocial development stages for adults approaching old age. It involves a concern for establishing and guiding the next generation (Erikson, 1979), the ability to transcend personal interests to provide care and concern for younger and older generations. This capacity develops around the question, "Can I make my life count?". Generativity, in this sense, can extend beyond potential parenthood to include activities adults engage in through various forms of social and professional involvement. Volunteering in an association is one such activity.

The life course paradigm, emerging in the 1970s and gaining prominence in the 1980s in aging study (Baltes & Mayer, 1999; Elder, 1994; Elder & Giele, 2009), offers valuable insights for linking biographical trajectory analysis with social structures, accounting for both social transformations and individuation processes. Elder and colleagues, along with other researchers, propose five fundamental principles: (1) the Life span development principle, (2) the Timing in lives suggest that the positioning of lives are situated in historical time and place, (3) the principle of Linked lives (individual trajectories unfold in interaction with close persons), (4) the Historical time and place, suggesting variations according to individuals' biological, psychological, and social ages; (5) the Human agency, emphasizing individuals' capacity to act in their lives (Sapin et al., 2007). This approach prevents reducing individuals to mere social roles while acknowledging the influence of social phenomena on choices made. In this vein, Riley (1979) provides valuable insights for studying aging. She emphasizes four specific principles: (1) aging is a process that starts at birth and ends at death; (2) it involves the interaction of biological, psychological, and social processes; (3) an individual's life course is traversed by social, environmental, and historical changes; (4) individuals are similarly affected by events, resulting in genuine social changes (Burney, 2022).

These theoretical approaches, briefly outlined here, have significantly contributed to an agentive perspective on aging adults. They also highlighted the importance of considering individuation processes within their social and cultural context, showing the relevance of focusing on "crises" as potential sites of identity transformation and development and identifying conditions for such development, related to both individual and institutional resources. However, these works have faced criticism for several reasons. Notably, their "normative" dimensions, presenting certain patterns of change as better than others (Lalive D'Epinay & Spini, 2007; Sapin et al., 2007); their neglect of individual situation variability; and their reliance on the assumption of linear life courses, despite contemporary trajectories being much more variable (Valsiner & Connolly, 2003; Zittoun, 2008).

We suggest here to examine how a sociocultural and dialogical perspective can provide insights for studying development by seniors, emphasizing the importance of social and instrumental genesis of the psyche, of meaning-making, of emotions and of social interactions and dialogical movements.

5.3.3 A Sociocultural and Dialogical Perspective on Post-retirement Development

To better understand volunteer activity and its developmental aspects among retirees, we need a developmental theory that more thoroughly integrates the cognitive, relational, and emotional dimensions of the individuals with the context in which they live. In recent years, researchers have been working to develop a sociocultural psychology of aging, considering it a suitable theoretical framework for understanding this stage of life (Grossen et al., 2021; Gfeller & Zittoun, 2023; Hviid, 2022; Muller Mirza, 2024; Zittoun & Baucal, 2021). As it defines the individual as an active agent who makes sense of their experiences within constraining and influencing contexts, and who undergoes transitions and transformations throughout their life, it offers important conceptual tools.

Although primarily used for studying child development, rooted in Vygotsky's historical-cultural theories (1934/2019), a dialogical definition of development as an open and dynamic system may provide valuable insights for studying adults and the elderly. By revisiting the main dimensions defining psychological development from this perspective, we articulate several elements that will help our exploration.

Modes of action, thought, emotions, and individual identity are not ahistorical entities; they develop throughout life, linked to the accumulation of **material and semiotic tools** in a society that individuals learn from others and uniquely appropriate. These tools can change due to the different needs of individuals based on their life experiences and trajectories. They are artefactual or socially elaborated and transmitted. They are internalized, and in this process, the psyche restructures, reorganizing its functions (Wertsch, 1985). This process occurs from the outside in, from interaction with others to autonomous activity, involving a transformation: by appropriating the world, the persons transform themselves using psychological instruments. Thus adults through their life trajectory stabilize experiences, semiotically mediated, that can be more or less detached from the immediacy of the senses (Zittoun, 2023).

Another important process constitutive of development is **meaning making**. People engage in activities that make sense to them, in relation to socially shared meanings. Development occurs if the individual creates meaning (Zittoun & Baucal, 2021) and builds connections between the past, present, and possible worlds. In this process, continuity and a sense of stability are constructed (Bruner, 2003). The idea of meaning making is central to this perspective. It involves an orientation toward the future and thus a movement away from the here and now, as an existential tension to what has to come or could occur (Zittoun & Gillespie, 2016), which can also be called creativity or imagination. Meaning making can also be linked to significant relationships, social recognition, and a sense of belonging. In this definition, it can be articulated with the relationship between the self and society (Marková, 2016).

Development is defined not only in cognitive but also in **affective dimensions**. In a sociocultural approach, emotions are not separate from but constitutive of thought (Bruner, 2003). Vygotsky used the term *perezhivanie* (often translated as emotional experience) to explain this intertwining. Affects are linked to the personal meaning an activity holds for an individual and concern their agency (Clot, 2006). Vygotsky stressed that: "Behind every thought, there is an affective-volitional tendency, which holds the answer to the last why in the analysis of thinking. A true and full understanding of another's thought is possible only when we understand its affective-volitional basis" (Vygotsky, 1934/2019, p. 252). Scholars emphasize the importance of considering the sensory and affective experience in thought processes and the potential for individuals to engage (Muller Mirza & Tartas, 2023). In this perspective, pleasure—and in particular pleasure of thinking—has been conceived as an important ingredient of the developmental trajectory of people with different modalities, such as curiosity, deepening an activity, discovery, a dialogical pleasure, or enjoying one's own ideas (Zittoun, 2024).

Research within a sociocultural perspective views **social interaction** not merely as a developmental factor but as its matrix. It is by the actions in a sociomaterial world and its reaction that mind develops. Researchers study different dimensions of interaction, considering for example argumentation (Muller Mirza & Perret-Clermont, 2009) or dialogical movements in conversation (Grossen & Muller Mirza, 2019). Here, discourses are studied as responsive to broader social contexts beyond the immediate context (Grossen, 2009), with dialogism conceived as both a theory and an epistemological and ontological stance, viewing the Other as both a "real" Other and an inner characteristic of the human mind (Marková, 2016).

As regards older individuals, we can suppose that these dimensions continue to play an important role in their learning and development. From this theoretical frame, as our aim is to better understand how volunteering may serve as a privileged space for development among individuals over the age of 65, enabling them to creatively and meaningfully mobilize competencies acquired throughout their lives, we relate to the role of past experiences and competencies of the volunteers We suggest three general questions that will guide our investigation:

(1) How do individuals over the age of 65 mobilize and transform their competencies in volunteering contexts, and how does this process contribute to meaning-making?
(2) What connections can be identified between the competencies enacted by older adults in their volunteer activities and the experiences developed in other life domains?

(3) What role do emotions play in older adults' engagement in volunteering and in their perception of these activities as meaningful and creative?

To obtain relevant insights, it seemed essential to us to design an appropriate methodological framework that allows to focus on processes and "acted competencies".

5.4 Methodological Framework

In certain conditions an interview can grant access to the complexity of the psychological activity that occurs in engaging in an activity. With Clot, we thought that to study development, inherently dynamic and situated, an "indirect historical" method is necessary, focusing on the history of development: "Experience and consciousness are observable only in their development, not as products, states, or invariant structures but through the processes that make and unmake these sedimented forms" (Clot, 2006, pp. 183–184—our translation from French).

Therefore, a specific interview—that we called "narrative-explicitative"—was elaborated to study this activity and its potential development with the interviewee's help. The interviews had a dual purpose. Firstly, in the narrative part, the person was invited to recount their personal and professional journey and the meaning they attributed to their commitments. We aimed to understand the reasons behind their involvement in volunteering and how it fits into their unique trajectory. In the second part of the interview, the "explicative" part, the interviewer (Vittoria Cesari Lusso or the author of this article) used techniques inspired by the explicitation interview developed by Pierre Vermersch (Cesari Lusso et al., 2016; Vermersch, 1994/2003). The goal was to guide the person in a detailed description of a specific "meaningful" situation that illustrates his or her ability to manage and succeed in the volunteering, and actualized what we called "acted competences".

We assumed that verbalizing the different elements of an activity in a specific context is neither easy nor familiar—what we do and how often seems "normal" or "self-evident"—and requires the support of a trained interviewer. By "acted competence", we refer to the set of resources (cognitive, relational, affective, sensory perception) mobilized in a particular situation that yield satisfactory results for the person implementing them. This is not a repeated operational pattern but an action situated in the unique specificities of a situation (Cesari Lusso & Muller Mirza, 2022).

The instruction formulated to the interviewer at the beginning of the explicitative part looks like this: "So, if you agree, I propose that you take your time and that we look together this 'normal,' enormous activity and what it contains." "We enter a somewhat unusual conversation because the usual conversation is the one where you said, 'I do the accounting, it's normal,' but I propose that you think back to a moment this morning when you started the work…".

Through this method, we aimed to:

- Support the description of activity in its various components (cognitive, affective, relational) as situated in an institutional and relational context and the

interview. Our goal was to capture the multifaceted nature of actions, emphasizing how they are embedded within specific contexts.
- Implement sensitivity to the intersubjective processes of constructing a definition of the situation during the interview. Fostering an awareness of the mutual construction of understanding during the interaction was important for us from an ethical perspective and to better understand the intersubjective conditions of describing an activity and its complexity.
- Help the participants becoming aware of their own resources, thereby contributing to a developmental dynamic. The interview provided an opportunity for the participants to reframe their experiences from past actions to analyzable objects, potentially enabling new perspectives and applications in future interactions (Cesari Lusso & Muller Mirza, 2022).

5.5 Data and Method of Analysis

The analysis in this chapter is based on four transcribed narrative-explicitative interviews conducted via Skype, Zoom, or face-to-face, as the data collection period coincided with the COVID-19 pandemic between 2020 and 2021. Conducted by a researcher trained in explicitation interviews (the author or our colleague Vittoria Cesari Lusso), each session lasted approximately 60 to 80 min. With participants' consent, the interviews were recorded and transcribed.

We selected four participants from our corpus as we thought that their trajectories provided an interesting illustration of the processes at stake in volunteering. They are two women (Angela [70 years old] and Simone [65 years old]) and two men (André [70 years old] and Louis [85 years old]), had an average age of 72.5 years. They were characterized by high educational levels, good health, and multiple commitments, fitting into the social category of "engaged retirees" or "active seniors" (Repetti, 2018). Three of them (Angela, Simone and André) could be considered as leaders in their volunteer activities, holding responsibilities in organization, design, and management. Angela discussed her role in recruiting and supporting volunteers for reading in schools; Simone described her responsibility in organizing a photographic exhibition with other volunteers; André recounted his fundraising efforts for concert organization. Alongside, Louis shared his experiences of reading literary texts in a senior living facility.

Our analysis involved repeated readings of the transcriptions, a general content analysis to identify themes, and the selection of "explicitative" sequences where participants described their "acted competencies". We identified excerpts and defined process categories.

The results are illustrated with interview excerpts. In the final section, we analyze a longer excerpt, drawing on a dialogical analysis (Grossen & Salazar Orvig, 2011).

5.6 Results

Assuming that the period of retirement might be perceived as a rupture, this section presents the results of our analysis, focusing on how older adults engage in volunteering as a possible site of development and meaning-making. The analysis of the narrative-explicitative interviews reveals three interconnected aspects that characterize the participants' experiences of volunteering.

5.6.1 Weaving Experiences: Mobilizing Competencies from Diverse Life Domains

When seniors describe the competencies they used in a particular situation, experiences and knowledge from different times and places are invoked.

What individuals did and knew how to do in their previous activities is often considered a starting point for choosing a volunteer activity. However, this choice is not made in a linear relationship between the field in which the previous (often professional) activity was conducted and the domain of the volunteer activity. Instead, it involves a nuanced interplay between several dimensions: personal interest in an activity, a "cause", or a type of practice; previous experiences and what individuals claim to master or competencies that others have recognized in them (e.g., "a friend called me to ask if I wanted to get involved").

Let us refer to the example of Simone, who, after training in the health field, became the director of a university-level training institution in the capital of her canton. She also traveled around the world and developed an interest in photography. She chose to retire 2 years before the official retirement date. Once retired, she asked herself: "What should I do with all this?" She quickly became involved in several associations in the region where she currently lives. She stated that she intended to "contribute", using her organizational competencies and cultural interests, to enliven her village and create connections with the nearby city:

> So, I thought I could bring organizational, relational, and other competencies to the table. After all, the required competencies aren't very difficult if you have relational networks, organizational, and structural abilities, and even budgeting and communication competencies. For me, it's quite easy (Simone).

She said that it was important for her to relate different domains of her past:

> For me, it's about how to connect the two [professional and volunteering activities]; it seemed important to me and this idea of promoting local culture through organizing conferences, cultural visits, etc. (Simone).

Angela, who was a social worker professionally and engaged in institutions for the elderly and children with disabilities, explains her choice to recruit and support volunteer readers for children in her canton's schools. While reading was part of her family environment (she reads stories to her grandchildren), she mainly used her organizational and coordination competencies developed in her professional sphere for this activity:

> I limit myself to coordinating the group. (…) I felt that I had competencies for this from my previous work, and I read books to my grandchildren the most. (…) And I feel more useful in this role of coordination and volunteer recruitment, which is also done very seriously (Angela).

We observe that the decision to engage in an association and a specific field is oriented by the awareness of existing competencies which are then mobilized in the activity of volunteering.

The interviews with Simone and Angela provide interesting illustrations of this process: resources used in other contexts are remobilized in the volunteer activity, but creatively, as they are updated according to the specificities of the new context.

Simone indicates how her previous experiences, particularly in management, enable her to organize the projects she coordinates. When asked to provide a concrete example where displaying these competencies had a favorable issue, she cites organizing a photo exhibition, which she associates with project management:

> So, how to plan? Yes, definitely these project management competencies, because an exhibition for me is a project. I have a schedule planned months in advance, with stages, identifying decision points that need to go to the Committee, the president, or others. I identify different sub-groups of work, seek the competencies of people, etc. For me, project management is very useful in these volunteer activities. It's reassuring; if something needs to be done by a certain date, it will be done. And I always have a larger reserve of time than I did professionally, which I accept, but they aren't supposed to know that. They know I'll find solutions, that's what it means. I think that somewhere, the professional competencies I have allowed me to be reassuring regarding deadlines, budget, etc. In some way, I'm the guarantor of the organization process, the conduct of exhibitions, and that reassures many people (Simone).

Simone refers to actions she has previously implemented in other contexts, such as establishing schedules, stages, sub-groups of work, identifying decision points, recipients for each stage, and the competencies of collaborators. In the described situation, these "competencies" are remobilized but oriented *towards the others* ("the professional competencies I have allowed me to be reassuring"; "I'm the guarantor of the organization process", "that reassures many people") and *with more flexibility*, especially regarding the temporal dimension, as she says: "I always have a larger reserve of time than I did professionally".

The interview with Angela also highlights these processes of updating previous competences in a new environment. Her description of the actions implemented in supporting volunteer readers in a new institution provides insights into the intricate weaving of previous knowledge with the unique aspects of the environment:

> We generally have meetings during nap time when things are a bit calmer, with the director and two educators responsible for the group of preschoolers aged 2.5 to 4 years. We meet in a small room, and I explain… the competencies I might have include [embarrassed laugh] I don't know how to put it, perceiving the expectations behind the discourse, understanding what the expectations are, which might not be what we can offer, but this comes from my previous work where I conducted many interviews, allowing everyone to speak and also hearing what lies behind the discourse, etc. These are things I've tried to implement (Angela).

Updated, the competencies previously implemented elsewhere are *transformed*—they are set in motion. They are adjusted to the specificities of the current environment: the characteristics of the recipients (the Committee, the president, and other volunteers with their expectations and perceived competencies), and the activity's purpose defined around a personal sense (promoting local culture; enabling children's access to books and stories). The previous competencies, when mobilized, become an *instrument* of another activity, making this experience an occasion of learning and development.

Another interesting element that emerges from interviews is that the volunteer activity takes place in a context oriented towards an objective perceived as significantly different from the contexts in which the competencies were previously developed. One of the specificities of this context, according to the participants, is that the activity is not directed towards profitability or performance in terms of financial results and is also *free from time constraints*.

Simone speaks to this point:

> It means that the other people in this volunteer work, and myself, we are all at the same level. It's not a level of performance but rather about who has more information or interest in that area. If someone tells me they're not available on a certain day because they have their grandchildren, I have great respect for that person, saying we can change the day, we will find something else so they can also participate without frustration. Whereas in the professional world, if someone said they had another priority, I would be quite disturbed by that (Simone).

It thus appears that the meaning attributed to the situation ("doing things well and correctly for others") in a context where there are no (or different) perceived constraints, hierarchy ("we are all at the same level"), or time pressures, allows individuals to imagine appropriate responses and operate differently. It doesn't mean that there are no constraints, but that the constraints of the volunteering activity are articulated to another meaning than in the professional context.

André also provides an interesting example in this perspective as he insisted on the fact that as a volunteer the notion of profitability and "making money" is not the main purpose of the activity anymore:

> It doesn't translate in the same way at all in a very structured context like [the institution where he worked for many years]. Even though we were 45,000 when I joined and 28,000 when I left, you are still required to achieve a certain profitability. The need to be profitable means that the competences you provide are somewhat different.
>
> (…) You need competences to be performant in a company, which is not at all like those you use as a volunteer. That's also what I liked about volunteering. It's not for making money. As a volunteer, you don't offer your performance in the same way. You are motivated by doing things well and correctly, for others (André).

5.6.2 Values and Self-representations: Identity Continuity Through Volunteering

In the previous examples, we have already seen how the choice to engage in a volunteer activity is made with an awareness of one's competencies—what can be offered, what can be useful for the collective—even though this choice is sometimes also fueled by a desire for discovery and learning. From the interviews, there also emerges a sense of what could be read as guiding principles that seem to direct the person's choices in the volunteer activities, but more generally throughout their life.

For Angela, for instance, her role as coordinator of volunteer readers in daycare centers seems underpinned by a concern for *caring for vulnerable children*, echoing her professional activities in institutions where the focus on relationships with others was central.

> What particularly motivated me when starting as a coordinator was to emphasize, in what we might call less privileged neighborhoods. I'm not saying we'll teach them French through books, but we are an additional drop in the stream of learning French, and the teachers told us we contribute to that because the children then borrow books from the small corner of the library—it's something that becomes familiar (Angela).

Or in André's case, where the notion of *loyalty* manifests itself as much in the reports he writes for fundraising efforts or when he consolidates the sponsor network for organizing concerts in the association he works for as it does in other situations in his private life:

> But you see, all this, and perhaps in life in general, there is the question of loyalty (…). I understand loyalty in the message I send to the widow of one of [my old friends], and I specify that in these 54 years of friendship, firstly it's humor, and secondly, it's loyalty. But loyalty in all of this is important. Loyalty and retention in fundraising. Loyalty is also part of all the steps I've mentioned, it might be a bit mercenary, but there is the question of donors' loyalty because they are eager to support a worthwhile project (André).

Here too, the connections between activities are not straightforward transfers or determinism. However, underlying themes emerge, and it seems as if a "melody," the melody of their lives, plays and guides certain choices (Zittoun et al., 2013).

We observe how, referring to Clot's words: "activity thus places the subject not only in a triadic space [ego-alter-object] but also in a history that succeeds or fails in transforming the past into a means of living the present" (Clot, 2006, p. XIX).

5.6.3 Emotions and Creativity: The Role of Pleasure in Meaning-making

From the analysis of interview sequences focusing on the competencies implemented, a recurrence of the term "pleasure"was observed.

Here is an illustration from the interview with Angela. She discussed the importance of pleasure not only in her own activity but also in supporting her attention to the activity of others, which she believes should also be driven by pleasure:

> Once these three trainings are done we often still receive calls from participants who still have questions, or doubts as well about their ability to start, and my job is to reassure them, to tell them you must first have pleasure in order to give pleasure to the children. It's important because in an activity like this, in any activity, if there's no pleasure, it's better not to do it, so I wouldn't want to send my readers to the slaughter, so I must feel how they will be welcomed (Angela).

The next excerpt is taken from the interview with Louis, who works as a reader for elderly people in a senior living facility. He spoke not only of his love for literature, which he shares with the residents but also of the pleasure that this reading gives him.

> They also really like—I really like Maurice Genevois in his three works he wrote about animals. And, for example, I read them about the squirrel. In 8 pages, it appears that on the fifth page, but the rest is so beautiful, so poetic, so enlightening that it gives, they love it because for me, as these are texts that I enjoy, I manage to convey, how should I say, my attachment, my vision, my happiness, in reading it (Louis).

In this excerpt, we observe the emotion that "ricochets" between his own love for the subject ("I really like Maurice Genevois in his three works"; "these are texts that I enjoy"), the pleasure of reading he wants to transmit ("I manage to convey my happiness in reading it"), and the pleasure he observes in the residents ("they love it"). The emotion of joy traverses and touches all elements of the activity (objects as well as people), making it difficult to identify a single source from which the emotion arises and transforming this situation into an emotional experience (Muller Mirza & Tartas, 2023; Vygotsky, 1925/1971).

The activities in which volunteers are engaged thus seem to be "affected", permeated by a strong emotion, that of pleasure, which psychologists have shown influences learning and development processes, as a dynamic tension seeking an object, which may generate a positive affective experience (Zittoun, 2023). Emotion engages the sense of an activity, representing this movement of appropriation of a living environment by a person. In this context, the notion of pleasure seems to be linked by the participants to the activity of volunteering in contrast with a professional activity associated with time and administrative pressures.

5.6.4 Interactions and Dialogical Moves: The Interview as a Potential Space of Development

Beyond examining the skills deployed by senior volunteers and their underlying meanings, experiences, and emotions, a further level of analysis focuses on the interaction itself between researcher and participant. Specifically, the interview process can be understood as a dialogical space where meaning-making and development may occur through the very act of verbalizing one's experience to another. As Vygotsky (1934) posits, development can arise from the tension between lived experience and its articulation through language and interaction.

In the present research, the interview was presented to participants as a means to better understand the activities of senior volunteers and to construct knowledge related to the competencies they enact. However, participants' reflections on the conversation itself suggest that the interview setting may also have served as a developmental space. At the end of their interview, some participants made comments about the conversation, expressing what it meant to them. Angela, for example, concluded by stating, "I left feeling comforted, it gave me back energy. It allowed me to see things that I trivialize". Such remarks indicate that the act of narrating and reflecting upon one's experience in a relational context may contribute to new insights, emotional relief, or enhanced awareness, suggesting that the interview process itself can be a site of meaningful engagement and transformation.

Let's revisit our intentions as researchers. The narrative-explicitative interview can be defined as a social activity that brings together one researcher and one participant, a senior volunteer. Discourse is one of the means through which the participant will present what she does and her "competencies" in the context of her involvement as a volunteer. It is an asymmetric situation in which both interlocutors have different roles: the participant reports on what she experienced, her feelings, thoughts, etc. (as an expert of her life), and the researcher will work on the participant's report (as an expert of the method). In Bakthin's words, this situation is a dialogue that is not only composed of speech (external dialogue) but there is an internal dialogue, that can be grasped (1) at the level of the dialogue in praesentia and (2) at the level of the dialogue in absentia (where each participant's discourse is made up of and through other discourses or voices) (Grossen, 2009):

> Within the arena of almost every utterance an intense interaction and struggle between one's own and another's word is being waged, a process in which they oppose or dialogically interanimate each other. (Bakhtin, 1934/1986, p. 354)

By leading individuals to describe a concrete situation as they experienced it at a specific time and place, guiding them in verbalizing the various actions (perceptions, affects, decision-making, etc.) that were implemented, rather than the "discovery" of a mental object previously inaccessible, during the interview, the re-discovery or rather the re-creation of this psychic object takes place in a new context that makes it see differently. Dialogical movements thus allow, if we follow Clot and before him Vygotsky, not to recover an intact past but rather to relive it in the present action, which sometimes results in what can be called "consciousness", in Vygotsky's sense, that is, a "social contact with oneself" (Clot, 2006, p. 179).

In the continuation of this section, I propose an analysis highlighting the dialogical movements between external dialogue (interlocution phenomena) and internal dialogue (internal dialogization which refers to the relationships between a statement and other discourses) (Grossen & Salazar Orvig, 2011; Grossen & Muller Mirza, 2019). In this perspective, a discussion is an intermingling between dialogue in praesentia and dialogue in absentia (Grossen & Salazar Orvig, 2011). We consider the dialogical order of the interview a different order than that of conversation or interaction—as offering a scene "where subjects meet, themselves and others, as well as their stories, environment, and circumstance" (Clot, 2006, p. 115—our translation from French).

By following this proposition, that internal dialogism entails "dialogical relationships" (Bakhtin, 1934), that is, minimal differences, contradictions, or oppositions between the various voices making up any discourse, we focus on these encounters, oppositions, contradictions that we perceive as potential developmental indicators.

By using a dialogical analysis to examine the potential developmental dimension of the experience of volunteer activities for seniors, we draw inspiration freely from

Grossen and Salazar (2011) and Clot (2006) (for another type of dialogical analysis of focus groups where we were particularly interested in dialogues "between situations" and discourses (Linell, 2009), conducted with volunteers, see Muller Mirza, 2024).

Here, we will be particularly attentive to:

1. Certain dialogues (external dialogue) between the volunteer and the interviewer playing the role of discursive and argumentative spaces in which others' words can become sources and resources for elaborating thought;
2. Traces of self-dialogism, when the speakers seem to be in dialogue with themselves, making visible the inner debate and where they symbolically split between an "I" and a "me" (Grossen, 2009);
3. The temporal movements of the narrative, which move from the past of the action to the present of its enunciation, and to possible futures, in the past of the past or in the future of the present. We also consider these movements as potential drivers of development.

Let us take a sequence from an interview with Angela.

Angela chose to describe the situation in which she accompanies two volunteers in a nursery to describe the competencies she puts into action. One particular point draws our attention.

The researcher is very attentive to guiding Angela in describing a lived experience, hence singular. At the beginning of the sequence, Angela says, "We are received in a small room and there I explain either I start by explaining who we are and what we do or I let the person who receives us tell us how the nursery works how many children". The phrase "either I start… or I let…" informs the researcher that Angela is mentioning several types of situations. She then prompts Angela to return to the evocation of the chosen situation by asking her, "for example, this time". Angela responds that she "couldn't say it could be me or the director". She explains, "it's quite spontaneous". This expression, indicating that the action occurs in the moment, without premeditation, catches the attention of the researcher who sees it as something to delve into and presents it to Angela, inviting her to elaborate on what she means by spontaneous: "when you say 'it's quite spontaneous', there is already a competence behind it, to grasp what is appropriate to say". Angela picks up the thread and indicates what she does when she acts "spontaneously": "who wants to start, so I try to perceive". She tries to perceive who wants to start. This information seems important to her as she continues after the researcher's intervention, echoing but changing the temporal modality, as from the present used by Angela ("I try to perceive"), she moves to the past tense as if the action had actually been carried out: "so you perceived". Angela picks up the proposition: "what I perceived is that the educator duo was very motivated". Beyond 'who wants to start', Angela states that what she does when she "perceives" is to define somewhat the mindset of the people who will welcome the volunteers. Later, she will say, "and so the competencies that maybe I have is [slight embarrassed laughter] I don't know how to say it, it's to perceive the expectations behind the discourse what are the expectations that are maybe not those that we can offer".

These few turns of speech reveal not only (1) the "sociocognitive", argumentative, intersubjective work involved in describing an activity, which eludes memory as it seems to occur under the expert injunction of "it depends"—meaning that the specificities of the here and now situation are caught by the volunteer, but also (2) how one's words, through the repetition of the other's words, collide and reopen the meaning of the experience: what I do is not "simply" coordinating a reading activity by volunteers, but rather setting up the conditions of my coordination activity which are crystallized in this ability to "perceive the expectations behind the discourse". This is a capacity that proves difficult to articulate ("I don't know how to say it") to another—who may not understand it (which can be read behind the 'embarrassed laughter')—while having contributed to its enunciation.

The second dialogical dimension that interests us is the utilization of self-dialogues. These are, of course, "addressed self-dialogues" if we follow the definition of dialogue as a heterogeneous space where "any discourse is fundamentally dialogical, as it is determined by a response which is not already uttered but requested and anticipated" (Bakhtin, 1934/1986 quoted by Grossen, 2009) and a discourse is always a response to previous (real or virtual) discourse. They are not very numerous and discrete in the sequence. But we observe this type of movement in Angela's following statements: "surely it rejoiced me"; "probably I had to say to myself"; "it comes back to me now"; "it's interesting"; "I don't know how to say it". Here, the person realizes, in discourse, this return to her own experience and thought in motion, and inscribes a sort of gap with reality, characteristic of thought.

A third dimension may also provide us with information, that of the use of verb tenses. At the end of the sequence, Angela returns to what she considers "her" competencies, and plays with the tenses of experience. We are struck here by how much it is the narrative present that governs the entire statement with the use of verbs in the infinitive ("to grasp desires", "to make sure", "to please oneself", etc.). Angela here leaves the description of a particular situation she experienced at a moment in a particular place; she speaks on another register of what seems to correspond to a timeless order, which traverses all her actions. This is reinforced by the use of the adverb "always" when she says, "what I always want to convey," associated with an expression that reflects a personal and affective relationship to the described action: "I want to". Two disjunctions can be observed: when she anchors herself again in the *hic et nunc* of the interview situation by stating "I don't know how to say it" (addressed both to the researcher and to herself), and when she mentions the "work she did before". It's as if this past experience solidifies the current activity in an eternal yet dynamic present, oriented towards the future of the activity: "ensuring that the project can start without pressure".

These different elements, which would require further exploration with the analysis of other sequences, lead us to propose, according to Vygotsky and other authors, that this conversation between researcher and participant, a dynamic dialogical space, becomes a psychological instrument. Thought here reassumes its primary role, which "consists in determining our way of living and our behavior, changing our actions, directing them, freeing us from the concrete situation" (Vygotsky, 1934, cited by Clot, 2006, p. 242—our translation from French).

5.7 Conclusion

Some studies in geriatric psychology have shown that volunteering, under certain conditions, has a positive effect on the well-being of individuals over the age of 65 who engage in it. At a stage in life where identity is often fragilized due to retirement, volunteer activities directed towards others and oneself can play a role in supporting generativity processes.

In this text, drawing from data produced within the framework of the VIVRA research project, we aimed to better understand the potential developmental ingredients of volunteer activity for participants. To achieve this, we adopted a sociocultural and dialogical approach to defining lifelong development. The objective was to understand individuals as situated within both a social and historical context and a unique biography, examining how they mobilize cultural tools and their resources in sense-making processes that are central to development. We implemented an original methodological approach aimed at examining development as *situated* and dynamic.

Based on the analysis of four narrative-explicative interviews, our findings highlighted the ways in which participants creatively mobilize skills acquired throughout their lives, weave these competencies into new contexts, and find meaningful ways to enact them. Furthermore, the findings illustrate how volunteering becomes a space where personal values, self-representations, and emotional experiences intersect, thereby contributing to a sense of identity continuity and fulfillment during this post-retirement period.

The analysis of the narrative-explicitative interviews reveals three interconnected dimensions that characterize the psychosocial processes in the participants' experiences of volunteering:

1. The complex weaving of experiences: The competencies mobilized in volunteering are not isolated from prior experiences. Instead, they are the result of a complex interplay between various competencies developed across different life domains. This interweaving process appears to be central to how older adults make sense of their volunteering activities.
2. Values and self-representations: The competencies enacted through volunteering are strongly tied to values and self-representations cultivated over the lifespan. For many participants, volunteering provides an opportunity to express, affirm, or even transform these core aspects of their identity.
3. Emotions and creativity: Emotional experiences, particularly pleasure, play a significant role in how participants invest in their volunteer activities. This emotional dimension often underpins the perceived meaningfulness of volunteering and fosters a sense of creativity and fulfillment.

We can suggest that activities carried out by volunteers, to the extent that they are informed by prior knowledge linking past, present, and possible futures, and are imbued with personal meaning and powerful emotions related to pleasure, resemble what Clot calls "living activities" (2006).

These findings contribute at various levels. They urge us to move beyond the usual representations of individuals over 65 as passive and useless. Engaged people play a significant role in society, particularly in care-related domains where state institutions are less present. They bring in-depth, expert knowledge and contribute to maintaining social and intergenerational links in often neglected and invisible areas.

Our work also provides elements of discussion on adult development after retirement from a sociocultural perspective in psychology, an emerging and promising field in our view, as it allows for a close examination of the situated experiences of the individuals encountered. It also contributes to the discussion on methodological tools that seek not only to make visible the competencies of individuals but also to co-construct a developmental space that unfolds between the participant and the researcher.

However, we must be critical and vigilant before drawing conclusions: it is not about defining volunteering as the sole place of fulfillment; other activities are sources of pleasure and development in retirement. It is also important to be sensitive to what could be a form of social injunction to productivity and social utility even after retirement. Literature provides critical insights into volunteering, which can be seen as unpaid work. It is also important not to overlook the fact that this study was conducted with individuals from a particular social category (affluent, with previously recognized competencies). It would be important to conduct these analyses with individuals from different socio-economic backgrounds.

From this exploration, however, we retain an important element, emphasized by those individuals for whom awareness of finitude serves as a driving force for their engagement: that of pleasure. One participant concluded her interview discussing her commitment as a volunteer by playing with the words "envie" (desire) and "en-vie" (alive), which sound almost equivalent in French. A reminder that it would be beneficial to instill this hint in all our activities at every stage of life.

Acknowledgements The data presented in this chapter are taken from a research project funded by the Leenaards Foundation in Switzerland. The author is very grateful to the associations and the participants for their cooperation that made this project possible. I also wish to extend special thanks to the members of the VIVRA team and in particular to Vittoria Cesari Lusso who deeply contributed to the reflection I developed in this text.

References

Anderson, N. D., Damianakis, T., Kröger, E., Wagner, L. M., Dawson, D. R., Binns, M. A., Bernstein, S., Caspi, E., Cook, S. L., & Team, T. B. (2014). The benefits associated with volunteering among seniors: A critical review and recommendations for future research. *Psychological Bulletin, 140*(6), 1505–1533. https://doi.org/10.1037/a0037610

Bakhtin, M. (1934/1986). *Speech genre and other late essays*. University of Texas Press.

Baltes, P. B., & Mayer, K. U. (Eds.). (1999). *The Berlin aging study: Aging from 70 to 100*. Cambridge University Press.

Bruner, J. S. (2003). *Making stories: Law, literature, life*. Harvard University Press.

Burnay, N. (2022). *Parcours de vie* (pp. 79–90). https://doi.org/10.4000/books.septentrion.140749
Caradec, V. (2008). Les mécanismes de la transition identitaire au moment de la retraite. *Spirale—Revue de recherches en éducation, 41*(1), 161–176. https://doi.org/10.3406/spira.2008.1232
Caradec, V. (2017). L'*épreuve* de la retraite Transformations sociétales, expériences individuelles. *Nouvelle revue de psychosociologie, 23*, 17–29. https://doi.org/10.3917/nrp.023.0017
Cesari Lusso, V., Iannaccone, A., & Mollo, M. (2016). Tacit knowledge and opaque action in the processes of learning and teaching. In *Reflexivity and psychology* (pp. 273–290). Information Age Publishing Inc-IAP.
Cesari Lusso, V., & Muller Mirza, N. (2022). La quête de l'*intersubjectivité* dans l'entretien de recherche sur les *compétences*. *Expliciter, 133*, 1–28.
Clot, Y. (2006). *La fonction psychologique du métier*. PUF.
Cook, S. L. (2011). An exploration of learning through volunteering during retirement. *International Journal of Volunteer Administration, 28*, 9–19. http://www.ijova.org/
Cumming, E., & Henry, W. (1961). *Growing old. The process of disengagement*. Basic Books.
Elder, G. H. J. (1994). Time, human agency, and social change: Perspectives on the life course. *Social Psychology Quarterly, 57*(1), 4–15. https://doi.org/10.2307/2786971
Elder, G. H. J., & Giele, J. Z. (Eds.). (2009). *The craft of life course research*. Guilford Press.
Erikson, E. H. (1959). *Identity and the life cycle. Selected papers (1959th ed.)*. International Universities Press. http://www.archive.org/details/identityandtheli011578mbp
Erikson, E. H. (1979). *Dimensions of a new identity*. Norton & Co.
Erikson, E. H., Erikson, J. M., & Kivnick, H. Q. (1986). *Vital involvement in old age*. Norton.
European Values Study (2018). https://europeanvaluesstudy.eu/
Fassa, F., Cesari, V., Muller Mirza, N., & Repetti, M. (2023). *Bien vivre sa retraite avec les autres. Engagements, compétences et qualité de vie à l'ère du lifelong learning. Quelques constats de la recherche à discuter*. Universités de Lausanne et Genève, HETS-Valais.
Fassa, F., Repetti, M., Muller Mirza, N., Cesari, V., & Iannaccone, A. (2018). *Bien vivre sa retraite avec les autres. Engagements, compétences et qualité de la vie à l'ère du lifelong learning*. Fondation Leenaards.
Gergen, M. M., & Gergen, K. J. (2001). Positive aging: New images for a new age. *Ageing International, 27*(1), 3–23. https://doi.org/10.1007/s12126-001-1013-6
Gfeller, F., & Zittoun, T. (2023). A new housing mode in a regional landscape of care: A sociocultural psychological study of a boundary object. *Human Arenas. Advance Online Publication, 8*(2), 461–479. https://doi.org/10.1007/s42087-023-00363-5
Grossen, M. (2009). Interaction analysis and psychology: A dialogical perspective. *Integrative Psychological and Behavioral Science, 44*(1), 1–22. https://doi.org/10.1007/s12124-009-9108-9
Grossen, M., & Muller Mirza, N. (2019). Interactions and dialogue in education: Dialogical tensions as resources or obstacles. In N. Mercer, R. Wegerif, & L. Major (Eds.), *Routledge international handbook of research on dialogic education* (pp. 597–609). Routledge.
Grossen, M., & Salazar Orvig, A. (2011). Third parties' voices in a therapeutic interview. *Text & Talk – An Interdisciplinary Journal of Language, Discourse & Communication Studies, 31*(1), 53–76. https://doi.org/10.1515/text.2011.003
Grossen, M., Zittoun, T., & Baucal, A. (2021). Learning and developing over the life-course: A sociocultural approach. Introduction to the special issue. *Learning, Culture and Social Interaction, 37*, 100478.
Hviid, P. (2022). Aged experience—A cultural developmental investigation. *Learning, Culture and Social Interaction, 37*, 100386. https://doi.org/10.1016/j.lcsi.2020.100386
Lalive d'Épinay, C., & Spini, D. (2007). Le grand âge: un domaine de recherche récent. *Gérontologie et Société, 30123*(4), 31–54. https://doi.org/10.3917/gs.123.0031
Linell, P. (2009). *Rethinking language, mind, and world dialogically*. Information Age Publishing.
Marková, I. (2016). *The dialogical mind. Common sense and ethics*. Cambridge University Press.
Muller, M. N., & dos Santos Mamed, M. (Eds.). (2021). *Dialogical approaches and tensions in learning and development. At the frontiers of the mind*. Springer. https://link.springer.com/book/10.1007/978-3-030-84226-0

Muller Mirza, N. (2024). Argumentation and reasoning in people older than 65. A sociocultural and dialogical analysis of focus groups on senior volunteering. In F. Arcidiacono & J. Convertini (Eds.), *The psychology of argumentation and reasoning* (pp. 211–237). Nova Science Publishers.
Muller Mirza, N., & Perret-Clermont, A.-N. (Eds.). (2009). *Argumentation and education*. Springer.
Muller Mirza, N., & Tartas, V. (2023). Learning in dialogues through aesthetic experiences: Some theoretical and methodological issues. In C. Damsa, A. Rajala, G. Ritella, & J. Brouwer (Eds.), *Re-theorising learning and research methods in learning research* (pp. 65–80). Routledge.
OFS. (2023). https://www.bfs.admin.ch/bfs/fr/home/statistiques/population/naissances-deces/esperance-vie.html
Oris, M. (2020). Vieillissement démographique et bien-être des aînés: progrès et inégalités. In *Bulletin de l'Académie suisse des sciences humaines et sociales* (Vol. 2, pp. 32–35).
Repetti, M. (2018). *Les bonnes figures de la vieillesse*. Antipodes.
Riley, M. W. (Ed.). (1979). *Aging from birth to death*. Westview.
Sapin, M., Spini, D., & Widmer, E. (2007). *Les parcours de vie. De l'adolescence au grand âge*. Savoir suisse.
Serrat, R., Scharf, T., Villar, F., & Gómez, C. (2020). Fifty-five years of research into older people's civic participation: Recent trends, future directions. *The Gerontologist, 60*(1), 38–51. https://doi.org/10.1093/geront/gnz021
Tournier, I. (2022). Learning and adaptation in older adults: An overview of main methods and theories. *Learning, Culture and Social Interaction, 37*, 100466. https://doi.org/10.1016/j.lcsi.2020.100466
Tremblay, D.-G., & Lazzari-Dodeler, N. (2017). Les retours en emploi post-retraite: Les fins de carrière du futur? *Vie et Vieillissement, 4*(2), 21–32.
Valsiner, J., & Connolly, K. J. (2003). The nature of development: The continuing dialogue of processes and outcomes. In J. Valsiner & K. J. Conolly (Eds.), *Handbook of developmental psychology* (pp. ix–xviii). Sage Publications.
Vermersch, P. (1994/2003). *L'entretien d'explicitation*. ESF. Translated in English in 2007. *The explicitation interview*. Independently Published.
Vygotski, L. (1934/2019). *Pensée et langage*. La Dispute.
Vygotsky, L. S. (1925/1971). *The psychology of art* (original work published in 1925, published in 1971 in English).
Wertsch, J. (1985). *Vygotski and the social formation of mind*. Harvard University Press.
Zittoun, T. (2008). Learning through transitions: The role of institutions. *European Journal of Psychology of Education, XXIII*(2), 165–181.
Zittoun, T. (2023). *The pleasure of thinking*. Cambridge University Press.
Zittoun, T. (2024). The pleasure of thinking in human development. *European Journal of Developmental Psychology, 22*(3), 375–394. https://doi.org/10.1080/17405629.2024.2333949
Zittoun, T., & Baucal, A. (2021). The relevance of a sociocultural perspective for understanding learning and development in older age. *Learning, Culture and Social Interaction, 28*, 100453. https://doi.org/10.1016/j.lcsi.2020.100453
Zittoun, T., & Gillespie, A. (2016). *Imagination in human and cultural development*. Routledge.
Zittoun, T., Valsiner, J., Vedeler, D., Salgado, J., Gonçalves, M. M., & Ferring, D. (2013). *Human development in the life course: Melodies of living*. Cambridge University Press.

Chapter 6
Moving House in Older Age: Challenges and Resources for the Sense of Self-continuity

Fabienne Gfeller and Michèle Grossen

> Young people usually move to a bigger flat, you see, whereas we, the elderly, it's the other way round (Mrs Molteni).

6.1 Introduction

Moving house is an experience that each of us is liable to make. Whereas it can be experienced as pleasant or even banal for families in repeated mobility (Zittoun & Levitan, 2019), it is certainly an important transition for older people as it involves facing finitude (Verdon, this book; Verdon & Rexand-Galais, 2021), anticipating some limitations due to age (Racin, this book), or, in many cases, living in a smaller place that fits present and hopefully future needs and abilities (Thalineau & Nowik, 2009). This, in turn, implies getting rid of meaningful objects and pieces of furniture, and leaving a place filled with personal memories. This both concrete and emotional experience challenges the sense of self-continuity (Erikson & Erikson, 1998) and requires developing resources.

The study presented in this chapter aimed at understanding how older people who were about to move into an assisted living flat coped with this transition. Assuming that objects and more globally the material environment, notably the living place, are an integral part of psychic life (Searles, 1960; Tisseron, 2003) and play a role in keeping a sense of self-continuity, we examine how the participants in

F. Gfeller
Institute of Psychology and Education, University of Neuchâtel, Neuchâtel, Switzerland
e-mail: fgfeller@proton.me

M. Grossen (✉)
Faculty of social and political sciences, University of Lausanne, Lausanne, Switzerland
e-mail: michele.grossen@unil.ch

T. Zittoun, F. Gfeller (eds.), *Ageing, Learning and Development*, Lifelong Learning Book Series 36, https://doi.org/10.1007/978-3-032-11057-2_6

this study came to the decision to move and how they sorted their personal belongings in preparation for the move. We show the diversity of the resources they mobilized to keep self-continuity and to experience moving house as an opportunity for learning and development. To tackle this issue, we first introduce some elements of a large research field on moving house in older age and draw on a sociocultural and dialogical approach to conceptualise the notion of Self.

6.2 Moving House in Older Age: Theoretical Challenges

Moving is an important transition that may entail changes at various levels (Prentice et al., 2023): change of neighbourhood, village or town; change of immediate physical, geographical environment, social relationships, activities (such as sport) and habits. Such a transition may have different meanings for older people. Thalineau and Nowik (2009) found that residential mobility shortly after retirement tends to be oriented toward pleasure and represents an idealised mobility, whereas residential mobility occurring some years after retirement represents an "adjustment mobility" triggered by: "The awareness that physical strength is weakening, the occurrence of a health problem affecting the person or his or her spouse, the death of a spouse" (p. 101, *our translation*). Moving into an assisted living flat pertains to this second category.

Research on moving in older age has mainly focused on transition into a nursing home or other long-term settings and shown that one of the challenges older people must overcome is to develop a sense of home in their new environment and to keep self-continuity (Bigonnesse & Chaudhury, 2020; Droz-Mendelzweig & Bedin, 2022; Rowles & Chaudhury, 2005). The concept of home has received renewed interest with demographic ageing. Often taken for granted, this concept does not have a unified definition, but can be defined as a place, a relationship and an experience (Gillsjö et al., 2011), which is altogether emotional, cognitive, relational and imaginary, and results from home-making practices that involve adaptation and change (Pazhoothundathil & Bailey, 2020). Hence, it is "a complex blend of emotional, cognitive, behavioural and social bonds to a particular place" (Cooney, 2012, p. 189). Linking a place to a feeling (being at home), these definitions emphasize that the sense of home has both an objective dimension related to a geographical environment (a given space with its affordances and practicality) and a subjective dimension: the person's experience of a given space. Moreover, Gillsjö et al. (2011) showed that among older people (six in their study), the experience of home was a conflicting one, as it oscillated between a place they "cannot imagine living without" and a place they "might be forced to leave".

Moving in older age does not only imply leaving a familiar place with its related memories, habits, social relationships and practices, but also, for most people, entering their last dwelling in life (Mallon, 2007). It raises a feeling of loss and grief (Droz-Mendelzweig & Bedin, 2022), threatens the sense of home and presents a challenge: that of (re)creating a sense of home. Establishing material, relational and symbolic continuities between home and the nursing home is a way of "reducing the gap between two universes and demonstrating a strategic or tactical anticipation of ageing" (Mallon, 2007, p. 255, *our translation*). It creates a sense of security, comfort and predictability (Cooney, 2012). Participating in the decision to move and choosing a place to live seems to favour the creation of a sense of home (Cooney, 2012). Reproducing habits in the daily routine of the nursing home or through objects that link the new housing with the old one is an active mode of creating a sense of home and facing the transition (Mallon, 2007; Zittoun et al., 2021). The materiality of space and objects frame the residents' behaviour by constraining but also expanding it through thoughts, representations and memories. At stake here is a sense of control which concerns, among others, the decision to move and the choice of the items and furniture to take along (Prentice et al. 2023).

Among personal belongings, so-called *cherished* ("valued" or "treasured") *objects* play an important role in creating a sense of home (Cooney, 2012; Pazhoothundathil & Bailey, 2020). Kroger and Adair (2008) defined these as "those physical objects that hold a special meaning for the individual […] It [cherished object] holds a meaning for the owner that may defy rational explanation, but provides the owner with a sense of pleasure, comfort, attachment, or well-being." (p. 6). Their study sheds light on the linking functions of these meaningful objects: links to cherished relationships, past events, Self in previous life phases or historical periods. In a study carried out in a nursing home, Zittoun et al. (2021) found that residents actively achieved a sense of home by creating one or several spheres of experience, that is, "a pattern of activities, modes of engagement, feelings, relations, and so on, that is sufficiently recurrent for a person to feel the same across time and space" (p. 2). Some residents complied with the various institutional rules and procedures, others made compromises and others still created new spheres of experience through the development of new activities, habits and relationships. Present spheres of experience were also linked to previous and distant ones thanks to symbolic resources (Zittoun, 2013), such as photographs, paintings, religion, furniture, which allowed older people to work out self-continuity.

This emphasis on the role of objects may be linked to the Self theory developed by William James (1890/2012). Indeed, James argued that the Self of a man [sic] includes, "(…) his clothes and his house, his wife and children, his ancestors and friends, his reputation and works, his lands and horses, and yacht and bank-account" (p. 291). In other words, the materiality of the environment pertains to human development and learning (Searles, 1960; Tisseron, 2003). In the same vein, a basic assumption of sociocultural psychology (Vygotsky, 1934/2012) is that signs, tools and technologies mediate human-environment relationships, shape the development of human cognition and are in turn transformed through human activity (e.g., Iannaccone et al., 2024; Säljö, 2021, 2022; Valsiner, 2014).

Through his theory of language, Mikhail Bakhtin (1981) also contributed to a theory of the Self. Opposing Russian formalism, he defined language as a living discourse, which is always addressed to an addressee, whether present or not, and which echoes former speakers' voices (see also Linell, 2021). Thus, dialogue is not just a conversation between two or more speakers, but refers to the Others' voices echoed in a single speaker's utterance. This view matches Mead's theory (1934/1967) which assumed that the Self develops through social interactions, the Other being a mirror through which the person (Ego) can treat him- or herself as an object as if he or she was somebody else. In a recent dialogical trend, Marková's theory assumes that the Self and the Other (Ego-Alter) are interdependent and form "an irreducible dialogical ontological unit" (Marková, 2016, p. 108). This is what Marková calls the dialogicality of the mind. Other dialogical theories assume that the Self is made of multiple and heterogeneous facets and is therefore fundamentally conflictual (e.g., Hermans & Gieser, 2012; Marková, 2023).

Drawing on Bakhtin and his circle (Bakhtin, 1984; Vološinov, 1929/1986), Grossen and Salazar Orvig (2011; see also Salazar Orvig, 2005; Salazar Orvig et al., 2023) made a distinction between three aspects of dialogue: (a) *external dialogue*, which refers to the compositional structure of speech, such as a turn-taking system or types of interventions (questions, assertions, responses); (b) *internal dialogue*, which refers to the way in which the points of views of different enunciators combine, confront, oppose or complement each other - Internal dialogue concerns the various voices expressed within any discourse and how they circulate in a dialogue between two or more persons (*dialogue in presence,* François, 1988) or in the discourse of a single speaker who mentions voices of absent third parties (*dialogue in absentia)*, whether real persons or virtual (media, scientific discourse, laws, proverbs, etc.) - ; (c) *auto-dialogue*, which refers to what Bakhtin (1984) called the "dialogic relationships of a speaker to his own discourse" (p. 182) and can notably be identified in discourse through self-reported speech, mitigators, or other linguistic clues indicating the opposition between different voices (Grossen & Salazar Orvig, 2023).

To these three aspects which can be identified through discourse analysis, we add a psychological aspect: *inner dialogue*, which, according to Marková (2006) refers to humans' "capacity of speaking to themselves and of having a symbolic dialogue with the Alter that may not be immediately present" (p. 135), that is, with an "inner Alter". Inner dialogue cannot be directly observed. As Greco (2017) underlined in her study of individual reasoning taken as an inner dialogue: "(…) because adults' inner speech is not externalised, it cannot be accessed directly (…) Methodologically, there is no way to escape this problem; thus, inner dialogue in a pure form remains inaccessible" (p. 338). In view of this impossibility, the analysis of auto-dialogue, that is, of the various, and more or less conflicting, voices echoed in a speaker's discourse, can be considered as one of the methodological tools (Gillespie & Cornish, 2010) liable to capture inner dialogue, even though auto-dialogue is not an equivalent of inner dialogue, since in the former the speaker's discourse is addressed to somebody (here the interviewer), thus oriented towards his or her addressee's responsive understanding (Bakhtin, 1986). However, identifying the various and conflicting voices echoed in auto-dialogue allows us to capture at least some aspects of the heterogeneity and conflictuality of the Self. On a methodological level, this method makes our own interpretations visible and therefore open to debate.

From this brief presentation we draw three main conclusions. First, research on moving house in older age has mainly focused on transition into nursing homes and investigated the role of cherished objects once the move had already taken place. Second, moving house has a special meaning in older age and threatens the sense of self-continuity. Cherished, that is, meaningful, objects are liable to support persons in their search for self-continuity. By linking past, present and future, they act as resources that help persons to face the transition. Third, although research on moving in older age mentions identity and self-continuity as core concepts, a more explicit theory of identity is needed.

Confronted with these limitations, we draw on a sociocultural and dialogical approach to the Self to analyse the data collected in a study which is original in two respects: it involves older persons moving into a special type of adapted flat described below; it consists of interviews which were conducted before the move. These interviews focused on the decision to move and on the sorting of objects to be taken along, thrown, given away, or sold.

6.3 Presentation of the Study

The study presented in this chapter is part of a larger research project on housing modes for older people, called HomAge, a regional dialogical case study (Zittoun, 2020) carried out between 2019 and 2024, in a French-speaking canton of Switzerland (approximately 178′000 inhabitants). In this section we present the political context of the canton, the study and the procedure of data collection and analysis.

6.3.1 Flats with Referent: A New Policy

In 2012, the canton in which the study took place introduced a new socio-sanitary policy, which followed a trend observed in other Swiss cantons and European countries. This policy moves away from institutionalized housing modes, such as nursing homes, and encourages ageing in place (Gfeller et al., 2021, 2022). Among other innovations, it promotes the construction of so-called *flats with referent* (in French: *appartements avec encadrement*; Magestrini, 2021), a form of sheltered housing for older people that is a complementary offer to nursing homes.

Flats with referent are private flats or houses that are accessible to people with reduced mobility and include a common room, an alarm system and the part-time presence of a professional referent, whose role is to foster social life in the building, to organize collective activities or support them, and to propose individual visits to the tenants once or twice a month. The professional has to ensure that the tenants and their relatives receive the support they need in everyday life, for example by referring them to a food delivery service.

Flats with referent are constructed by private and public actors, while the role of the canton is to promote such buildings, to provide financial support under certain conditions and to grant a label to these dwellings if they meet certain criteria. They aim at: (a) responding to new needs and demands of the ageing population; (b) preventing social isolation; (c) favouring intergenerational relationships as much as possible by setting these flats in intergenerational buildings or neighbourhoods; (d) reducing the healthcare costs for an ageing population; (e) regulating, at least minimally, the flat market for older people.

Currently (October 2024), 623 flats have received the cantonal label and 1377 are planned by 2030. They are typically 2.5 to 3.5 room flats, measuring between 50 and 70 square metres, but developers can make other choices depending on the target population. They were initially intended for people aged 60 and over, so as to favour mutual help between younger and older inhabitants. However, the inhabitants are on average older than expected and are generally in their 80s.

6.3.2 The Study

The data are taken from a longitudinal case study which focused on a building called Beaulieu. Situated in a village, this building comprises 34 two-and-a-half to three-and-a-half room flats with moderate rents. Each flat has a beautiful view of a lake and vineyards. The building is owned by a non-profit foundation which launched the project in 2008 and received the label of the canton. Since the beginning of the project, the persons interested in renting one of these flats could put down their names on a registration list, without any commitment at this stage.

The study started in 2020 when the building was still under construction. It stopped 2 years later, when all the tenants had been living there for 1 year. The field work was carried out by the first author and relied on recurrent observations, field notes, as well as formal and informal interviews with different stakeholders: tenants, members of the foundation, professional referents, an activity therapist, the head of the cantonal housing office, employees of the cantonal home care office, and politicians. In this context, four series of semi-structured interviews were conducted with the (future) tenants at different moments of the moving process: 2–3 months before the move; 2–4 weeks before the move; 4–8 weeks after the move; 11–12 months after the move. In this chapter, we analyse the first series of interviews and explore the resources used by the future tenants to keep a sense of home and preserve self-continuity. More specifically, we examine how they experience and face their decision to move and how they proceed to the sorting of the objects and furniture required by the restriction of space.

6.3.3 Procedure: Data Construction and Analysis

The first series of semi-structured interviews took place between March and April 2021 (during the COVID pandemic). At that time, we contacted the 20 individuals or couples who were about to move (and announced it officially to the foundation). Three of them refused or could not be reached, and two interviews were not included because the persons were under 65 and moved to this building because of long-lasting physical impairments unrelated to age. All participants signed an informed consent form.[1]

The interviews took place in the participants' home and lasted between 45 and 120 min (65 on average). Out of the 15 interviews analysed, four were carried out with couples, one with a woman whose husband did not attend the interview, and ten with women living alone. The participants' age ranged from 68 to 93: three persons were between 68 and 72 years old, five between 74 and 79, ten between 80 and 89 and one was 93. All participants have children. Twelve persons or couples live in the same commune as Beaulieu, the three others live in the same canton. They have lived in their current house or flat for between 6 and 61 years. All participants except one are moving to a smaller place; 8 of them have a private garden.

After an extensive and repeated reading of the 15 interviews, extracts concerning the decision to move and the sorting of objects were selected.

For the analysis of the decision to move, we proceeded in two steps. First, we identified: the participants' attitudes towards the move; their description of the flat; their description of the organization of the move; the mention of their age, of health problems or physical (dis)abilities; the report of interpersonal discussions or conflicts about the move; the resources used to face the transition. Second, we carried out a dialogical discourse analysis in which we identified self-reported speech and internal dialogue in order to account for the conflictuality of the Self.

For the analysis of the sorting of objects, we identified all the objects mentioned by the participants, including indefinite items such as "all this", "everything" or "these things", and we systematically noted the actions taken or planned about these items (e.g., keeping, giving, or throwing away), their destination (e.g., a granddaughter), their history (e.g., a grandmother's belonging), the characterization of the object (e.g., "beautiful"), the person's attitude toward the item (e.g., "I like it"), the activities related to the object (e.g., playing tennis), and interpersonal conflicts (e.g., when a participant wants to keep an item while her daughter considers it useless).

[1] The design of the study has been validated by the Ethics Committee of the University of Neuchâtel (Ref 59/2020).

6.4 Deciding to Move

How did the participants come to the decision to move? To answer this question, we first account for the process leading to their decision to move. Then we describe the contrasted emotions they experienced at the prospect of moving. Finally, we analyse how the participants face the tensions raised by this impending move.

6.4.1 The Process Leading to the Decision to Move

Most of the participants are, as we already mentioned, residents living in the same village or nearby. Consequently, they heard about Beaulieu while it was still being planned and were able to follow the progress of the project for years. They had time to get information, talk with their family or friends, sometimes also with members of the foundation which launched the project. Some participants enrolled very early on the registration list, as did Mr. Ponti[2] who signed up 10 years ago, with the idea of anticipating the future:[3]

[1]
well, I signed up, I said to myself "if I sign up now, when I need a flat, something more suited to my age and physical condition" (…) I said to myself "I'll sign up now and when we can't stay here anymore, we might go and see this thing" (Ponti, 62[4])

As the registration list did not commit them, the Pontis, as others, had plenty of time to think about moving and to confirm their interest in this flat. Enrolment on the registration list was only a first step, and the time elapsed until the final decision enabled them to make up their mind. Some registered persons were still uncertain, but one or more circumstances made the decision necessary, typically too many burdens related to household and gardening, health issues, age, a feeling of loneliness, or obstacles to mobility such as stairways.

Not all participants, however, registered early. Some of them registered 1 year ago or even less. They did it after having talked with other registered persons or because they experienced difficulties or had an accident. In such cases, the registration coincided with the decision to move, as for Mrs. Mayor who registered 1 year ago after an accident:

[2]
I was in great shape, etc. and I walked a lot and I didn't see old age coming yet, I said to myself that it was all going to continue like that. I didn't even think about it. And then I had an accident (Mayor, 15)

[2] All names are pseudonyms.

[3] See Appendix 1 for the excerpts in original language.

[4] These figures locate the quotations in our corpus.

Mrs. Accola was not willing to move but was urged by her children. She finally agreed after having visited one of these appartements. Her decision was more a matter of resignation, even though, like others, she now recognises the advantages of moving house.

Beyond the process leading to the decision to move, two major observations are worth being mentioned. Firstly, the decision to move resulted from many discussions, above all with their children who, according to the participants, encouraged them in their reflections, even if the move sometimes gave rise to tense discussions; Mr. Aebi, for instance, reports having been "upset". Except in one case in which a participant's sister objected that she was too old to move, no family member seems to have disagreed with the project to move. In some cases, the members of the foundation also played an important role by underlining the benefits of a life in such a flat, commenting the flat plans, showing the flat or sharing their enthusiasm for the project. The participants' friends and acquaintances who were already on the registration list also advised them to move. Moreover, most participants knew at least one future tenant, which encouraged them to register too. Hence, the decision to enrol on the list and then to move is both an individual and collective process. It involves voices expressing encouragements, emotional support and arguments in favour of the move, and more rarely also apprehensions, fears, or even disagreements. This is in line with what Mallon (2007) observed about moving into a nursing home (see also van Hoof et al., 2016). Secondly, beyond these many discussions, all the participants, except Mrs. Accola, point out that moving is their own decision, even when they previously mentioned having been incited by their children or friends, or by health problems. Some do not want to be a burden to their children, others anticipate the possible consequences of ageing, but in all cases, they are keen to show that they were in control of their decision and that they have taken ownership of the reasons that make it a reasonable decision.

All these elements show that, faced with the challenges of ageing, the participants needed time to make up their mind. The duration of the building's construction enabled some of them to mature a decision, so that the long period between enrolment on the registration list and the move itself offered an opportunity for reflection and elaboration of the rupture of self-continuity presented by this transition. However, even though at the time of these interviews, the participants had decided to move, they expressed mixed emotions at the prospect of moving.

6.4.2 Moving: A Mix of Contrasted Emotions

Except for three future tenants who express only pleasure at the prospect of moving, the participants report both pleasure and worry. Mrs. Ermel, for instance, says that she and her husband are happy to move, but underscores the difficulty of this period and begins to cry. Mrs. Ponti provides a vivid description of this confusion of emotions:

> [3]
> so we decided to go, well, and I went through all states of mind, first looking forward and then feeling very sad after a few days of anxiety (Ponti, 14)

Beyond the anxiety raised by the concrete preparation of the move, these numerous expressions of mixed emotions testify to the participants' awareness that this transition entails different challenges:

(a) *Challenges to their social relationships:* Mrs. Ponti worries that the space reduction might impact her relationship with her husband:

> [4]
> (...) that's what I said to my husband, "but do you realize that we're going to be together all the time", here we can go upstairs, there's one of us in an upstairs or downstairs room (Ponti, 150)

Others fear being obliged to talk to people and losing their peace and quiet. Others still regret that, because of space reduction, they will no longer be able to invite as many people as they used to.

(b) *Challenges to self-continuity:* In line with the previous point, many participants mention elements of self-definition at stake in social relationships:

> [5]
> I don't really talk to people, yes I do talk but I hear them and I don't tell them too much (Monnet, 52)

One participant also mentions that the media's categorisation of so-called flats for the elderly makes her feel old.

(c) *Challenges to their habits:* Some participants anticipate changes in the organization and unfolding of their daily activities:

> [6]
> it'll be different, the kitchen block is to the north, there's no door you'll have to get used to it because here we have nooks and crannies everywhere and then we'll miss the windowsills (Ermel, 137) (...) no radiator to put things to dry (Ermel, 158)

(d) *Challenges to their geographical landmarks*: Mrs. Joly says she will miss the view she has from her kitchen window.

The participants also mention what they need to learn: to mix with people, to manage the available space, to be tidy or to use a new cooker. They mention the activities that will allow a continuity with their present habits, such as looking at the lake, flowering the balcony, gardening, using the (shared) terrace, or continuing to welcome their grandchildren. They imagine new activities, the most frequent being meeting people, and, despite their long list of what they are about to lose, underscore some advantages they will gain, typically reducing the household maintenance burden (which imply gendered relational, emotional and identity issues that can notably be reactivated by retirement, as discussed by Siaugues and Verdon, 2020), having more comfort, taking over abandoned activities or starting new ones, such as playing card games.

All these mixed emotions can be interpreted as manifestations of a threat to self-continuity, an observation leading to a new question: how do the participants cope with the fears, apprehensions and expectations raised by the prospect of moving house?

6.4.3 Facing the Risk of a Rupture in Self-Continuity

To examine this question, we carried out a dialogical discourse analysis which consisted in identifying the voices echoed in the participants' discourse, that is, auto-dialogue, bearing in mind, however, that the participants' discourse is addressed to the interviewer. To do so, we considered self-reported speech and other linguistic clues referring to the voices of absent third parties.

6.4.3.1 Self-reported Speech

The use of self-reported speech is a recurrent characteristic of the participants' discourse:

> [7]
> but if one feels a little blue, a little bit, a little hole there, then I say to myself "my goodness, it's nothing at all, do you realise how beautiful nature is, how lucky you are" (Mayor, 67)

Mrs. Mayor's discourse echoes two voices: the first includes herself through a generic positioning *(one feels)* and expresses a dysphoric feeling (*blue, hole)*; the second—the reported speech— is an answer to this voice; it addresses herself as if she were another person *(you)* and offers a different perspective on the move (*it's nothing at all...how lucky you are*).

Different voices are sometimes confronted within the self-reported speech itself:

> [8]
> since last year, I've aged a lot too, and then I said "it'll be better though, it'll be easier in a 2-room flat" (Molteni, 84)

At first sight, Mrs. Molteni's self-reported speech presents only the benefits of a move (*it'll be better; it'll be easier in a 2-room flat*) and the mention of her ageing works as an argument to justify her decision to move. However, her reported speech contains a hedge (*though*, i.e., *quand même* in French), which downgrades, modulates, the assertion "it'll be better" and casts doubt on it.

These auto-dialogues can be viewed as *argumentative interactions*, that is: "a situation of discursive confrontation in which antagonistic answers to a question are constructed" (Plantin, 1996, p 11, *our translation*). This argumentation has a double addressee: the speaker him- or herself and the researcher to whom the speaker attributes a certain understanding of his or her discourse. In this sense, auto-dialogue appears to be both a form of self-persuasion, and a way of persuading the researcher that he or she considers having made the right choice.

These argumentative interactions are expressions of dialogical tensions between different voices and, on a psychological level, can be interpreted as clues of psychological conflicts raised by the prospect of moving.

6.4.3.2 The Voices of Absent Third Parties

The participants' discourse also includes voices of absent third parties. Some are allocated to specific individuals; others refer to a "generalized Other" (Mead, 1934/1967), that is, to indefinite people, and to others still whom we call, for want of a better term, a "divine voice".

The Voices Attributed to Specific Individuals

These voices are above all those of the participants' children and consist mostly of a set of arguments in favour of the move, sometimes complemented by encouraging or reassuring words:

> [9]
> well, I'm going to miss here, but my children told me "well, you can always come back" (Mayor, 32)

The children's voice (*well, you can always come back*) opposes Mrs. Mayor's voice (*I'm going to miss here*) with a reassuring argument referring to the fact that her house will not be immediately occupied.

The children's discourse, as reported by their parents, seems to be reassuring but also attuned to their parents' emotional state. Mrs. Ponti reports that after having visited her future flat with her daughter, she received an encouraging message (*you'll be fine in this flat*) to which she answered:

> [10]
> (…) "Thank you for the encouragement, but I'm overwhelmed with sadness", and then she (her daughter) replies "so am I" (Ponti, 126)

The children's voices, as they are reported by their parents, are arguments in favour of moving house and show empathy for their parents' emotions. Their voices can be viewed as social resources to face transition.

The Voice of the Generalized Other

On a theoretical level, identifying the voices of the generalized Other is questionable. Indeed, if, we assume with Bakhtin (1986) that "the utterance (…) reflects (…) others' utterances, and, above all, preceding links in the [discursive] chain (…)" (1986, p. 93), then any discourse refers in one way or another to a generalized Other.

Nevertheless, we think that, on a methodological level, identifying such voices gives us clues about the conflictuality of the Self. Two discursive elements may be relevant to point to these indefinite voices.

The first is the use of deontic statements, such as "one must" or "one should" (*il faut,* in French), which correspond to the "expression of the compulsory or permitted nature of the planned experiment" (Salazar Orvig, 2003, p. 286), as in these three examples:

[11]

- and then we say to ourselves "this *will have to* work [...] that's it" (Monnet, 24)
- there will maybe be advantages and disadvantages, yes, *one has to* get used to it, that's true (Marti, 15)
- one *has to* get into the mood (Somaini, 12)

By using a deontic modality, the participants take the position of a generalized Other and impose an obligation on themselves. The deontic modality works as a voice that argues against another unformulated voice made of reservations and objections.

The second consists of statements referring to *doxa* (Amossy & Herschberg Pierrot, 2021), that is, to commonplaces, clichés, banalities or even stereotypes, which are also elements representing the voice of the generalized Other. Mrs. Accola recounts:

[12]
now that my husband's gone, *it's only logical for the children to take over* (Accola, 19)

The statement "it's logical for the children to take over" is a commonplace taken for granted and works as an argument that justifies moving house. The same appears in Mrs. Erni's discourse:

[13]
maybe once I was a bit nostalgic and said "but still", but no- but not even- no no no no *you have to live with the times you have to move forward you shouldn't live in the past* (Erni, 101)

The statements "you have to live with the times", "you have to move forward", "you shouldn't live in the past" are all introduced by a deontic (*you should*); they are commonplace ideas that oppose Mrs. Erni's dysphoric emotions at the prospect of moving (*I was a bit nostalgic).*

The Divine Voice

Two participants referred to God's voice. Mrs. Accola reports having consulted a religious calendar containing quotes of the Lord:

[14]
you know I have calendar sheets every day, and one day I got "don't worry, I'll be with you". So I stuck it by my bed, and a few weeks later I got "don't be afraid, I'll take care of you" or something like that. I said "well, this time I'm going [...]" (Accola, 77–79, 82)

Mrs. Accola's self-reported speech (*well this time I'm going*) is a response to the quotes of the calendar, which are themselves a reassuring and protective response to her fear of moving.

Mr. Ponti refers to a Bible episode to account for the psychological elaboration he had to do to accept moving:

[15]

"[…] being a Christian, I've taken this time to let things go, because I say to myself Abraham, he too had cows, everything in abundance for a time. And one day the Lord said to him "now give this to your brother and go somewhere else", where there was nothing. So I take it psychologically, in that sense, and for me it's today, I live now, I don't live what came before, I don't live what's going to happen, we project ourselves, but I live today (Ponti, 17–20)

In both cases, religion supports self-continuity and takes the function of a symbolic resource.

6.5 The Sorting Process

Moving into a smaller place requires the persons, firstly, to sort out their furniture and other objects, and to decide what to take or what to leave; secondly, to imagine their future home and plan the arrangement of their belongings so as to, hopefully, recreate a sense of home. The way in which they carry out these two tasks shows how moving into a flat designed for older people calls into question both their past and future life, challenges self-continuity and confronts the future tenants with uncertainty.

Mrs. Molteni's case provides an extreme example of a person for whom sorting objects raised much uncertainty and a series of conflicting issues:

[16]

Mrs M: I've got some armchairs here; do I take them or not? I've got some smaller armchairs upstairs, rattan armchairs. Do I take those? Do I take these? It's always that, it's always that.

FG: You have to decide whether to take your favourites or the more practical ones

Mrs M: Ah well yes, the favourites too, but the favourites may not be enough, and then I still have to see the space, that's always the problem (Molteni, 206–211)

Mrs. Molteni is confronted with a dilemma: which set of armchairs should she keep? While the researcher's question introduces two conflicting criteria "favourite" and "practical", she associates "favourite" with two other conflicting criteria: the fact that one set might not be *enough* on the one hand, and space constraints *(I have to see the space, it's always the problem)* on the other hand.

The Somainis also face a dilemma: their piano needs to be tuned but this will be only worthwhile if it is played in the future, whereas not moving it means giving up for good an activity that had a personal meaning and belonged to the person's self-definition.

Faced with the uncertainty raised by such dilemmas, the persons used different resources: taking action, imagining the future home, postponing the decision, handing it over, and relativising the importance of objects.

6.5.1 *Taking Action*

One frequent resource to face uncertainty consists in taking concrete action by gathering or checking information, such as measuring furniture or counting the number of plates needed in the future home. Some of these actions rely on other people; for example, Mrs. Joly's son, an architect, has scaled the furniture on pieces of paper. Sorting objects requires hard work, as two extreme examples illustrate: Mrs. Chappuis measures the size of each drawer and cupboard of her future kitchen to decide what kitchen utensils to take, while Mrs. Somaini is rereading the books she does not remember well to decide which ones to keep.

6.5.2 *Imagining the Future Home*

For the participants, preparing the move means anticipating a future arrangement of the objects and imagining their life within this new space. Some persons plan an arrangement of the selected items liable to recreate a sense of home:

> [17]
> now I don't know if I want to take this piece of furniture, or if I want to take the one upstairs, *but those two don't go together*, (Molteni, 295)

Others consider the density of furniture in the flat to be a key issue:

> [18]
> if you take the shelving unit and you have the living room until you find something smaller, it's already quite full, and then there's the table by the kitchen, well that's full, so the china cabinet *I thought was too much* (Ermel, 27)

Imagining the future flat has sometimes broader repercussions since, for some participants, sorting items entails a reflection about their longevity, thus showing their awareness that the move is due to age, to actual or imagined physical impairment and the dependency it might imply, and to one's finitude (Baars, 2017; Molony, 2010; Racin, this book; Verdon & Racin, 2021). Mrs. Muller's statement is typical of many other comments about limited life expectancy:

> [19]
> because it's quite a big move, you have to sort through a lot of stuff, and I say to myself "if I've made the effort to move, to sort out all my stuff, (...) *[I hope] I can stay for a few years; I'm not asking for much, 2 years will be enough* (laughs) (Marti, 76, 78)

6.5.3 Postponing the Decision and Handing it Over

The date of the move combined with the quantity of items to be sorted prompts most participants to make rather quick (if not immediate) decisions. However, some of them don't need to clear out their home immediately, which enables them to postpone any decision. Mrs. Molteni reports that her son urges her to hand over the sorting process and to wait for what happens next:

> [20]
> my son said "you leave everything here and then we'll see. We tell the family to come and have a look, if anyone wants anything they can take it, and if they don't then we'll see what we do with the rest" (Molteni, 293–294)

Mrs. Mayor reports that her son gave her similar advice. Mrs. Mayor and Mrs. Molteni are over 90 and own a fairly large house. They both express much anxiety at the prospect of moving house and seem stuck in the sorting process, or unable to undertake it. The amount of work (whether practical or emotional) together with their limited capacities make the transition particularly difficult and reduce their control over the situation.

6.5.4 Relativizing the Importance of Objects

The sorting process offers people an opportunity to think about the meaning they give to their personal belongings:

> [21]
> and then I say to myself "but what are these earthly things? you get attached to them, *but as you move on, you get detached too",* you say to yourself "but what are they worth? Am I really that attached to them?" I do my housework, I like it to be tidy, but sometimes I say to myself "but there are so many other things in life that are just as pleasurable, visits, or going out and talking to someone" (Accola, 180)

Mrs. Accola positions herself in line with a generalized Other for whom objects are not, or less, important (*as you move on, you get detached*). Her self-reported speech takes the form of an aphorism and is a response to what she said earlier in the interview (i.e., her attachment to the objects she has collected over the years). It is also a self-persuasive argument addressed to the researcher.

6.6 The Outcomes of the Sorting Process

The sorting process we just described leads to different outcomes: keeping objects, transmitting them, giving or making a transaction, throwing objects away and sometimes purchasing new objects.

6.6.1 Keeping Objects

Objects can be kept for their practical function (e.g., tables, chairs, plates) so that keeping them hardly calls for a decision. Nevertheless, most participants have too many similar practical items for the available space (e.g., several tables). Taking them depends on different characteristics of the object. Instead of keeping her "beautiful" and "rather expensive" (her words) plates with golden edges, Mrs. Marti chooses to keep ordinary white plates because they are dishwasher-safe. In so doing, she gives priority to a practical aspect over aesthetic and economic values. In other cases, functional objects, for instance an exercise bike or a tablet computer with game applications, are kept because they express an intention to maintain an activity in the future living place, thus supporting self-continuity.

Beyond these practical and functional aspects, many objects are kept for their aesthetic value; usually, they are quite briefly labelled as "beautiful". Others are kept for their emotional resonance. They notably remind of past activities. Even though these activities are not carried out anymore, keeping related objects enables the person to maintain continuity with a former meaningful activity, for example a vase that recalls a porcelain painting activity. A flowerpot for gardening takes on a specific meaning for Mrs. Accola:

[22]

Mrs. A: that's my life a little bit

FG: the garden?

Mrs. A: the garden, flowers, so that was what I liked. Besides, I had a father-in-law who always said to me "[first name] (…) "you should have been a landscape gardener" because I love flowers so much, and being outside. Otherwise, I don't go out much

FG: and that's something you will take with you? Flowers?

Mrs. A: ah yes, I hope I can have at least one (…) but then if I can at least have a geranium, or a coloured flower, then that would help me a lot (Accola, 89–94)

For Mrs. Accola, gardening is an important part of her self-definition (*it's my life a little bit*), a quality formerly acknowledged by her stepfather, and which pertains to her sense of self-continuity. For Mrs. Ermel, television supports self-continuity:

[23]

I am not ashamed to say that I love TV (Ermel, 239)

Some objects enable the person to keep a link with loved ones, in particular deceased relatives. Mrs. Ermel keeps pictures of her great-grandmother and a chest of drawers that once belonged to her grandmother.

Still other objects support the imagination of new activities that could be set up in the collective life of the new building. Talking about the clothes she wants to take, Mrs. Marti intends to organize a fashion show as a collective activity.

All these reasons are of course not mutually exclusive, as shown by the next example in which Mrs. Jungo talks about a green play mat for card games:

[24]

oh yes yes yes this one comes along (laughs) first of all it's beautiful. (…) I had a brother-in-law who was disabled, he sold card mats for the disabled people's association, so it's really a beautiful mat, it's thick like this, it's not the little thing, so this one I'll take it, for wheelchairs it was, it's quite expensive but it doesn't matter it was for them (Jungo, 96–98)

This play mat condensates many meanings: it is altogether a means for a loved activity, a valuable, aesthetic and high-quality object, a link to her brother-in-law, and a sign of a good deed she did.

All these examples have a common point: the objects are resources that support the persons' sense of self-continuity by relating their past to their future.

6.6.2 Parting from Objects

Many objects are discarded because of space reduction. However, parting from them arouses varying emotions among the participants. Moreover, with this action, objects acquire new meanings ranging from garbage to gifts.

6.6.2.1 Emotional Resonance of the Separation

In many cases, there is no trace of any particular emotional attachment to the object. The reasons mentioned to throw them away are notably that:

(a) These objects are too big or unsuitable for the dimensions of the future flat, as the Somainis' wardrobe:

[25]
(…) no it's much too big, it takes too much space in the room (Somaini, 115)

(b) They are considered old or damaged:

[26]
I have carpets upstairs, and they're 38 years old, they're so worn out that they have holes (Molteni, 48)

(c) They are judged useless in the context of a flat with referent:

[27]
(…) I'm going to remove some plates and crockery that we keep just in case, as usual (…) (Erni, 52)

In any case, the participants need to part with many meaningful objects. These meanings are mentioned in a story or information about the object, or through emotions related to the object. For instance, as the researcher and Mrs. Molteni walked around her house, Mrs. Molteni pointed to a nightstand:

[28]
(…) my father made it (…) (Molteni, 380)

Separating from this nightstand means separating from an element linked to a deceased parent, getting rid of an object which supported self-continuity and also interrupting intergenerational transmission.

Similarly, Mr. and Mrs. Ermel have an important collection of slides related to their lifelong passion for mushrooms and plants, an activity they had to stop because of their declining health condition. They need to throw away many objects related to this past activity, a difficult separation that takes them one step further away from their passion.

Mrs. Accola, who used to read a lot but had to reduce because of her declining sight, still hesitates to take her library:

[29]

FG: and would you like to take the library?

Mrs. A: maybe I'll take it

FG: do you like to read?

Mrs A: I have read a lot, (...) I always have a book with me, but I can no longer read for a long time because I superimpose the letters, so now I read for a while, sometimes I read for a while in the morning, I read for a while in the evening, but not for hours and hours, (Accola, 123–125)

Taking her bookcase or not is related to Mrs. Accola's past Self as an assiduous reader as well as to her present and future Self for whom this loved activity is becoming more and more difficult.

6.6.2.2 Trajectory of the Object: Giving or Selling Objects

Some objects are given to relatives, in particular children, grandchildren and their partners. Reasons to give an object are not only its financial or practical value, such as a desk chair that Mrs. Aebi gives to her grandson-in-law, but also its aesthetic value, such as crockery that Mrs. Molteni gives back to her daughter who offered it:

[30]

it was beautiful crockery, beautiful (...) (Molteni, 279)

Giving items can also consist in inviting relatives to help themselves to a set of objects:

[31]

one day I'm going to put all my vases on my table, I have many, many, many vases, and I'll tell my daughters and granddaughters to come and choose what they want (Marti, 124)

By giving objects to their children, the participants show their concern for their children's possible needs or wishes, but also, and more fundamentally, their desire to transmit something to their children, to leave a trace of themselves.

A lot of objects are given to charity or second-hand shops. This means giving anonymously to unknown persons, as if objects have enough value not to be thrown away, but not enough to be kept or transmitted to a relative. This is typically the case of books, except for Mrs. Joly who gave her art books to a niece, a goldsmith, because she was aware that it might be of interest for her. Other objects stay in place, until they are taken over by the next tenant or by the family members who will live in the house.

Some objects, for example furniture or small objects (such as silver cutlery) are sold. The participants try to sell them to second-hand dealers, on the internet (often with their children's help) or put posters in their neighbourhood, with pictures and prices of the furniture. Mrs. Molteni's daughters went to a car boot sale to sell some objects.

Other transactions are only indirectly financial. Reporting that his grandson took a workbench and a few other objects, Mr. Aebi adds:

[32]
(...) I said "you bring me a good bottle of wine" *(laughs)* (Aebi, 42)

Mrs. Marti negotiated an arrangement with the owner of her present flat: she would leave a corner buffet in the living room in exchange for payment of her last electricity bill.

As they try to give or sell objects, some participants are aware that the objects might be refused:

[33]
(...) we ask him (their son) whether he wants them, if he does not well then we know what we have to do (Ermel, 17)

Some participants don't find anyone interested in their objects despite their attempts to sell or give them. This applies to the Ermels who did not find anybody interested in their slides of plants and mushrooms, and have to conclude that they are "out of date". They are disappointed, as if such lack of interest called their passion into question, hence a part of themselves and of their life. More rarely, it happens that relatives or friends ask for an object that was about to be thrown away. For example, a Aebis' granddaughter asked whether she could keep the wardrobe they wanted to throw away.

These examples show that by giving or selling objects, the participants delegate the future of their belongings to others. In this sense, accepting an object, or asking for it, appears to validate not only the object itself but also the donors and has the side-effect of strengthening the relationship between donor and recipient.

6.6.3 Compromises

Some objects are subject to a compromise: they are kept, but not in their entirety or not under their initial form. For example, the participants decide to keep only part of certain functional objects (such as dishes, cups or cutlery) because it is sufficient for their everyday life and because the restricted space will not allow them to invite many people at a time. Several participants see such compromise as the sign of a change in their role in the family: they will no longer be those who organize and welcome family gatherings.

Some objects are kept at the expense of a transformation. The Ermels took a cutting of their more than five-metre-long plant to grow it anew. They also digitalized their slides of mushrooms and plants (see extract [18]). In these examples, throwing away part of the object seems unavoidable but still difficult. The rest of the Ermels' plant for example must be composted:

[34]
and it hurts me to destroy this thing (Mr Ermel, 327)

Mrs. Joly's son suggests that she buys cupboards, but she considers it is not worth buying new furniture at her age. They finally find a compromise: she agrees to buy them if her son takes them when she dies.

6.6.4 Acquiring New Objects

The move is also an opportunity to buy new objects, in particular furniture. Several participants buy a few items that are more adapted to the flat's size. Only Mrs. Monnet intends to replace most of her furniture. Two participants see the move as an opportunity to buy more ergonomic chairs. Mrs. Molteni for instance chooses a series of rotary chairs which help her sit close to the table.

Some acquisitions are imagined but are not realized. Mrs. Chevalley fancies buying a beautiful round table, but renounces because of the flat's size.

6.7 Discussion

The analysis of the interviews conducted with older persons who were about to move into a flat with referent located in a newly-built facility, showed that for most participants the decision to move was a long-lasting process which took several months or even years, during which the persons thought about their ageing and its possible implications. This duration has an important consequence: that of enabling the participants to perceive themselves as the authors of their decision to move. The participants emphasised that they were in control of their lives, even when the move was suggested by the children or prompted by undesirable circumstances. This did not prevent them from feeling mixed emotions. Even though most of them said they were looking forward to moving, they also reported "stress", sleeping difficulties and all kinds of worries, and mentioned the various challenges ahead: challenges to their social relationships, self-continuity, habits, and geographical landmarks. More generally, they commented on their age or, for some, on their life expectancy, suggesting that they experienced this move as an important transition in their life trajectory and a threat to their sense of self-continuity. The future tenants showed that they had some resources to face uncertainty and the emotions raised by this change. They took and found multiple opportunities to discuss their decision with acquaintances, friends, or villagers. They shared their thoughts and hesitations with their children who, as significant others, encouraged them, provided emotional support and took an active part in the organisation of the move. Some members of the foundation which launched the Beaulieu project put a lot of effort into this project and were also keen to see it come to fruition. One member of the foundation took a leading role in providing information, answering questions, reassuring, answering many calls in which the future tenants shared their worries. All these social supports worked together, each on its own level, and created a framework which scaffolded the emotional, cognitive and behavioural experience of this transition.

The analysis of self-reported speech and of the various voices echoed in the participants' discourse enabled us to show that the participants' discourse often took the form of an argumentative interaction where reassuring arguments were opposed to their own counterarguments that pointed to uncertainty, worries, fears, "stress", etc. These argumentative interactions can be seen as the expression of psychological conflicts that the person tries to resolve by persuading the researcher that he or she took the right decision and, through a sort of mirror effect, by self-persuasion. The participants also echoed the voice of absent third parties or generalized Others (for example sayings from popular wisdom) that brought arguments in favour of moving. These voices can be seen as inner Alters that act as a resource and have a scaffolding function, as dialogues with other people may have.

Cultural elements also acted as symbolic resources and, as such, contributed to working through emotions. This was however quite rare since only two participants mentioned that a cultural element, the Bible and religious quotes, helped them decide and accept the move.

In brief, these results show that the decision to move cannot be categorised into a simple dichotomy between a decision taken by the individual vs. imposed by others. Even though the persons claimed to have freely decided, the process of their decision appears to be distributed: it is the complex outcome of a given contextual configuration made of material elements (such as the building coming out of the ground, the available space), social elements (dialogues with various people) and personal resources (the ability to take the role of an Other and offer oneself encouragements, the use of symbolic resources).

In contrast to previous research which highlighted the role of personal belongings on elaborating a new sense of home (van Hoof et al., 2016) and preserving personal identity in the transition into a nursing home (Cooney, 2012), our analysis shed light on the object sorting process that took place before the move. Although the future tenants could keep many objects (more than if they were to move into a nursing home), the space reduction required them to sort their belongings and to give priority to some objects. This sorting process led the participants to revisit their life narrative, the activities they had been practicing and the people they had lived with or met over their life. Coming across forgotten objects in a corner of their home reminded them of what they had stopped doing, what they would not do anymore and whom they had lost over the years, thus confronting them with the finitude of human life (Baars, 2017).

However, sorting objects is not just turned toward the past, it also involves imagination of the future (Zittoun & Gillespie, 2016). It implies both decisions about what to do with former relations and activities, and projections on the activities to be maintained or developed in the future home. In this regard, sorting personal objects equated to taking a stock of their life.

Confronted with many conflictual options during the daunting task of sorting their belongings, the participants acted in different ways: they took action (e.g., by measuring objects or drawing plans); they imagined the future (e.g., by anticipating the collective activities that could be initiated in the building or by visualizing the layout of the furniture in the flat); they handed over all decisions concerning sorting which, however, threatened their feeling of control; they relativized the importance of objects in general by evoking a voice that undermined the significance of material possessions (a voice that acts as a promoter sign, i.e., an abstract sign that guides the "ranges of possible future meaning-making"; Valsiner, 2007, section Regulating the Subjective Future: The Promoter Sign, para. 2.). All these actions can be seen as resources to deal with the uncertainties inherent in sorting objects and, more generally, in moving house.

Moreover, the sorting process led to transforming, ascribing and renegotiating the meanings of objects (on transformations of the meanings of objects, see Valsiner, 2014, Chap. 7), as when a piece of furniture became waste, when an object to be thrown away became a gift or when a compromise between keeping and throwing the object was found. This shows that, despite the material affordances that constrained the possibilities for action, the participants demonstrated a know-how and an imagination that oriented and opened their scope of action.

6.8 Conclusion

This study shows that, from the point of view of the older people concerned, moving into a flat with referent is a difficult decision in many respects. It happens at a specific stage in a life trajectory, confronts the person with his or her ageing and finitude, goes together with the loss of a home in which many people have been living for many years, requires practical organisation and sorting out belongings in order to fit the available space. In the case we studied, people had, as we showed, plenty of time to decide whether to move or not; they were able to discuss with various persons, their children in particular who supported them throughout the decision-making process.

This slow decision process is, however, partly related to the specificities of our research field and many questions still need to be investigated. First, our study took place in the initial phase of implementation of flats with referent in the canton. Consequently, at that moment, most people did not know what a "flat with referent" was. We might wonder what will happen in a few years when people are better informed and have various feedback on the way these flats actually work. Second, as the Beaulieu building was built in a small village, most participants stood in a familiar geographical and social environment. We might qualify this situation as “ageing in place” (Forsyth & Molinsky, 2021), but our results show that even under these conditions, moving is… a move and a rupture in one’s life trajectory. On a city scale, this would not be very different, as a change of neighbourhood also represents a change in physical and social environment. Third, the owners of the Beaulieu building were highly motivated and implicated. A few members of the foundation gave a lot of their time to provide information and support, which raises a critical question: should support be provided? If so, which support? provided by whom? when? with what agency left to the persons concerned? Fourth, all the participants in our study had children who, as we showed, played a scaffolding role. All older people, however, do not have children. In Switzerland, 21% of the people aged between 65 and 80 do not have children (Knöpfli & Meuli, 2020) and might not benefit from such support.

These open questions underline that whereas for the participants the decision to move is a developing process, so it is also for the project of flat with referent: they will develop thanks to the ability to learn from experience and from what works as expected and what does not work.

Acknowledgments We would like to thank the Swiss National Science Foundation (project 10001C_182401 dir. by Prof. Tania Zittoun) which supported the HomAge project. We also address our warmest thanks to all the persons (policy makers, members of the Foundation, future tenants in particular) who agreed to participate in this study.

Appendix 1: The Excerpts in Original Language

[1]

boh je me suis inscrit je me suis dit, si je m’inscris maintenant, quand j’aurai besoin d’un appartement, de quelque chose qui serait plus adapté à mon âge et à ma condition physique, (…) je me dis je m’inscris maintenant et quand on pourra plus ici, on pourra éventuellement aller voir ce truc (Ponti, 62)

[2]

j’étais en pleine forme, etc. et je marchais beaucoup et je voyais pas l’âge venir encore, je me disais que tout ça allait encore continuer comme ça. J’y pensais même pas. Et après j’ai eu un accident (Mayor, 15)

[3]

alors on a pris la décision d’y aller, voilà, je suis passée par tous les états d’âme, d’abord me réjouir après une grande tristesse après quelques jours d’angoisse (Ponti, 14)

[4]

(…) c’est ce que je disais à mon mari « mais tu te rends compte qu’on va être tout le temps ensemble », ici on peut monter, il y en a un qui est dans une pièce en haut ou en bas (Ponti, 150)

[5]

moi je discute pas tellement avec les gens, oui je discute mais j’entends je raconte pas trop. (Monnet, 52)

[6]

ça sera différent le bloc cuisine c'est au nord il y a pas de porte il faudra s'habituer parce qu'ici on a des recoins un peu partout et pis alors il va nous manquer les rebords de fenêtre (Ermel, 137)(...) pas de radiateur pour mettre les choses sécher (Ermel, 158)

[7]

mais si vous avez un petit blues, là un petit peu, un petit trou là, alors je me dis « mais mon Dieu mais c'est rien du tout, tu te rends compte la nature comme c'est beau quelle chance tu as » (Mayor, 67)

[8]

déjà depuis l'année passée, j'ai beaucoup vieilli aussi, et puis j'ai dit « ça ira quand même mieux ça sera plus facile un 2 pièces » (Molteni, 84)

[9]

bon ben je vais regretter ici mais mes enfants m'ont dit « ben tu peux quand même toujours revenir » (Mayor, 32)

[10]

(...) « je te remercie pour l'encouragement mais je suis envahie d'une immense tristesse » puis elle me répond « moi aussi » (Ponti, 126)

[11]

- pis on se dit « faudra que ça ça joue, ça ça joue, voilà » (Monnet, 24)
- il y aura peut-être des avantages et des inconvénients, oui il faut s'habituer c'est vrai (Marti, 15)
- il faut se mettre dans l'ambiance (Somaini, 12)

[12]

maintenant du fait que mon mari est parti, c'est logique que les enfants reprennent

[13]

peut-être une fois j'avais un petit peu de nostalgie en disant « mais quand même », mais non mais même pas non non non il faut vivre avec son temps il faut aller de l'avant faut pas vivre avec le passé (Erni, 101)

[14]

vous savez j'ai des feuillets du calendrier tous les jours, et un jour j'ai eu « Ne t'inquiète pas, je serai avec toi ». Alors je l'ai collé près de mon lit, et quelques semaines j'ai reçu « N'aie pas peur, je prendrai soin de toi » ou quelque chose comme ça. J'ai dit « ben cette fois-ci j'y vais[...] » (...) (Accola, 77–79, 82)

[15]

(...) étant chrétien, j'ai pris ce temps de lâcher les choses, c'est parce que je me dis Abraham, lui aussi il a eu pendant un certain temps des vaches, des- tout en abondance. Et un jour le Seigneur lui a dit « maintenant tu donnes ça à ton frère et tu vas ailleurs », où il y avait rien. Donc, je prends ça psychologiquement, dans ce sens-là, et pour moi c'est aujourd'hui, je vis maintenant, je ne vis pas ce qui était derrière, je ne vis pas ce que va arriver, on se projette mais je vis aujourd'hui (Ponti, 17–20)

[16]

Mme M.: là j'ai des fauteuils est-ce que je les prends est-ce que je les prends pas. J'ai des fauteuils en haut plus petits, des fauteuils en rotin. Est-ce que je prends ceux-là? est-ce que je prends ceux-ci. C'est toujours ça c'est toujours ça.

FG: faut voir si vous prenez vos préférés ou bien les plus pratiques

Mme M.: ah ben oui les préférés aussi seulement les préférés veulent peut-être pas suffire, puis il faut toujours que je vois la place, c'est toujours ça le problème (Molteni, 206–211)

[17]

maintenant je sais pas si je veux prendre ce meuble-là, si je veux prendre celui qui est en haut, mais ils vont pas ensemble ces deux, (Molteni, 295)

[18]

si on prend la paroi et qu'on a le salon en attendant qu'on trouve quelque chose de plus petit, c'est déjà bien plein, et après il y a la table vers la cuisine, ben c'est plein alors le vaisselier moi je trouvais que ça faisait trop (Ermel, 27)

[19]

parce que c'est quand même un déménagement assez important, il faut trier beaucoup de choses hein, et je me dis si j'ai fait l'effort de déménager, de trier toutes mes affaires, que je puisse rester quand même quelques années (...) je demande pas trop, 2 ans et voilà, ça suffira [rire] (Marti 76, 78)

[20]

mon fils m'a dit « tu laisses tout là, et après on verra. On dit à ceux de la famille de venir voir, si y en a qui veulent quelque chose ils prennent, pis sans ça ben on verra ce qu'on fait avec le reste ». (Molteni, 293–294)

[21]

pis après je me dis mais qu'est-ce que c'est que les choses de la terre? on s'y attache, mais à mesure qu'on avance, on se détache aussi, on se dit mais qu'est-ce que c'est qu'est-ce que ça vaut? est-ce que franchement, j'y tiens j'y tiens, je fais mon ménage, j'aime que ce soit en ordre, mais des fois je me dis mais il y a tellement d'autres choses dans la vie, qui font aussi plaisir, des visites, ou sortir et parler avec quelqu'un (Accola, 180)

[22]

Mme A: c'est ma vie un petit peu ça

FG: le jardin?

Mme A: le jardin, les fleurs, alors ça c'était quand même ce que j'aimais. D'ailleurs j'avais un beau-père qui me disait toujours « [prénom] vous auriez dû être décoratrice de jardin » comment est-ce qu'on dit il y a un nom, pour faire les platebandes les jardins, paysagiste « vous auriez dû être paysagiste » parce que j'aime tellement les fleurs, être dehors. Autrement je sors pas beaucoup

FG: Et ça c'est quelque chose que vous allez prendre avec à Beaulieu? des fleurs?

Mme A: ah oui j'espère que je pourrai avoir au moins une, mais je sais pas si je donne de l'eau, parce que j'ai qu'un petit balcon il est pas grand, mais alors si je peux avoir déjà un géranium, ou une fleur de couleur, alors ça m'aiderait beaucoup (Accola, 89–94)

[23]

j'ai pas honte de le dire moi je suis très télé (Ermel, 239)

[24]

ah oui oui oui celui ci il vient avec [rires] d'abord il est beau. oui je l'avais acheté mais il y a quand même, j'avais un de mes beaux-frères qui était handicapé, il vendait des tapis de cartes pour l'association des handicapés, alors c'est vraiment un beau tapis il est comme ça épais, c'est pas le petit machin, alors ça ici je prends, pour les chaises roulantes c'était voilà. il est assez cher mais c'est pas grave c'était pour eux. (Jungo, 96–98)

[25]

(...) non elle est beaucoup trop grande, ça tasse la chambre celle-ci on va l'enlever, (Somaini, 115)

[26]

en haut je dois, j'ai des tapis en haut, et ils ont 38 ans ils sont au bout quoi, ils ont des trous carrément. (Molteni, 48)

[27]

je vais encore un peu enlever des assiettes, de la vaisselle qu'on garde si jamais, comme d'habitude, (...) (Erni,52)

[28]

(...) c'est mon père qui l'a faite (...) (Molteni, 380)

[29]

FG: et la bibliothèque vous aimeriez bien la prendre

Mme A: peut-être je vais la prendre

FG: vous aimez bien lire

Mme A: j'ai beaucoup beaucoup lu, (...) j'ai toujours un livre en train, mais je peux plus lire tellement longtemps parce que je superpose les lettres, alors je lis un moment, des fois je lis un moment le matin, je lis un moment le soir, mais pas des heures et des heures, (Accola, 123–125)

[30]

c'était de la belle vaisselle c'était beau (...) (Molteni, 279)

[31]

bon un jour je m'en vais mettre sur ma table tous mes vases, j'en ai beaucoup beaucoup beaucoup, et je dirai à mes filles et mes petites-filles de venir choisir ce qu'elles veulent (Marti, 124)

[32]

(...) j'ai dit tu m'apportes une bonne une bouteille de vin [rire] (Aebi, 42)

[33]

(...) on lui demande s'il veut, s'il veut pas ben voilà alors on sait ce qu'il nous reste à faire (Ermel, 17)

[34]

ça me fiche malheur de le détruire ce machin (M. Ermel, 327)

References

Amossy, R., & Herschberg Pierrot, A. (2021). *Stéréotypes et clichés* (4th ed.). Armand Colin.

Baars, J. (2017). Aging: Learning to live a finite life. *The Gerontologist, 57*(5), 969–976. https://doi.org/10.1093/geront/gnw089

Bakhtin, M. (1981). Discourse in the novel. In M. Holquist (Ed.), *The dialogic imagination: Four essays by M.M. Bakhtin* (pp. 259–422). University of Texas Press.

Bakhtin, M. (1984). *Problems of Dostoievsky's poetics*. University Minnesota Press.

Bakhtin, M. (1986). *Speech genre and other late essays*. University of Texas Press.

Bigonnesse, C., & Chaudhury, H. (2020). The landscape of "aging in place" in gerontology literature: Emergence, theoretical perspectives, and influencing factors. *Journal of Aging and Environment, 34*(3), 233–252. https://doi.org/10.1080/02763893.2019.1638875

Cooney, A. (2012). Finding home': A grounded theory on how older people 'find home' in long-term care settings. *International Journal of Older People Nursing, 7*, 188–199. https://doi.org/10.1111/j.1748-3743.2011.00278.x

Droz Mendelzweig, M., & Bedin, M. G. (2022). The perimeter of the home in old age: Reflecting on the sense of home in a sheltered housing facility during the COVID-19 pandemic. *Journal of Aging and Environment, 37*(2), 202–218. https://doi.org/10.1080/26892618.2022.2041144

Erikson, E. H., & Erikson, J. M. (1998). *The life cycle completed (extended version)*. W. W. Norton.

Forsyth, A., & Molinsky, J. (2021). What is aging in place? Confusions and contradictions. *Housing Policy Debate, 31*(2), 181–196. https://doi.org/10.1080/10511482.2020.1793795

François, F. (1988). Continuité et mouvements discursifs: un exemple chez des enfants de trois ans. *Modèles Linguistiques, 10*(2), 17–36.

Gfeller, F., Grossen, M., Cabra, M., & Zittoun, T. (2022). Réformes politiques face au vieillissement démographique: Diversité des perspectives dans la mise en œuvre d'une politique socio-sanitaire. *Revue pluridisciplinaire d'Education par et pour les Doctorant-e-s, 1*(1), 38–48. https://doi.org/10.57154/journals/red.2022.e990

Gfeller, F., Zittoun, T., Grossen, M., & Cabra, M. (2021). *L'offre de logement pour personnes âgées dans le canton de Neuchâtel. Évolution, état des lieux, tensions. (Rapport de recherche)*. Université de Neuchâtel. https://www.unine.ch/ipe/home/recherche/personnes-agees/homage.html

Gillespie, A., & Cornish, F. (2010). Intersubjectivity: Towards a dialogical analysis. *Journal for the Theory of Social Behaviour, 40*(1), 19–46. https://doi.org/10.1111/j.1468-5914.2009.00419.x
Gillsjö, C., Schwartz-Barcott, D., & Von Post, I. (2011). Home: The place the older adult can not imagine living without. *BMC Geriatrics, 11*(1), 10. http://www.biomedcentral.com/1471-2318/11/10
Greco, S. (2017). Using argumentative tools to understand inner dialogue. *Argumentation, 31*, 331–358. https://doi.org/10.1007/s10503-016-9408-4
Grossen, M., & Salazar Orvig, A. (2011). Dialogism and dialogicality in the study of the self. *Culture and Psychology, 17*(4), 491–509. https://doi.org/10.1177/1354067X11418541
Grossen, M., & Salazar Orvig, A. (2023). L'analyse dialogique du discours appliquée à l'entretien clinique: un point de rencontre interdisciplinaire. In L. Kloetzer & M. dos Santos Mamed (Eds.), *La perspective dialogique en psychologie: réflexions méthodologiques* (pp.19-48). Antipodes.
Hermans, H. J. M., & Gieser, T. (Eds.). (2012). *Handbook of dialogical self theory*. Cambridge University Press.
Iannaccone, A., Cattaruzza, E., & Schwab, E. (Eds.). (2024). *Expériences sociomatérielles. Objets, interactions, espaces*. Alphil.
James, W. (2012). *Principles of psychology* (Vol. 1). Cosimo. 1890 puis 1983 chez Harvard University Press (Original work published 1890).
Knöpfel, C., & Meuli, N. (2020). Vieillir sans famille. Une étude exploratoire. Haute école spécialisée de la Suisse du Nord-Ouest. https://www.im-alter.ch/uploads/media/default/0001/01/Alt-ohne-Angehoerige-Kurzbericht_fr-korr.pdf
Kroger, J., & Adair, V. (2008). Symbolic meanings of valued personal objects in identity transitions of late adulthood. *Identity, 8*(1), 5–24. https://doi.org/10.1080/15283480701787251
Linell, P. (2021). Languaging and dialogue beyond linguistics and conversation analysis. In N. Muller Mirza & M. dos Santos Mamed (Eds.), *Dialogical approaches and tensions in learning and development* (pp. 49–65). Springer.
Magestrini, L. (2021). Les appartements avec encadrement en droit neuchâtelois (Doctrine). In *Recueil de jurisprudence neuchâteloise* (pp. 17–39). Faculté de droit de l'Université de Neuchâtel, Tribunal cantonal.
Mallon, I. (2007). Entrer en maison de retraite: rupture ou tournant biographique? *Gérontologie et société, 30*(121), 251–264. https://doi.org/10.3917/gs.121.0251
Marková, I. (2006). On "the inner alter" in dialogue. *International Journal for Dialogical Science, 1*(1), 125–147. https://ijds.lemoyne.edu/journal/1_1/IJDS.1.1.125A.Markova.html
Marková, I. (2016). *The dialogical mind: Common sense and ethics*. Cambridge University Press.
Marková, I. (2023). *The making of dialogical theory: Social representations and communication*. Cambridge University Press.
Mead, G. H. (1967). *Mind, self and society*. The Chicago University Press. (Original work published 1934).
Molony, S. (2010). The meaning of home: A qualitative metasynthesis. *Research in Gerontological Nursing, 3*(4), 291–307. https://doi.org/10.3928/19404921-20100302-02
Pazhoothundathil, N., & Bailey, A. (2020). Cherished possessions, home-making practices and aging in care homes in Kerala, India. *Emotion, Space and Society, 36*, 100706. https://doi.org/10.1016/j.emospa.2020.100706
Plantin, C. (1996). Le trilogue argumentatif. Présentation de modèle, analyse de cas. *Langue Française, 112*, 9–30. https://www.persee.fr/doc/lfr_0023-8368_1996_num_112_1_5358
Prentice, K., Hand, C., Misener, L., & Hopkins, J. (2023). Older adults' relocation transitions: Relation of place, leisure and identity. *Activities, Adaptation & Aging, 47*(2), 146–170. https://doi.org/10.1080/01924788.2022.2056679
Rowles, G. D., & Chaudhury, H. (Eds.). (2005). *Home and identity in late life. International perspectives*. Springer.
Salazar Orvig, A. (2003). Eléments de sémiologie discursive. In S. Moscovici & F. Buschini (Eds.), *Les méthodes en sciences humaines* (pp. 271–296). Presses Universitaires de France.

Salazar Orvig, A. (2005). Les facettes du dialogisme dans une discussion ordinaire. In P. Haillet & G. Karmaoui (Eds.), *Regards sur l'héritage de Mikhaïl Bakhtine* (pp. 35–66). Encrage. https://hal.science/hal-04440793

Salazar Orvig, A., Grossen, M., & Meystre, C. (2023). De la douleur à la colère: mise en discours des émotions et travail thérapeutique. *Langages, 3*(231), 79–92. https://doi.org/10.3917/lang.231.0079

Säljö, R. (2021). Sign-making, inscriptions and access to epistemic practices: Development in a designed world. In N. Muller Mirza & M. dos Santos Mamed (Eds.), *Dialogical approaches and tensions in learning and development. At the frontiers of the mind* (pp. 67–83). Springer.

Säljö, R. (2022). Development, ageing and hybrid minds: Growth and decline, and ecologies of human functioning in a sociocultural perspective. *Learning, Culture and Social Interaction, 37*, 100465. https://doi.org/10.1016/j.lcsi.2020.100465

Searles, H. (1960). *The nonhuman environment in normal development and in schizophrenia.* International Universities.

Siaugues, C., & Verdon, B. (2020). « Que faire du travail domestique la retraite venue? » Tribulations des passages et des scènes chez les femmes à la retraite. *Travailler, 43*(1), 137–159. https://doi.org/10.3917/trav.043.0137

Thalineau, A., & Nowik, L. (2009). Être en « milieu de retraite » et choisir de vivre ailleurs. *Lien Social et Politiques, 62*, 99–109. https://doi.org/10.7202/039317ar

Tisseron, S. (2003). Nos objets quotidiens, de l'identité à la mémoire. In J. R. Filiod (Ed.), *Faire avec l'objet. Signifier, appartenir, rencontrer* (pp. 14–23). Chronique Sociale.

Valsiner, J. (2007). *Culture in minds and societies: Foundations of cultural psychology.* Sage. https://doi.org/10.4135/9788132108504

Valsiner, J. (2014). *An invitation to cultural psychology*. Sage.

van Hoof, J., Janssen, M. L., Heesakkers, C. M. C., van Kersbergen, W., Severijns, L. E. J., Willems, L. A. G., et al. (2016). The importance of personal possessions for the development of a sense of home of nursing home residents. *Journal of Housing for the Elderly, 30*(1), 35–51. https://doi.org/10.1080/02763893.2015.1129381

Verdon, B., & Racin, C. (2021). Ambivalence, emprise, soutien. De la difficulté d'entourer le patient âgé à « suffisamment bonne » distance. *L'Évolution Psychiatrique, 86*(1), 5–16. https://doi.org/10.1016/j.evopsy.2020.09.002

Verdon, B., & Rexand-Galais, F. (2021). À propos de « super-vieillissement ». Idéalisation, hypomanie, renoncement. *Gérontologie et société, 166*(3), 201–214. https://doi.org/10.3917/gs1.166.0201

Voloshinov, Y. N. (1986). *Marxism and the philosophy of language*. Harvard University Press.

Vygotsky, L. (2012). *Thought and language*. The MIT Press. (Original work published 1934).

Zittoun, T. (2013). Religious traditions as means of innovation: The use of symbolic resources in the life course. In H. Zock & M. Buitelaar (Eds.), *Religious voices in self-narratives making sense of life in times of transitions* (pp. 129–148). Walter de Gruyter.

Zittoun, T. (2020). Generalising from a regional case study: A dialogue with a hill. *Culture & Psychology, 26*(1), 62–77. https://doi.org/10.1177/1354067X19888187

Zittoun, T., & Gillespie, A. (2016). *Imagination in human and cultural development.* Routledge.

Zittoun, T., Grossen, M., & Tarrago Salamin, F. (2021). Creating new spheres of experience in the transition to a nursing home. *Learning, Culture and Social Interaction, 28*, 100458. https://doi.org/10.1016/j.lcsi.2020.100458

Zittoun, T., & Levitan, D. (2019). A sociocultural psychology of repeated mobility: Dialogical challenges. *Studies in Psychology / Estudios de Psicología, 40*(1), 79–106. https://doi.org/https://dialnet.unirioja.es/servlet/articulo?codigo=6939279

Chapter 7
The Dynamics of Dependency in Old Age: Psychoanalytic Perspectives

Céline Racin

7.1 Dependency Put to the Test to Age Well

Those who are ageing today can enjoy the fact that the spotlight is entirely on them, observing and supporting an ageing process that is described as 'capable' or 'healthy'. While longer life expectancy opens up a promising future in so far as technological and medical progress means that we can expect better living and health conditions in later life, the concentration of demographic growth at the top of the age pyramid nevertheless poses urgent societal challenges that require a major reorganisation of the way we live together. The way in which public policy responds to this social reality is particularly revealing about the philosophy and social representations of ageing. In recent years, for example, the financing of additional health expenditure linked to the foreseeable advance of life over death has led to a paradigm shift in public policy: the management of risks linked specifically to old age (rather than ageing) has given way to the anticipation and prevention of "health problems of a population perceived negatively as a consumer of care and services" (Déchamp-Le Roux, 2012, p. 82). In OECD countries, there has been a proliferation of projects to promote active and healthy ageing, the "successful" ageing that our idealistic societies have made the new goal. In recent decades, there have been many examples of collective concern about the well-being of people as they age and the risk of this growing segment of the population becoming increasingly frail. Examples include the *Active Ageing Project* (World Health Organization, 2002), the *Healthy Ageing Project* (2004–2007), the *European Year of Active Ageing and Intergenerational Solidarity* (2012) and, more recently, the Law of 8 April 2024 on measures to build a society of good ageing and autonomy (France), the European

C. Racin (✉)
Centre de Rercherche en Psychopathologie et Psychologie Clinique (CRPPC), University Lumière Lyon, Lyon, France
e-mail: celine.racin@univ-lyon2.fr

T. Zittoun, F. Gfeller (eds.), *Ageing, Learning and Development*, Lifelong Learning Book Series 36, https://doi.org/10.1007/978-3-032-11057-2_7

Innovation Partnership on Healthy and Active Ageing (EIP on HAA), launched following the publication of the European Commission's Green Paper on Ageing on 27 January 2021, the *UN Decade of Healthy Ageing* [2021–2030] (World Health Organization). At the same time, these initiatives reflect a desire to control demographic risks and the social and economic risks that they entail, which translates into a call for healthy ageing. The challenges posed by an ageing population have a significant impact on employment, influence intergenerational power struggles, challenge established economic models and raise philosophical questions about the meaning of life and the right to a "dignified" end to life and death. They also test the collective solidarity needed to reduce social inequalities in the face of illness, dependency and death. In these efforts to reshape society, concerns about the long-term financial equilibrium of the social protection system, for example in the context of the economic and financial crisis, sometimes overshadow the changing relationships between age groups, which are in danger of breaking up. While more generations are now living together, they also seem to be living together less frequently, and this goes hand in hand with an increase in loneliness, particularly among young adults and the elderly, which has been observed for some years (Parant, 2005).

"Live to a ripe old age, but in good health". *Those who are ageing today only need to 'behave'*… otherwise they will become dissidents from the socio-economic and cultural ideals of autonomy, independence and control that today make activity the model of normality; otherwise they will incur a debt to the next generation, an imaginary debt that cannot be avoided and that they will never be able to fully pay off. "We must therefore 'age well' in order not to jeopardise the new social pact that would tend to bind generations and different age groups in their relationship to social productivity and utility, which would be the sources of happiness, efficiency and social order (Déchamp-Le Roux, 2012). Not to be a burden on society because of the social cost of caring for dependents, not to be a burden on one's children and grandchildren, is thus a paradigmatic concern of our time, one that cannot be satisfied by external reality alone, as this concern also reflects highly mobilised projective movements. An example of this is an advertising campaign for a mutual health insurance company, for example, in which ageing subjects wear an emblematic penance: "*It's not my fault that life expectancy is increasing*", carefully concealing the underlying guilt under the guise of a reactionary formation. This ideology of "ageing well" is still very much constrained by a biomedical approach to *ageing* and is based on three essential pillars, to which different models give different prominence: intervening in the biological determinants that contribute to prolonging longevity and reducing and preventing morbidity by combating frailty; preserving cognitive performance; maintaining social interactions (especially, more recently, with a strong emphasis on digital technology). Although social and environmental resources are regularly cited to justify the success or failure of this programme, the large multidisciplinary research network organised around *Successful Ageing* since the 1960s (Baltes & Baltes, 1990; Havighurst, 1961, 1963; Rowe & Kahn, 1987, 1997, 1998) still regularly cites individual resources, which helps to perpetuate the confusion between 'ageing well' and 'successful ageing'.

The praise of an intense life, a contemporary ideal, has certainly become a "modern obsession", as Tristan Garcia puts it (2016). Intensity thus supports the pole that vectors the pursuit of happiness, understood as Freud emphasised "in the narrow sense of the word", the idea of experiencing "strong feelings of pleasure", achieved "predominantly or even exclusively" in relation to the other pole, which wants "pain and displeasure to be absent" (1929, p. 262). A whole range of values—performance, beauty, energy, mobility, surpassing oneself, initiative, conquest, seduction, flexibility, change, speed, pleasure for oneself—are conveyed by these incentives. In a dual movement, these incentives seem to guide and support a community and continuity of identifications, investments and ideals that underpin some elements of the "narcissistic contract" (Aulagnier, 1975) of "ageing well". The "means of acting on oneself" and the "staging of oneself" (Ehrenberg, 1995) suggested in this way concern the body at the highest level, in particular the desiring and enjoying body, which becomes the site of exaltation of phallic claims and manic defences against lack, castration, loss, separation and the unthinkable extinction of death.

It seems that the ageing body is ultimately a body under surveillance, firm, supple, aesthetic, dynamic, sexualised, obliged to respect the "pact on the negative" (Kaës, 2009) of castration, loss and the work of death, of which the body bears the stigmata, in a defensive illusion that can sometimes prove psychologically costly and exhausting for the subject. For René Kaës, it is through this negation pact that "an unconscious agreement on the unconscious is concluded and, in some cases, imposed, so that the bond is organised and maintained in the convergent or unequal complementarity of the interests of its subjects, so as to ensure the continuity of the investments and benefits linked to the subsistence of the function of the common ideals, the contract or the narcissistic pact" (2009, p. 121). Securing the subject's membership of the social group requires that he or she be assigned a place that is prescribed but that still allows for deviations, unless the narcissistic contract turns into a humiliating "narcissistic pact", which we associate with what Michel Billé and Didier Martz (2010) have denounced as the "tyranny of ageing well". Clearly, these social representations, however normative they may be, are not sufficient to capture the unique psychological effects of the narcissistic renegotiation of ageing subjects. While the ego's quest for the ideal in later life may find support in the socially valued ways of fulfilling certain desires conveyed by the ideology of 'ageing well', the fact remains that ideal representations of ageing remain vectored by the constitution of the ideal instance in early childhood, based primarily on the parental psyche, and its many readjustments as the trials of different ages are worked through. Our aim is to draw attention to the way in which, in certain situations, the ideology of 'ageing well' follows the path opened up by the 'ideology of happiness for all', which continues to serve a paradoxical and universalising conception of autonomy, closely confused with independence, against which the value of a 'successful' life is measured. However, by modelling an innate, ability-based conception of autonomy, these approaches are clearly incompatible with taking into account the anthropological dimensions that situations of dependency bring to the fore, namely the reminder of the fundamentally *temporal* nature of the human being and his irreducible *physicality*, at the heart of which lies the figure of a human being who is also vulnerable, fallible and embedded in a network of interdependencies.

7.2 At the Root of Dependency: Development Dynamics

It is precisely the fundamental asymmetry of dependency relations, with the risk of subjection and the threat to the autonomy of the subject that has given this concept a negative connotation in our societies, which are dominated by a legal and political conception of the rational moral subject capable of self-determination. This conception of the human being, despite the proposed shifts in emphasis, remains extremely widespread, so that *to be* in our societies is *to be autonomous*, and the question of dependence has long remained the question of the struggle for emancipation and the affirmation of the power of the subject. However, as Nathalie Maillard reminds us, "man has not always interpreted himself in this way. Autonomy is an attribute that 'arrives' to man in specific historical conditions, at the time of the modern Enlightenment" (2011, p. 24). Other perspectives, inspired in particular by the ethics of care, support the consideration of new moral categories and new conceptions of the human being. These categories allow us both to criticise the notion of autonomy and to reshape it in the light of a reconsideration of experiences that are a constant reminder of the fragility of existence, such as early childhood, old age, serious illness, disability and social insecurity. From this perspective, dependency is no longer seen as an obstacle to the emancipatory ideal of the struggle for autonomy, but as a possible and therefore potentially positive response to the anthropological vulnerability of the human being, just as it can, in another way, be the vector of increased vulnerability and the opportunity for relations of domination. In this way, Marie Garrau and Alice Le Goff specify that "this vulnerability refers to the relational dimension of an existence marked by passivity and exposure, which relations of dependence do not primarily limit, but support and protect" (2010, p. 7). In this sense, the dichotomy between dependent and non-dependent people (independence being the essential ground of autonomy in its classical conception) becomes obsolete: dependence is, as Pascale Molinier puts it, "the human condition" (2009). This approach also makes it possible to avoid the opposition between activity (confused with autonomy) and passivity (confused with dependence) at the manifest level, and to understand dependence not as something *to be suffered*, but as an organisation that makes sense for the psyche, as the (possible) affirmation of a subjective position, even if it is not reducible to the power and self-control highly valued in our societies. In this sense, vulnerability, far from being an obstacle to autonomy as a presumed and naturally available capacity, is ultimately consubstantial with it and works on it from within, requiring eminently relational 'empowerment' mechanisms.

Whether it is defined as the condition of a person who "needs someone to survive, because he is unable to carry out, definitively or for a prolonged period of time, the actions necessary for life due to impairment of vital functions" (Delomier, 1973,

p. 9), or as "a more or less accepted constraining relationship with an entity, an object, a group or an institution, real or ideal, resulting from the satisfaction of a need" (Memmi, 1979, p. 32), or again, among care theorists, as "a necessary and potentially positive relationship" (Garrau & Le Goff, 2010, p. 13), dependence leaves no choice but to have another person present. However, the situation of powerlessness that arises in the absence of this other person—the inability to provide for one's own needs and to protect oneself from danger—is not imposed on older people without their having experienced it at some point in their lives. The construction of the subjective relationship that each of us has with the question of dependence is inaugurated in the bosom of the primordial biological experience of *helplessness* in the human infant. This state of helplessness describes "the condition of a being who, left to his own devices, is incapable of helping himself" (Laplanche, 1987, p. 97). Freud makes this experience of primordial distress (Hilflosigkeit) a crucial point in the psychic construction and development of the subject, and describes the consequences that are fundamental to the subject: "*The influence of the real external world is strengthened*, the differentiation of the ego from the id is prematurely favoured, the dangers of the external world are heightened in their significance, and *the value of the object*, which alone can protect against these dangers and replace the lost intrauterine life, is *enormously increased*" (1926, p. 269) (emphasis added). Thus, from the very beginning of life, the human infant, because of its fundamental neoteny, encounters a state of dependence within which it is indefectibly driven to seek a connection with the other, in ways that are nonetheless unique to each individual. These modalities relate in particular to the way in which the subject deals with the psychological problems inherent in this "fundamental anthropological situation", organised under the "primacy of the Other" (Laplanche, 1997), from a primitive interpsychic experience marked by the seal of loss and passivity. Indeed, "the need for the presence of a third party to guarantee the continuity of life is a paradoxical reminder of the vulnerability of the subject and gives rise to fears about the consequences of the absence of this other or of his distance. The fundamental asymmetry of dependent relationships also puts to the test the subject's ability to tolerate the action of the other in relation to him or her, for him or her, without feeling overwhelmed, threatened in his or her sense of individuality, in his or her possibilities of expressing subjectivity and exercising autonomy" (Racin, 2023). The ways in which we relate to others, and the place that dependency occupies as a psychic reality, are therefore closely linked to the ways in which we deal with the fundamental anxieties that arise in the face of threats of loss and passivity.

Thus, from the initial psychic distressborn of primordial biological experience of *helplessness*, affective dependence settles indefinitely in the background of our psychic life, a more or less noisy tenant *on whose support* and *against which* the subject's investments are gradually modelled, whether these investments are narcissistic investments (turned towards the self, the continuity of the subject and the permanence of his investment in himself) or towards others. "We can never avoid dependence, but we can hope that it will eventually take on a moderate intensity that is acceptable to our narcissism. Some people go so far as to believe that they can 'choose' the way it manifests. In fact, there are forms of dependency that seem more attractive to narcissism, that give themselves the mask of freedom, that blur the role of the other, of the other subjects that cross our lives" (Roussillon, 2004, p. 421).

So there are dependencies that do not speak their name, quiet dependencies that are invisible in the background of our psychic life, based on a minimal acceptance that we cannot be everything, all alone, all the time, just as there are noisy dependencies that manifest themselves, even behaviourally, in particularly turbulent object relationships. Some dependencies can be experienced with confidence in a circle of friends and family whose reliability has been proven in the face of the threat of large sums of money, just as some dependencies simply cannot be recognised and remain denied or even denied against a background of division. In this respect, the borderline and paranoid paradigms are emblematic of the use of various forms of narcissistic defences to deny otherness in the face of the fear of being 'caught' in the other, fuelled by the threat of dependency. Some dependencies are surprising in that they arise where they are not required by external, biological and social reality, and worrying when they arise against the background of an internal, subjective need to guarantee the permanence of the object in order to safeguard narcissism (as in the case of addictive behaviours). The modalities of object relations that emerge in situations in which the need for security resurfaces and the significance of the object is heightened—a need that, as Freud argued, is paid for by the fear of losing the object's love and the threat of being abandoned to one's fate (1938)—offer a particularly favourable promontory for the clinical objectification of addictive phenomena. In this sense, any new (or newly revealed) threat to the subject's physical integrity (re)generates the need for the other. This is particularly the case in situations of long-term care. In this context, a whole range of pre-existing psychological positions, raised by the challenges of dependency, may find a point of call for re-actualisation, for movements of reorganisation or disorganisation.

In this sense, our aim is not to determine whether a subject is seized by the issue of dependency or not. Otherwise, of course, such a concept runs the risk of reducing the notion of dependency to a psychopathological model, or even, in the case of ageing, to a predetermined biological and developmental destiny, defined under the aegis of social norms that erect bitterly compartmentalised categorisations that contribute to reinforcing the phenomena of marginalisation and exclusion. We recognise dependency as a way of relating to others, with a latent and manifest content, which is part of the experience at every stage of life, through the many trials of differentiation, lack, separation, loss and passivity that punctuate human development, in variations and oscillations along the continuum of the normal and the pathological, so dear to Freud.

In the course of ageing, this concern enables us to gain a better grasp of the psychic work mobilised in a situation of dependency, also known as "dependency work" (Racin, 2019, 2022), in order to understand the way in which elderly subjects in care appropriate what constitutes their dependency and the help provided to them. This perspective allows us to hear the different forms of the psychic reality of dependency that support the transformation of narcissistic and object investments required at this moment of vulnerable passage. It sheds light on the way in which the subject comes to terms with this moment of transition and enables us to understand the psychic function performed by long-term care facilities and the figures of care who are encountered there. In an effort to remain as close as possible to the diversity of clinical reality and the polysemy of dependency situations, the aim is to specify the clinical and psychopathological forms and their possible inflections, in the course of a development that constantly oscillates between a tendency towards dependency and a tendency towards independence.

7.3 The Importance of Distinguishing Between Risk and Vulnerability in Ageing

Today, reaching the age of 80 is no longer an achievement. The paradox lies in the fact that a number of men and women over this age today, born at the beginning of the last century, marked by the murderous events whose sad memory now dominates history, could not have hoped for much more than to reach their 70th birthday. Today, the over-80 s are the fastest growing demographic group and reaching old age is now a "statistical norm" (Lalive d'Épinay & Spini, 2008). However, this period of life is far from being a new golden age: it allows people to postpone the prospect of death for longer, but unlike the imagined golden age of old age, it is still strongly associated with the prospect of irreversible losses, as the study by Jutta Heckhausen et al. (1989) on the perception of expected gains and losses in the course of development by different age groups has already shown. Current demographic projections strongly support these social representations, with analyses based on data from the 'Handicaps-Incapacités-Dépendance' (HID) survey predicting a rapid increase in the dependency rate for men and women over the age of 75, with the average age of onset of dependency set at 78 for men and 83 for women, and tending to fall further. Within this group of people affected by dependency—understood as the need for help to perform certain essential acts of daily life due to constraints inherent in the state of health but also in the material environment—the sex ratio is clearly to the disadvantage of women, who are more numerous in the group of elderly people but also more often affected by dependency than men (two thirds of people said to be dependent are women) (Duée & Rebillard, 2006). However, as we have stressed, dependency does not confine a group of people to a homogeneous category, just as not all people over the age of 80 are affected by activity limitations to the extent that they need to be compensated for by the action of a third party. The social construction of a demarcation at the age of 80 essentially underlines the increased prevalence of certain chronic conditions and physical and cognitive impairments at this age, and thus the increased risk of experiencing disabling functional limitations. Thus, while "the quality of life of the elderly has improved significantly over the decades [...], advancing age can unfortunately also be characterised by the onset of diseases specific to the elderly and by an increase in co-morbidities, making the very old more fragile and, for some, leading to dependency [...]". The onset of an acute illness can lead to a cascade of decompensation of one or more functions in an elderly person already suffering from one or more chronic illnesses" (Muller et al., 2004, pp. 172–173).

However, if our understanding of the phenomena of ageing is too closely linked to the prospect of functional decline, there is a great risk that the experience of older people will be studied only in terms of the threats inherent in old age, and that the deeper meanings of these experiences, as well as their great diversity, will be overlooked. We feel that research along these lines often contributes to a normative approach to the ageing process (as in the case of research that distinguishes between so-called 'pathological' ageing, characterised by medical conditions, and so-called 'normal' ageing). Others strongly promote models of successful ageing. This is the case of the theory of John Rowe and Robert Kahn (1987, 1997), which promotes an individual who is voluntary and responsible for his or her own ageing, and who is able to escape the trappings of normal ageing, characterised by a 'typical' decline with age, a perspective that has been strongly criticised for the optimism and elitism it conveys. The "developmental theory of human adaptation" of Margret and Paul Baltes (1990), as a counterpoint to this dichotomy between the virtues of an "independent" ageing process and the vicissitudes of a "dependent" ageing process, defends, albeit not without a certain fatalism, the irrevocability of a deficit process common to all forms of ageing in different degrees and causalities. From their point of view, we should prepare for it rather than try to change it, by observing principles that allow us to include dependency, when it occurs and cannot be avoided, in the register of adaptive resources available to the individual to cope with losses during the ageing process (Baltes, 1996).

It must be said that this pioneering work, which takes a categorical approach, leaves in the shadows the future of men and women who do not meet the criteria for *successful* ageing and who are more likely to be dependent. There is not space here for an exhaustive inventory of the dominant theories of ageing in international research. In most cases, however, we find it regrettable that the authors do not look more closely at the ways in which people move from one form of ageing to another. This descriptive, categorical approach, far from reflecting the subjective experience of the subjects concerned, who do not allow themselves to be so easily pigeonholed, also considerably reduces the possibility of proposing heuristic hypotheses capable of shedding light on the phenomena of ageing from the prism of a processual dynamic.

All too often, as Christel Colin (2003) points out, there is still a too rapid and systematic assimilation between the appearance of functional limitations (called "incapacities" in Wood's sequence) and limitations in activities leading to the need for assistance (called "disadvantages" or "handicaps" in Wood's sequence). This is all the more true given that an increasing number of studies, such as those carried out a few years ago by Emmanuelle Cambois and Jean-Marie Robine (2003), emphasise the wide range of factors underlying the dynamic process of this transition from functional limitations to dependency: In addition to the nature of the disability, social factors are widely implicated in this perspective, as well as the inter-individual differences identified in the way these disabilities are "managed". This last point opens up a very fruitful opportunity for the psychoanalytic clinic and psychopathology to shed light on the psychological dynamics at work in this transition.

Anxious to account for the "diversity of individual trajectories that seem to break the framework of life course models" (Lalive d'Épinay & Spini, 2008, p. 42) The Swilsoo study (Swiss Interdisciplinary Longitudinal Study on the Odlest Old), conducted by the Centre interfacultaire de gérontologie at the University of Geneva under the direction of Christian Lalive d'Épinay (sociologist) and Dario Spini (social psychologist), was guided by the conviction that more attention should be paid to the under-researched experience of old age. This study, entitled *Les années fragiles: la vie au-delà de quatre-vingts ans* (2008), is sufficiently rare in the field of qualitative research on ageing to warrant its mention here. In the study of the factors that determine and organise what the authors call the "architecture of old age", the concept of frailty occupies a nodal position in the identification of thresholds likely to mark the transitions between the various forms of ageing. The concept of frailty is far from universally accepted and has been used in a variety of ways in the scientific literature, even to the point of being equated in some guidelines with a phase prior to dependency. The French position is currently in line with the dominant international perspective of John Campbell and David Buchner (1997), in which the syndrome of geriatric frailty is understood as a constellation of many conditions, certainly without a precise scientific meaning, rather than as a specific clinical entity (Hamerman, 1999). The introduction of this concept, which refers to the reduction in physiological reserve capacity which alters the mechanisms for adapting to stress, in the absence of functional impairment, has helped to define, in life-course epidemiological study models (*Life course epidemiology*), the contours of factors that would represent a future risk of exposure to functional limitations and, consequently, dependency, which are regularly observed or revealed by the occurrence of adverse events such as falls (Rolland et al., 2011). In support of this concept, the authors of the study suggest that the process of *fragilisation* is the common denominator for all forms of ageing and represents "the dynamic that unites the three health states of old age [...]: a process initially in *statu nascendi* in *independent* old people, when frailty is not expressed or only in mild forms; a manifest process then, when it creates a risky situation and imposes a series of constraints on old people whom we call *frail* at this stage; finally, a severe process that generates forms of irreversible and chronic incapacity (*dependent* old people)" (Lalive d'Épinay & Spini, 2008, p. 38).

On this basis, the study seeks to identify the ways in which people move from one of these forms of ageing to another according to the above sequence, and to explore the nature of the determinants of these transitions. The conclusions of the study confirm the great diversity of trajectories and the bio-psycho-social determinants that shape them. They also highlight the fact that dependency is not an inescapable feature of old age, which suggests that we should move away from the idea that ageing inevitably passes through the three stages that follow the sequence of 'preserved independence—frailty—dependency'. In doing so, the authors invite the research community to focus more precisely on the transitions from independence to frailty or from frailty to dependency and, ultimately, to focus more specifically on the experience of *frailty* that is most common to all, regardless of the chronological age of the ageing subjects. They therefore encourage studies aimed at specifying the different forms of this dynamic, which would make it possible to understand why some subjects become dependent as they age, while others end their lives, even in old age, without ever having encountered the need for major assistance to meet their needs and enable them to continue living.

The interest of this study for our purposes lies in the fact that it allows us to shift our understanding of old age from relatively disjointed categories to a dimensional approach that emphasises the dynamics of the ageing process, approached from the angle of *fragility* specific to these ages of life. We are certainly in favour of this perspective, but with a number of conditions. The first condition is that independence and dependence should not be reified as "states", "pure" forms that exist only as abstractions (we are never, in the final analysis, completely independent or dependent), but rather as *tendencies*. Tendencies between which subjects constantly oscillate, in more or less pronounced, more or less manifest amplitudes, defining a continuum on which they are never completely fixed, but which can undergo stabilisations, possible, but always susceptible to destabilisation. Here we return to Winnicott's famous proposal of an evolutionary continuum, in the course of which development moves from dependence *to relative* independence, a formulation that underlines both the direction of a movement and the insistence on a conception of independence as an unattainable horizon rather than a definitive state. The second condition, which follows from the first, is that the continuum should not be turned upside down by reversing the poles on the pretext of age, as if it reflected a chronological sequence (even if it merges with it to some extent at the beginning of life) driven first by an inexorable movement towards independence and then by an equally irreducible movement towards dependence with age. This representation is similar to the sequence used in the study by C. Lalive d'Epinay and D. Spini and can be modelled as follows:

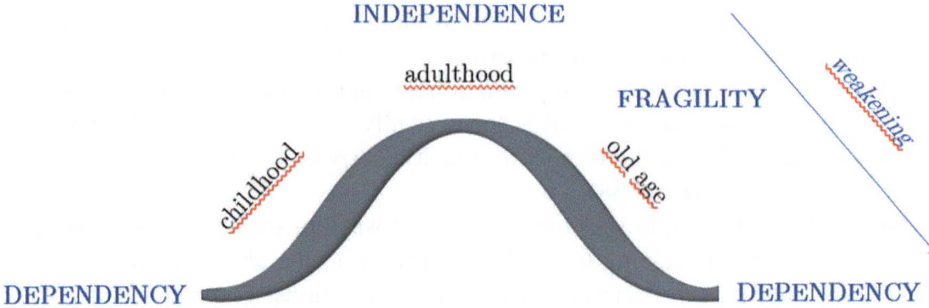

We propose to take full account of the perspective that allows us to consider possible regressions on the continuum from absolute dependence to relative independence. In this sense, pre-existing psychic positions of dependence are always likely to be brought out into the open (unveiled?) when the passage of life inflicts its tremors on the psychic edifice. We must therefore consider the process of fragility as one of the forces that act as a privileged attractor of a retrograde movement on this continuum, as one of the factors likely to intervene in the implementation of these regressions, but which never completely diverts the subject from the paths open to independence, which would otherwise condemn it to the vanishing point of dependence. Independence, in this way, always exists as a horizon in a possible future, and the movement, even if it appears counterintuitive and thwarted, remains that of dependence towards independence, in a way that is always complex and singular for each subject:

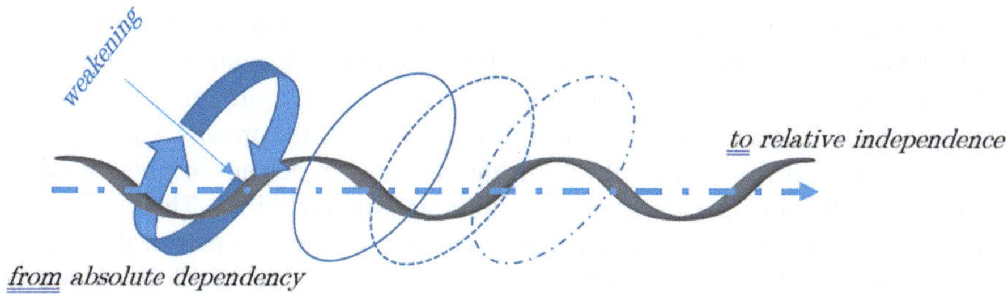

The third condition relates directly to the nature of the process of frailty, defined in the study as "the progressive and inevitable loss of physiological and sensorimotor reserves with advancing age" (Lalive d'Épinay & Spini, 2008, p. 110), which can be accelerated by exposure to multiple biological, social or psychological risks. It is important here to focus on the distinction between the concepts of risk and frailty, and thus between the dimensions of frailty and vulnerability, which are manifest at the physical and sometimes cognitive level of the older person, but can also be understood at the psychological level. These are issues inherent in psychopathology. They are the focus of much attention in relation to prevention issues raised in the social and clinical fields, and are particularly relevant to child development. However, it should be recognised that development is a dynamic process that does not stop at the threshold of old age and is therefore likely to influence the ageing process in its own way. While the multidimensional concepts of frailty and vulnerability in the elderly have gradually become part of the ethical, social and medical vocabulary, specific psychological aspects must necessarily be taken into account to shed light on the clinical and psychopathological problems encountered in this population. However, from a psychological point of view, the concept of vulnerability remains poorly defined. Stanislas Tomkiewicz and Michel Manciaux define it as "a state of reduced resistance to harassment and aggression". Vulnerability can be permanent or temporary" (1987, p. 737). From a psychoanalytic perspective, this definition leads us to associate vulnerability with a greater sensitivity on the part of the subject to internal and external stimuli, which can lead them to have a traumatic value, remembering that "it is not the event itself that is traumatic, but rather what we integrate from this event. We then speak of a potentially traumatic event, which depends on the way in which the subject integrates the events with which he or she is confronted. From an economic point of view, trauma is linked to an excess of excitement or demands that cannot be processed or managed by the resources available to an individual at a given moment. This image distinguishes trauma (excitations that penetrate the psyche and remain encysted there) from stress (which is more a deformation than an invasion of the excitatory barrier)" (Laurent et al., 2015, p. 115).

Vulnerability also builds an additional bridge to the dimension of fragility by introducing the notion of otherness. All in all, vulnerability testifies to the existence of an underlying fragility that is expressed in interaction with the environment, which unearths imprints of the subject's history and reveals traces of his or her psychological dynamics, which therefore need to be assessed. It is not the result of the individual alone, but seems to be linked to interactions with the environment throughout life. The framework of interactions means that the process of vulnerability has to be thought of in terms of circular causality, with each new frightening situation for a vulnerable person implying additional vulnerabilities. Thus, while we believe that frailty and the potential vulnerability it implies are part of the ageing process, as a result of the biological weakening and psychological changes that occur at this time, dependency is not a systematic expression of this: we see it as a risk associated with advancing age, characterised by circumstances and events that are far from being exerted on an inert subject. It is only by taking into account the interplay of these different elements that we can approach the libidinal economy that organises the psychic and relational configuration of the elderly person in relation to his or her dependency. This perspective is particularly fruitful for understanding the singular impact of the individual's confrontation with his or her dependency, whether new or increased. It is possible to define certain risk parameters for dependency, such as the onset of pathology and disability during the ageing process. However, as Colette Chiland points out, between what we know about risk before the fact and what we discover about a person's vulnerability after the fact comes the person's organising action, i.e. a story "which cannot be described only from the outside as a series of observable events" (1978, p. 378), but must also be understood from the inside in order to try to understand how a person does or does not give weight and meaning to the events he or she goes through.

C. Lalive d'Epinay and D. Spini argue that the transition from independence to frailty and the transition from frailty to dependence have very different consequences for the subjective feelings of the people who experience them, which they explain as follows:

> These two transitions are very different in nature. The first can be described as soft, in that [...] the process of frailty is initiated before the defined threshold of frailty status is crossed. [The transition from independent to frail is certainly associated with a deterioration in health, but this is gradual; in most cases it does not mark a break between before and after, and the person can remain hopeful of improvement. On the other hand, the transition to dependency, marked by the onset of serious incapacity, has strong, immediate implications for daily life, most of which are irreversible. (2008, p. 306–307)

And so it is with the metamorphoses of the body, nonchalantly passed over in silence for the possible seizure of conscience, with the muted sensations and perceptions that make up this "bass continuo of little miseries", as Henri Danon-Boileau and Gérard Dedieu-Anglade elegantly put it (2012). They seem to elude the reckoning of a watchful ego, scrupulous about the affronts it receives. The body bends, twists, staggers, shudders, contorts, memory and the senses may play a few unfortunate tricks, but without compromising the movement of desire towards the outside world and the investment of oneself. Sometimes, however, it is the potential space for the fulfilment of desires that comes up against the limited amplitude of a resisting articulation, colliding with the slightest clue that might signal the precariousness, vulnerability or betrayal of the body. The affront of a doorknob that refuses, of a garment that resists the passage of a hesitant joint, of a bed or an armchair that shies away from its supporting function, of a floor that unfurls its annoying lengths, of a saucepan that gives in to the pull of gravity, of a bus step that is vertiginously close to altitude, of a bathtub surface that competes with the adventurous floor of an ice rink, of papers and everyday matters that elude the effort of organisation.... So many limitations that some subjects may feel abandoned by the body, betrayed, condemned to inactivity and strangers in their own world, while others will cherish every remaining possibility of action as a pearl of culture that allows them to continue living and to expect pleasure from it. It is not so much the loss, which is an inescapable fact of life, as its irreversibility as we age, which forces the psychic apparatus to undergo a series of changes. Nor is it so much the manifest weight of the event—even if its 'reality' remains to be recognised—as the narcissistic investment of the episode experienced in the body and its unconscious conflictual resonances, which indicate its possible traumatic charge. In this respect, the clinic for memory disorders is very illustrative of a rupture in the continuous feeling of existence and of ageing without damage, which is likely to appear with the impression of less cognitive mobilisation (Verdon, 2007). However, there are certain events in the ageing process which inevitably lead to the urgent need to face the prospect of "loss of self", which until then could be avoided and postponed. The occurrence of a somatic event, whether insidious or sudden, is sometimes one of those heavy blows to the body that betray the passage of time and its effects. When the weakening dynamics associated with the ageing process take their toll on the body, medical observation often reveals a health profile known as "polypathological" (Muller et al., 2004), characterised by a weakening or even deterioration of cardiovascular, osteo-articular, sensory, endocrine-metabolic and visceral systems and functions, in heterogeneous configurations. Epidemiological studies unanimously highlight the increasing prevalence of chronic diseases, functional disabilities and dementia with age (Henrard & Ankri, 2003). The challenge is therefore to consider both the genesis of and the encounter with these somatic changes, in a creativity that also depends on the subjectivity of the subject in terms of this risk-vulnerability interaction related to the onset of dependency.

From this perspective, we can say that while the illnesses and disabilities that increase with age undeniably have a bio-physio-chemical or mechanical origin, the fact remains that the singular experience of encountering dependency, indeed, can only be understood in terms of transaction, some of which open the way to an elaborate resumption of the various metamorphoses of the body within the psychic work of ageing, while others more unfavourably compromise the possibility of a work of subjectivation of this experience. Among the many ways in which people grow old, the transition from hospitalisation in a geriatric ward to long-term care in a residential institution is one of the riskiest experiences for older people, requiring close attention to the psychic work that is likely to be mobilised.

7.4 Clinical Vignette: Bertrand[1]

At the age of 85, Bertrand had already been hospitalised several times in the previous 2 years, but this latest hospitalisation, during which I met him as part of a research project, following a fall at home in the context of incipient cognitive impairment and cardiac hyperfragility, heralded a new era for him, marked by the prospect of significant changes in his daily living environment in the form of a move to a nursing home (although the alternative of returning home with increased support had long been maintained). Prior to his hospitalisation, Bertrand lived alone in an upstairs house with no bedroom on the ground floor. He walked alone with a stick and was still driving a year ago. He received help from a few professionals (a nurse to administer his medication and an occasional home help), had meals delivered to his home and received help from his children with his administrative affairs, but refused any specific help with daily tasks, particularly personal care. In Bertrand's case, the castration anxiety was primarily focused on his intellectual abilities, the basis of his inventiveness, an anxiety that was reinforced by his awareness of the reduced efficiency of his cognitive functions.[2] Bertrand proudly describes himself as "self-taught", endowed with "ingenuity" and a "passionate temperament", which has enabled him to pursue a "successful career" and take on responsibility. The guarantee of his "masculinity", which occupies an important place in his concerns, lies not so much in the performance of the body, he tells us, but in the "intelligence" of the body, its "ability" to verify in reality the hypotheses that an insatiable curiosity never ceases to inspire. Bertrand gives me an immediate example of this, not without a certain jubilation, when he explains how he solved the problem—insoluble for hospital nurses—of a lamp that was no longer working. "I can use my arms and legs", he says as he painfully observes: "I realise I can't do what I did two months ago. You see, everything costs you, everything causes problems. And then I can't walk". At the hospital, Bertrand noticed that there were "no young people" and was surprised, even though he didn't feel "old" but "disabled". Deprived of certain abilities that once allowed him to "help out" and gain the approval of those around him, Bertrand now fears that he will lose control over the things that affect him.

[1] Some elements of this clinical vignette have been used in a publication in the journal *Neurologie-Psychiatrie-Gériatrie* from the point of view of the problems of refusal of help and care in dementia (Racin, 2019).

[2] The cognitive assessment supports the hypothesis of a cortical disease of the Alzheimer type.

Bertrand also feels powerless in the face of the suffering of his peers on the ward, a mirror that reflects back to him the threatening image of a worrying future: "I've already called for help, you know. You do it without thinking. […] I've always been active, I've always done things myself, I've always been independent". Bertrand feels "useless" and wants to regain his independence, for which mobility is the key. He marvels at his discovery of the walker, a very clever ally in its ability to support multiple functions ("it's amazing, it's also a stool!"). Bertrand would like to return home, but under conditions that would allow him to ensure the continuity of his previous investments and, in particular, the continuity of his links with his children, grandchildren and neighbours. From his point of view, his home should reflect the image of an active, independent man, capable of providing help and maintaining "interesting exchanges", which he felt was incompatible with the proposed refurbishment of his ground floor, on which his return was conditional (in particular, the installation of a care bed in the living room). We hear the extent to which Bertrand sees his home as a source of material and narcissistic investment, and the threat to the satisfaction he used to feel there, which could be taken away from him by younger people in positions of authority, as he used to manage a team of "young people" at the height of his career.

We meet Bertrand again 4 months after his discharge from hospital. He was still experiencing some episodes of somatic fragility and—according to the carers—was having difficulty adapting to his new nursing home lifestyle. The aids and the different forms of care seem to be a constraint. Bertrand regularly expresses his refusal to be touched during hygiene care and his annoyance at feeling deprived of control over things that concern him, a feeling exacerbated by an institutional system that promotes the systematic presence of a carer to ensure that daily tasks are carried out correctly, even though Bertrand shows himself capable of carrying them out alone. His attempts to gain control, for example by storing and doing his own laundry, sometimes lead to power struggles with some of the carers, to the point where he feels insecure, dispossessed and robbed. However, Bertrand has been able to form some bonds within the centre, helped by his regular participation in the activities on offer. When we met up with him again, after a resumption of contact complicated by organisational difficulties within the nursing home which meant that Bertrand was unavailable at the time of our visits, he had no recollection of our previous meetings, but readily accepted our presence. From the outset, the relationship was marked by Bertrand's libidinal investment, and he was seductive towards me, proudly escorting me to his room, "in all honour", as he was careful to point out, and taking me on many detours around the premises. This manoeuvre seemed designed both to conceal his difficulties in finding his way around the establishment and to mischievously show me off to the curious and scrutinising eyes of the other residents. "Now I can walk normally," says Bertrand. "You see, everything works normally. Except for the tiredness…". Bertrand finds the contrast with the hospital difficult to bear and denounces the extremely restrictive environment ("It's regulated, you see. I'm not allowed to do this, I'm not allowed to do that") and insufficiently supportive, where a warm and involved presence is sorely lacking. In fact, despite our invitations to talk about it, Bertrand seems to have little interest in the carers, whose identity and intentions are anonymous ("you never know who is who or what they've come to do"), leading to a new encounter with an unfamiliar and worrying environment.

Bertrand constantly waves the trump cards that allow him to stand upright in the face of the threat, in a movement that at the same time betrays the precariousness of these supports of phallic-narcissistic reassurance: he can dress himself, but many "vital" items are missing; he can tidy up "his home", but the furniture is inadequate, and his love of filing, once supported by his "predispositions" and his "methodical" nature, is no longer so secure, leading him to say: "I've lost my bearings here" and that he might need a woman to help him. "But they assumed I was an addict because I was a single man. Well, no, anyway, I'm here because I'm alone. I don't... I don't... I don't have, I don't have any, physically, any reason to be here. You see? In the midst of this world of "old people" whose pleasures are reduced to regressive means of satisfaction, the supreme asset imposing its superiority over all others is that to which Bertrand gives the name of "independence", this independence having become, to test the narcissism of small differences in the nursing home, the virtue of those who can "get around" and "climb the stairs" without needing to use a wheelchair or wait for the lift. The phallic claim now focuses less on intellectual capacity, as was the case in the hospital, and more on mobility, which allows them to stand up and carry themselves wherever they want, while the others are pinned down, immobilised and castrated in their means of action. This scene is played out every day in the restaurant's living theatre: this morning, for example, Bertrand arrives at the restaurant quite early, sees a few ladies already seated, but all alone, and says to himself in spite of himself: "Look, I'm going to do the rounds. So... from, from my seat I got up and then I went towards, towards... towards one, towards two, I said: "By the way, I've come to say hello to you, you're all alone in your little corner, so.... I'll say one or two words and that's... that's... that's... that's of no importance and it's a pleasure, you see. After that, that, that clears the atmosphere. And then he spotted this man who had arrived in a wheelchair, pushed by a third party, and had come to sit at the next table, a table for four. "I saw that it was a single man who already had three, three women at the same table. So nobody was talking to him, just an illustrious stranger from outside. Ah, I got up from my table and then... I have a table next to me, and then, because I don't have a trolley, I don't have a wheelchair, I don't have anything, I can move around easily. So I moved over and then I was at the table where he was, where he had just sat down. I tapped him on the shoulder and said: "Well, welcome. Are you new here?"

Bertrand's renunciation of the ways in which he was previously satisfied is not without its share of suffering. However, Bertrand's ability to deal with the problem of loss means that he is able to make a variety of investments in care and/or peer relationships, and to support investments that are sometimes even renewed in response to new proposals from the environment as part of the institutionalisation process.

7.5 Institutionalisation and Development in Old Age

For Bertrand, as for many of the people we meet, the new need for long-term care is a metaphor for confronting the complexity of growing old and the diversity of its forms, some of which offer an ambiguous mirror of a future marked by dependency. The theatre of institutionalisation thus seems to mark *paradoxical* thresholds between security and discontinuity, between tranquillity and anxiety about the future. This moment of passage, which forces us to mourn the loss of what *came before*, adds considerable material as well as psychological stakes to the event of entering the nursing home, as seen in the singularity of the experience. At this point, the hospital scene and the nursing home scene not only welcome this passage, but also frame it by offering their own ways of making sense of it, their own ways of figuration of the transformations that the subject is going through. The question of institutionalisation can thus be revisited by considering the effects of meaning produced by long-term care facilities in old age, which can support the process of subjective appropriation of the experience of dependency and be used to promote the ongoing development of the individual.

In this way, Bertrand, who had previously been rather solitary and not very comfortable in society, took on the role of mediator within the nursing home, which led him to occupy a privileged position within the group of residents, a source of narcissistic replenishment in the changes brought about by the institutionalisation process.

In some respects, institutionalisation can have an empowering function, provided that it is seen as a "process of stabilising the conditions of encounter between an elderly person facing a reduction in the means to carry out the activities necessary for life and a person willing to help them, to care for them" (Racin, 2019, p. 202, 2022; Talpin & Racin, 2023, p. 115). The value of this perspective is that it invites us to think about the conditions of encounter that make possible the work of care, which refers simultaneously to a set of psychological dispositions and activities that support life (Tronto, 1993). This formalisation allows us to focus our efforts on understanding the sources and forms of this *disposition* on the part of the carer, on the one hand, and the nature of the *process/work* involved on the part of the person being cared for, on the other.

A salutary recourse can thus be gained when the theatre of care becomes a story-maker, a producer of fantasy scenes, provided that care manages to escape the danger of fetishisation, the procedural requirement, which is not self-evident, that it can be inscribed in a transitional space where care possibly becomes a co-creation situated between the inside and the outside; not merely an objectively perceived attack or imposition of external reality against which the ego must defend itself; not also a 'subjective object' held within the subject's sphere of omnipotence, where the carer is at its mercy. This is not self-evident, because it presupposes a minimal masochistic contribution on the part of the caregiver (Rosenberg, 1982; Verdon, 2004), mirroring that of the elderly subject *in care*, without which no plasticity can be expected on the part of the caregiver to allow herself to be 'used' and 'deformed' in the slightest, and to give the subject another chance to experience other modalities of relating to the object. This presupposes that the care scene can support the construction of a possible play space in which the elderly subject can hope to constantly reconstruct the universe he or she needs and which is always partially slipping away. On this condition, we can hope that the elderly subject will never stop inventing, manipulating, fabricating and shaping a world for *himself*, dreaming up a project under the gaze of others through which he can sustain a desire that prolongs him, a consolation if ever there was one for the relative disinvestment in the fantasy of immortality put to the test in the course of ageing.

The emphasis on the register of *doing* ('manipulating', 'making', 'shaping') through which the subject experiences the pleasure of mastery, and the questioning of the *gaze*, are essential in considering the sources of narcissistic replenishment in the face of the failure and powerlessness that can sometimes be experienced in dependency. This obsession with care and in care plays an essential role in enabling the subject to experience the effectiveness of control, to experience a sense of pride and personal worth based on the recognition of what *has been done*.

But the importance of recognition for *doing* also highlights the transmission issues in the care relationship, the transmission of one person's 'know-how' to encourage the other person's 'power to do', which is how the narcissistic foundations are maintained. Recognition based on the uniqueness of everyday life, "which will be implemented in the gratuity of moments. With perhaps no satisfaction, no apparent return, no measurable result… but without denying the possibility that gratitude may arise, as if by surprise, for what has been shared and is still being shared" (Zielinski, 2014, p. 65).

In other words, this position, which can be experienced through the most ordinary everyday gestures (washing, dressing, cooking, tidying up, shopping, etc.), when the challenges of passing on these "skills" can be really taken on and developed on the care stage, plays a major role in the elderly person's sense of "autonomy". As Pascal Dreyer points out, this is reflected in the exercise of a form of sovereignty that involves the pursuit of "profound gestures", "these gestures, these seemingly insignificant but in reality profound gestures, structure the individual's relationship with himself, with others and with the space he inhabits [, which] connect each individual in daily life and in the present with a history (not limited to his own), with living or dead individuals with whom he maintains a relationship, and with his multiple experiences of space. These dense gestures are acts of creation. They bring dimensions of the past into the present and open the door to the future, to life. They contribute to a sense of continuity of self and connection with the environment" (2015, p. 90–91).

This challenge calls for a great deal of inventiveness on a daily and collective basis in order to renew every day the space of an intermediate area where each person can deposit something of their psychological reality and then reintroduce it into a movement that favours the appropriation of long-term care systems; to ensure that, in the face of the strong heteronomy inherent in residential life, traces of the past can be preserved, linking past and present (by rearranging the decoration of the nursing home bedroom, for example, using significant personal objects, photos, familiar furniture, etc.). Allowing even seemingly insignificant projects to continue to be dreamed and woven into the fabric of the ordinary, "even if they are usually not realised, so that the present does not run the risk of becoming immobile" (Pontalis, 2002, p. 93). To support an imaginary continuity, to thwart the illusion of the end of history that is all too often associated with life in these institutions (the elderly men and women we meet like to use the popular and disturbing expression "final resting place"). Finally, to ensure that the process of institutionalisation takes full account of the value of rituals, which are genuine co-creations, constantly renewed and redesigned (Racin, 2019), and which help people to exercise control over the things that concern them, over the space-time necessary for them to take place, by carrying out the little things of everyday life, at the pace that suits them, in the way that they want, according to the arrangements that they like. Here we come back to the recognition that is focused on *doing*, where the attention paid to others, the care that drives us to want the good of others, easily leads us to focus on incapacities and to impose a series of constraints in the name of 'caring'. This recognition can only unfold within a relational dynamic that allows the emergence of what is essentially the most essential for the individual, what is essentially waiting to be worked out and which threatens to collapse in the "dependency crisis" of old age.

References

Aulagnier, P. (1975). Le contrat narcissique. In *La violence de l'interprétation. Du pictogramme à l'énoncé* (pp. 182–192). Presses Universitaires de France.

Baltes, M. M. (1996). *The many faces of dependency in old age*. Cambridge University Press.

Baltes, P. B., & Baltes, M. M. (1990). Psychological perspectives on successful aging: The model of selective optimization with compensation. In P. B. Baltes & M. M. Baltes (Eds.), *Successful aging: Perspectives from the behavioral sciences* (pp. 1–34). Cambridge University Press.

Billé, M., & Martz, D. (2010). *La tyrannie du bien vieillir*. Le Bord de l'eau.

Cambois, E., & Robine, J.-M. (2003). Vieillissement et restrictions d'activité: L'enjeu de la compensation des problèmes fonctionnels. In *DREES, Études et résultats* (Vol. 261).

Campbell, J., & Buchner, D. (1997). Unstable disability and the fluctuations of frailty. *Age And Ageing, 26*(4), 315–318.

Chiland, C. (1978). Editorial. In E. J. Anthony, C. Chiland, & C. Koupernik (Eds.), *L'enfant dans sa famille. L'enfant vulnérable (1982)* (pp. 377–378). Presses Universitaires de France.

Colin, C. (2003). Que nous apprend l'enquête HID sur les personnes âgées dépendantes, aujourd'hui et demain ? *Revue française des affaires sociales, 1–2*(1), 75–101.

Danon-Boileau, H., & Dedieu-Anglade, G. (2012). *Une certaine forme d'obstination. Vivre le très grand âge*. Odile Jacob.

Déchamp-Le Roux, C. (2012). La prévention des risques liés au vieillissement: Un nouveau pacte social ? *Gérontologie et société, HS, 1*(5), 81–91.

Delomier, Y. (1973). Le vieillard dépendant. Approche de la dépendance. *Gérontologie, 12*, 19–24.

Dreyer, P. (2015). Habiter, entre résistance et réparation. In *Fondation AIA. Le grand âge: Une vie à construire* (pp. 84–97). AIA.

Duée, M., & Rebillard, C. (2006). La dépendance des personnes âgées: Une projection en 2040. *Données sociales - La société française, 7*, 613–619.

Ehrenberg, A. (1995). *L'individu incertain*. Calmann-Lévy.

Freud, S. (1926). Inhibition, symptôme et angoisse. In *Œuvres complètes: Vol. XVII (1923–1925) (1992)* (pp. 203–286). Presses Universitaires de France.

Freud, S. (1929). Le malaise dans la culture. In *Œuvres complètes: Vol. XVIII (1926–1930) (3e éd.: 2015)* (pp. 245–334). Presses Universitaires de France.
Freud, S. (1938). Abrégé de psychanalyse. In *Œuvres complètes: Vol. XX (1937–1939) (2010)* (pp. 225–306). Presses Universitaires de France.
Garcia, T. (2016). *La Vie intense. Une obsession moderne*. Autrement.
Garrau, M., & Le Goff, A. (2010). *Care, justice et dépendance: Introduction aux théories du care (1–1)*. Presses universitaires de France.
Hamerman, D. (1999). Toward an understanding of frailty. *Annals of Internal Medicine, 130*(11), 945–950.
Havighurst, R. J. (1961). Successful aging. *The Gerontologist, 1*(1), 8–13.
Havighurst, R. J. (1963). Successful aging. In R. H. Williams, C. Tibbitts, & W. Donohue (Eds.), *Process of aging: Social and psychological perspectives* (pp. 299–320). Transaction Publishers.
Heckhausen, J., Dixon, R. A., & Baltes, P. B. (1989). Gains and losses in development throughout adulthood as perceived by different adult age groups. *Developmental Psychology, 25*(1), 109–121.
Henrard, J.-C., & Ankri, J. (2003). *Vieillissement, grand âge et santé publique*. Éditions de l'École nationale de la santé publique.
Kaës, R. (2009). *Les alliances inconscientes*. Dunod.
Lalive d'Épinay, C., & Spini, D. (2008). *Les années fragiles: La vie au-delà des quatre-vingts ans*. Presses de l'Université Laval.
Laplanche, J. (1987). *Nouveaux fondements pour la psychanalyse: La séduction originaire (1994e éd.)*. Presses Universitaires de France.
Laplanche, J. (1997). *Le primat de l'autre en psychanalyse: Travaux 1967–1992*. Flammarion.
Laurent, M., de Tychey, C., Lighezzolo-Alnot, J., Bustany, P., Paysant, J., & Krier, M. (2015). Approche comparée de la résilience psychologique chez l'adulte après confrontation à un risque de mort. In C. de Tychey (Ed.), *Violence subie et résilience* (pp. 111–135). Érès.
Maillard, N. (2011). *La vulnérabilité: Une nouvelle catégorie morale?* Labor et Fides.
Memmi, A. (1979). *La dépendance. Esquisse pour un portrait du dépendant*. Gallimard.
Molinier, P. (2009). Vulnérabilité et dépendance: De la maltraitance en régime de gestion hospitalière. In M. Jouan & S. Laugier (Eds.), *Comment penser l'autonomie ? Entre compétences et dépendances* (pp. 433–458). Presses Universitaires de France.
Muller, F., Denis, B., Valentin, C., & Teillet, L. (2004). Vieillissement humain: Évolution démographique et implications médicales. *Nutrition Clinique et Métabolisme, 18*(4), 171–174.
Parant, A. (2005). Les enjeux du vieillissement de la population. *Revue française d'administration publique, 113*(1), 83–95.
Pontalis, J.-B. (2002). *En marge des jours*. Gallimard.
Racin, C. (2019). De la dépendance à l'institutionnalisation des soins de longue durée dans le grand vieillissement: Perspectives psychanalytiques autour des dynamiques du passage. *Revue de psychothérapie psychanalytique de groupe, 73*(2), 199–210.
Racin, C. (2022). Le psychologue clinicien en gériatrie. *Le Carnet PSY, 252*(4), 18–22.
Racin, C. (2023). Quelques ressorts du mécanisme de projection dans le « travail de dépendance » au cours du vieillissement. *Psychologie clinique et projective, 33*(1), 153–173.
Rolland, Y., Benetos, A., Gentric, A., Ankri, J., Blanchard, F., Bonnefoy, M., de Decker, L., Ferry, M., Gonthier, R., Hanon, O., Jeandel, C., Nourhashemi, F., Perret-Guillaume, C., Retornaz, F., Bouvier, H., Ruault, G., & Berrut, G. (2011). Frailty in older population: A brief position paper from the French society of geriatrics and gerontology. *Gériatrie et Psychologie Neuropsychiatrie du Viellissement, 9*(4), 387–390.
Rosenberg, B. (1982). Masochisme mortifère et masochisme gardien de la vie. *Cahiers du Centre de Psychanalyse et de Psychothérapie, 5*, 41–96.
Roussillon, R. (2004). La dépendance primitive et l'homosexualité primaire « en double ». *Revue française de psychanalyse, 68*(2), 421–439.
Rowe, J. W., & Kahn, R. L. (1987). Human aging: Usual and successful. *Science, 237*(4811), 143–149.

Rowe, J. W., & Kahn, R. L. (1997). Successful aging. *The Gerontologist, 37*(4), 433–440.
Rowe, J. W., & Kahn, R. L. (1998). *Successful aging*. Dell Publishing.
Talpin, J.-M., & Racin, C. (2023). *Psychologie clinique du vieillissement normal et pathologique (3ème éd. augmentée et actualisée)*. Dunod.
Tomkiewicz, S., & Manciaux, M. (1987). La vulnérabilité. In M. Manciaux, S. Lebovici, O. Jeanneret, A. E. Sand, & S. Tomkiewicz (Eds.), *L'Enfant et sa santé. Aspects épidémiologiques, biologiques, psychologiques et sociaux* (pp. 737–742). Doin.
Tronto, J. C. (1993). *Un monde vulnérable. Pour une politique du care (2009)*. La Découverte.
Verdon, B. (2004). Souffrance névrotique chez le sujet vieillissant. *Cahiers de psychologie clinique, 23*(2), 35–57.
Verdon, B. (2007). Diversité psychopathologique dans la clinique de la plainte mnésique de l'adulte vieillissant. *Psychologie et NeuroPsychiatrie du vieillissement, 5*(3), 209–223.
World Health Organization. (2002). *Active ageing: A policy framework* (No. WHO/NMH/NPH/02.8). World Health Organization.
Zielinski, A. (2014). Comment considérer la personne lorsque l'identité semble s'effacer? *Jusqu'à la mort accompagner la vie, 119*(4), 53–65.

Chapter 8
The Paradoxes of Ageing and Its Future

Tania Zittoun and Michèle Grossen

This book on learning and development in older age starts and finishes with a paradox: on the one hand, societal, technical and medical advances have allowed an impressive extension of the life expectancy, and because of the overall decline of the birthrate, a massive increase of the proportion of older persons in the society; on the other hand, while one person in four is soon over 65, little is known about these persons, in majority still considered as a mass of indistinct "persons in decline" constituting a "social burden" for the younger population.

Approaching people over 65—the average age of retirement in central Europe, where the studies presented here are conducted—the developmental, clinical, psychoanalytical or sociocultural psychologists in this volume address that problem by revealing another, more interesting paradox. Indeed "old" persons, people between 65 and 115 (!) are individuals who live their life and experience some challenges, as is anyone else along their trajectories. Their everyday life is usually both in continuation with what they did in the past, and requiring some changes; most people are reasonably open to transformation. Age can of course bring its lot of difficulties: certain activities cannot be realised anymore; for most people, their professional activities had to be ended; their body at times reduces its vigour; close persons and acquaintances may live further or die; and perhaps some aspects of one's mind or memory seems less infallible. However, the same ageing persons have not only the experience of adjusting to the transformations coming with ageing, but also the concern of staying who they are; they manifest and express their will for life, their desire to be active and creative, and their need to have significant and anecdotic

T. Zittoun (✉)
Institute of Psychology and Education, Université de Neuchâtel, Neuchâtel, Switzerland
e-mail: tania.zittoun@unine.ch

M. Grossen
Faculty of Social and Political Sciences, University of Lausanne, Lausanne, Switzerland
e-mail: michele.grossen@unil.ch

T. Zittoun, F. Gfeller (eds.), *Ageing, Learning and Development*, Lifelong Learning Book Series 36, https://doi.org/10.1007/978-3-032-11057-2_8

relationships with others. Also, very often, they are engaged with helping others to continue making the world a good enough, if not a better place. This existential, and concrete paradox, brings about a series of tensions, or even conflicts, between social discourses and representations on the one hand, and individual practices and aspirations on the other, that need to be accounted for, as well as implications for theorising older age, for research and practice.

8.1 Towards an Integrative Approach of Developing with Age

In theoretical terms, bringing sociocultural psychology and psychoanalysis together aims at proposing an integrative approach to development with age. Assuming that development occurs in the transactions between the person evolving until her last breath, and a constantly changing society, it aims at accounting both for the social and interpersonal dynamics, as well as for the intrapsychic ones, that shape the person. It brings to the fore the inherent dialogicality of human life, that is, the fact that, due to its historicity and situatedness, the human mind echoes the voices of so many others and experiences. This has as first implication that the person, as unique human being, can only emerge from, and through sets of conflicting tensions. Second, it also assumes that is also precisely also through such inherent conflictuality that the person keeps developing with age, even though she may encounter losses due to time. Third, it examines the nature of what develops with older age, for the unique persons: at the junction of the two traditions, it emphasises the changing dynamic of sense making, and the fundamental role of pleasure in these developments.

Authors in this volume all inscribe ageing in the unfolding of the course of life of humans, as these occur through the ages, yet with all the specificities of our contemporary world. Both psychoanalysis and sociocultural psychology admit that people only can be and become through their relationships with others. Whether they call it the necessary co-dependency of intersubjectivity and intrapsychic processes (Green, 2005) or the ontological dialogicality of the mind (Marková, 2016), they always admit the mediated nature of human life: people develop through close relationships with others, but also through social discourses and cultural artefacts that echo different and conflicting voices, and are thus part of their inner dialogues. Consequently, they assume that individual development is embedded within the social, material and symbolic environment. Such dialogical stance puts to the fore the relationality of human experience all life-long (Gillespie & Martin, 2014; Zittoun, 2022).

In line with this assumption, the studies presented in this volume go one step further and put to the fore the existential need for significant human relationships in older age. The development of people, and per extension of older persons, can only be understood when persons are apprehended in their lived environment, and in the light of their past trajectories in a multiplicity of material, social and symbolic environments. Hence, the experience of dependency an older person may have has to be understood in a long history of phases of relational dependency alternating with relative independency—an absolute dependency to the carer at birth, a relative independence from care yet more important to friends, etc. (Racin, 2025). Similarly, competences and skills have to be approached together with people's socially and technically shaped environment, and as part of their life trajectory (Muller Mirza, 2025) and epistemic practices (Säljö, 2025). The memory of an 85 years-old person is not only in "her brain"; it is also in her access to a photographic album or a notebook (Zittoun, 2025), in her discussions with old friends, through Wikipedia on their tablet, and through the books on the shelves. If competences are socially and materially situated activities, then to understand how a person displays her skills, we need to locate her within her social, material and symbolic environment. Thus, a person's former managerial skills do not exist—cannot be mobilised and acknowledged by others—after retirement, unless she engages in volunteering work, where its planning and budgeting abilities can be displayed by a transfer and a transformation in this new context (Beach, 1999; Muller Mirza, 2025). The same type of dynamics occurs regarding the sense of identity and self continuity: these are not experienced within the limits of the skin but emerge through dialogues with others, real and imaginary, in their familiar spaces, with preferred objects, or in specific landscapes and neighbourhoods (Gfeller & Grossen, 2025; Habermas, 1996; Zittoun et al., 2021). In older age, this process has a specificity: the fact that people have a long-lasting experience and have a longer view over time and history. They have seen the world change, for example from WWII or the tremor of the 60s', to the arrival of the tablet, the snow recess, or industrial transformations—this confers them a unique perspective on the present, and for many of them, a strong orientation toward the future of societies (Muller Mirza, 2025; Verdon, 2025). Such observations require to characterise people, and ageing persons, not only in the limits of their organic body, but within their whole lifespace (Lewin, 1943, 1951)—the situated experience, present, past and future, that are relevant in the here-and-now—that has also been coined a configuration of spheres of experiences or domains of conduct (Zittoun, 2025, 2026). This dialogical and situated perspective then calls for a series of assumptions for studying learning and development with older age.

First, on a theoretical plane, all approaches in this volume insist on the historicity of age: people develop in a changing societal environment; their ontogeny is always occurring via transactions with the world, through every microgenetic encounter they engage into. This, as a consequence, implies a rejection of static, category-based approaches to aging (Racin, 2025)—these that would classify people according to stable cognitive skills, enduring personality types, or states of frailty or dependency. Rejecting categories has many implications: it calls for a developmental perspective, for rejecting normative and prescriptive stances, and for the acknowledgment of the singularity of every trajectory of ageing. While it seems relatively easy to reject essentialisation—that can be found in ageism or generationism (Angus & Reeve, 2006; Binstock, 2010; White, 2013)—it creates a more complex question about the development of older persons. Indeed, to account for development in older age, it is all the more necessary to capture general social and cultural dynamics and individual singularities (Lewin, 1951; Zittoun, 2017); how to generalize without simplifying, that is, how to theorise so as to have a model flexible enough to account for the extreme variation of human learning and development in older age?

Second, the singular nature of these evolving configurations of spheres of experience over the course of a life brings to the fore the person's sense of continuity. If people's changing lifespace is extended in time and space, and is both materially and symbolically supported, how can people maintain a sense of who they are through time, a sense of integrity and self-continuity (Erikson et al., 1986)? This is where important affective and idiosyncratic components are brought to the fore in these chapters. Persons develop through basic investment in others and in themselves, which psychoanalysts call respectively objects investments and narcissistic investments (Racin, 2025; Verdon, 2025). Development in older age challenges these two forms of investments. Losing significant relationships, being exposed to others who reject older persons or have negative prejudices against them, as well as experiencing the weakening of one's body, may all challenge one's sense of identity, of being the same despite many changes. The risk is thus either to loose these investments to oneself and to let oneself go, or to try to fit these societal demands of remaining fit—and alienating "narcissistic pact" alimented by the societal injunction of "healthy aging" (Racin, 2025; Verdon, 2025). Development instead requires a degree of depressivity—the acceptance of loss—while reengaging these investments; there is therefore an actual "work of ageing" (Bianchi, 2020). The same type of work is required during the lifecourse every time one experiences a rupture and engages in the work of transitions—but older age brings people to face an accumulation of ruptures: professional retirement (Muller Mirza, 2025), moving home (Gfeller & Grossen, 2025), or renouncing one's preferred leisure time activity—mountaineering, or gardening, for instance (Zittoun, 2025). In each case, the person has to reinvest some aspects of herself, often validated by others (one's professional status, one's achievement, etc.); she therefore needs to transform these narcissistic and object investments. In summary, older people have to reconfigure the spheres of experiences which expose them to a variety of people and social discourses, while maintaining some significant affective investments which contribute supporting their sense of continuity.

Third, ageing is not only about loss; it is also about tension of realisation, and pleasure and meaningfulness, to be experienced in dialogue with others. Interestingly, all the authors in this volume emphasise the importance of pleasure—the pleasure and meaning of continuing one's work, of sharing one's knowledge (Muller Mirza, 2025), of moving home to a new place opening possibilities (Gfeller & Grossen, 2025), or of doing something that matters for others and society (Verdon, 2025); the pleasure of welcoming others (Racin, 2025), the pleasure of love, of contemplating the sky or of reconnecting with parts of one's pas long gone (Verdon, 2025); the pleasure of realising, and making sense of, the paradoxes of one's ageing (Zittoun, 2025)—all deeply social activities. Even if pleasure and meaningfulness are experienced as personal, they need at times to be shared with present or absent others (Zittoun, 2023).

This brings about another, fourth central feature of ageing. Assuming that conflictuality is a central feature of human mind (conflictuality between different voices or conflictuality between Ego and Alter), both sociocultural psychology and psychoanalysis observe that becoming older raises specific conflicts. Indeed, as they become older and are viewed and treated as "older persons", people are likely to experience conflicts between the various societal discourses and representations about what aging is or is not, should be or should not be, and their own needs and projects. This can have various consequences. Older persons may have to appropriate in a personal way what aging means to them (Caissie, 2011; Friedan, 1994; Woodward, 2002). They may feel tensions and conflicts within their daily relationships, and around them. On a more intrapsychic level, they can be crossed by tensions between their engagements in life and the forces that slow them down, tensions between their will to enjoy life and their experience of frailty (Gfeller & Grossen, 2025), or tensions between what they would like to do and what they think they are expected to do—which may be experienced consciously and unconsciously. In any case, these two lines of studies have demonstrated that people may find ways to contain, elaborate, semiotically mediate and express the tensions, conflicts or ambivalences, for themselves and with or for others, and thus, maintain their creativity alive (Verdon, 2025; Villa, 2010; Winnicott, 1991; Zittoun, 2025). These core affective challenges—the pain of loss, the maintenance of the will to live, the pleasure one can find in complex or simple things, meaningfulness—may be active all life-long if this pleasure directly or indirectly links the person to significant others and makes sense within shared cultural practices in which the person feels involved (Quinodoz, 2009). It is for these reasons that this conclusion prioritizes it.

Altogether, the present integrative theoretical proposition represents a paradigm shift in the way older age is conceived. Indeed, it proposes to radically turn away from theories and social representations seeing ageing as the characteristics of an isolated person who loses efficiency and performativity on a series of biological, physical and cognitive dimensions, modulated by a series of other functions such as one's "resilience" or good will to "compensate" age with appropriate training; it also refuses to see ageing as the problematic attribute of an indistinct mass of "costly" and "dependent" people. On the contrary, it examines the singularity of the person developing over their lifecourse, whose development is always emerging from direct or indirect dialogues with others in a social, material and symbolic environment, within a society shaped by discourses, beliefs and practices. This paradigm shift needs to be followed by an adequate methodology and has also empirical implications.

8.2 Approaching Ageing: Methodological Implications

There have been many ways of approaching ageing in psychology; as with other phenomena, methodology reflects the researchers' epistemological and theoretical assumptions. The authors in this volume have all quite deliberately kept away from some of the most standard methods of study.

As a reminder, ageing has been approached from a combination of phenomenology and secondary analysis of existing literature (de Beauvoir, 1970; Hall, 1922), before moving to more systematic research. In psychology, it is the beginning of lifecourse or lifespan approaches that have systematized the study of ageing, from the very qualitative and narrative interviews of older persons led by Erik Erikson as part of his enquiry on the cycle of life (Erikson, 1959; Erikson et al., 1986), to the attempts to document the changes of people's functions over time through systematic testing (Baltes & Mayer, 1999). The former line of studies has been extended in different approaches privileging first-person narration (Butler, 1963; Coleman et al., 2015; Freeman, 2011; Gubrium, 2011; Radtke et al., 2016), questioning what can be learned and generalized first, beyond single cases (Cornish, 2020), and second, beyond what can actually be told. The latter has developed more and more complex statistical treatment of the data, to come to see its own limits—the will to generalize decontextualizes so much the collected data that the results may become meaningless, too (Säljö, 2025; Tournier, 2020). A third line of studies has attempted to approach older people within their environments, through different qualitative and quantitative methods; here again, the importance of defining concepts that enable to move beyond specific cases—of people, of places—has always been a concern (Bigonnesse & Chaudhury, 2020; Golant, 2003; Lawton, 1985; Lieblich, 2014).

As all the authors in this volume assume the situatedness of ageing and its historicity, they approach people through specifically tailored qualitative methods, which aim to preserve the situated and developmental nature of the phenomena under study, and to account for actual practices. This means that they are all aware of the many transitions that older people keep experiencing, the tensions and conflicts they experience, as well as the specific social frames in which these unfold (Valsiner, 2007; Zittoun, 2009).

The methodological choices proposed here involve different temporalities (Gillespie & Cornish, 2010). Focused on specific transitions, some studies examine microgenetic dynamics on the background of people's lifecourse. The explicative-narrative interviews developed by Nathalie Muller Mirza and her team especially aim at zooming in and out of a person's trajectory to focus on specific skills and competences mobilized as people engage in voluntary work (Muller Mirza, 2025); the interviews analyzed by Fabienne Gfeller and Michèle Grossen, together with ethnographic observations, belong to a set of repeated interviews and examine transitions to a new home on the background of the persons' life trajectory (Gfeller & Grossen, 2025). Such longitudinal qualitative methodologies also enable to capture a longer time scale, that of ontogenetic development (Zittoun, 2025). Comparably, clinical psychologists also follow people for a longer period of their lives (Racin,

2025). Finally, to capture more sociogenetic transformations, authors adopt an abductive perspective, dialoging between existing literature and their expertise as theoreticians and practitioners, thus bringing to the fore general and core principles about aging (Säljö, 2025; Verdon, 2025).

There are, however, differences in the extent to which researchers consider their own implication and participation in the data collection or construction, as well as in the way they objectify their analysis. First, considering that behind the collection of any data, there is always a researcher who sets up a certain frame or asks certain questions (whether in a questionnaire or in an interview), we may wonder to which extent the transcript and the analysis take into account the interventions of the researcher (Grossen, 2015, 2021). In other words, to what extent does the analysis consider the addressivity of discourse, that is, the fact that, as Linell puts it: "Every act is addressed to somebody, whether this addressee is individual or collective, real, or imaginary, being another person (or group) or an aspect of one's own self" (Linell, 2009, p. 167). Addressivity presupposes that as she addresses somebody, the person anticipates what the comprehension of her addressee might be, and orients her discourse accordingly (Marková, 2016). To say that one is a strong, or dependent, or depressed, or youthful older person, is a way of presenting and positioning oneself toward another person, perceived as friends, specialist, younger person or expert (Gillespie & Martin, 2014; Goffman, 1956). Hence, it is not a mere reflection of the person's thinking or emotions, it is a social and discursive construction which, on a psychological level, may inform us about the various and sometimes conflicting voices that are echoed in the person's discourse (Grossen & Salazar Orvig, 2025). Second, while the contributions presented in this volume are all based on data collected in so-to-speak natural settings, the analyses of these data entail different degrees of interpretation. An analysis based on a theoretically-inspired analysis of clinical interviews (Racin, 2025) offers less access to the data than research based on abductive engagement with recorded and transcribed data (Zittoun, 2025) or written testimonies (Verdon, 2025), and both less than a systematic dialogical analysis of transcribed interviews (Gfeller & Grossen, 2025).

In any case, all approaches presented here respect the same epistemological stance; they respect the richness of lived experiences, in their singularity, in their environment, and in time. They all have also a strong theoretical anchorage. And it is therefore through each attempt to generate a dialogue between theories, past studies and current observations, that we observe the emergence of a more general picture, as sketched in the first part of this chapter.

In short, the studies presented in this book share certain epistemological assumptions that allow us to propose an integrative approach. A first shared fundamental premise is that dialogue between Ego and Alter (whether in face-to-face interactions or in inner dialogue/auto-dialogue) and the potential resulting conflict (or dialogical tensions) are an ontological characteristic of human mind. Another shared premise is that ageing, as any period of life, requires a careful balance between continuity and change, maintenance and recreation of oneself under new forms. The sociocultural approach to learning and development makes us particularly sensitive to ruptures people experience; as forms of crises in a life trajectory they are likely to trigger processes of transitions that entail learning, reexamination of aspects of one's identity, and sense-making. This is quite clear here when people enter new social settings: starting voluntary work (Muller Mirza, 2025), moving to a new home (Gfeller & Grossen, 2025), or to a nursing home (Racin, 2025). Comparable processes occur in more subtle ways as one has to find another way down the stairs because knees refuse to bent (Zittoun, 2025), or when the kettle suddenly becomes too heavy (Racin, 2025).

Although older persons may find all kinds of resources to facilitate these transitions, like at any other age, development and learning in older age involve some particularly significant core challenges, as highlighted by psychoanalysis. In effect, older persons find themselves exposed to two major forces: the negative social representations of older persons—ageism which tends to push people out of the public space, ignore their opinion, invite them to age politely and silently—and not too costly—and the depressivity which they may have to face due to necessary losses. To this, a physical or material environment that resists, or a social network that vanishes, may reinforce the feeling of falling and losing one's bases (Bonnet & Louchard Chardon, 2024). To counterbalance these challenges, older persons need more than ever to find resources that reinforce their sense of continuity, integrity, and support for the relationships to others (particular, specifically) and oneself.

In both approaches, research methods aim at accounting for the way in which the person appropriate sometimes divergent social discourses, that is, develop and transform them according to her own experience, her interpretation of the past and her projections into the future—this appropriation being constitutive of her uniqueness. This basic assumption considers that the person is in a state of continuous development within a society that is itself in constant transformation. It involves using methods that do justice to the person's perspective, pay attention to her practices and discourses in the various contexts in which she lives, and understand her discourse and (self-)representations in the context of social or interpersonal discourses. As a result, an integration between sociocultural and psychoanalytical perspectives brings to the fore the tensions and paradoxes of ageing: as older persons develop within their environments, they may experience difficulties and obstacles, yet they seem foremost engaged in activities that are meaningful to them, that correspond to their engagements, bring them pleasure, connect them to others, and enable them to link their past with the present, and the collective future.

8.3 Supporting Ageing: Implications for Policy, and Practice and Training

This integrative approach has consequences for practice: for policy making, for professional practice and care, and consequently, for training.

First, *at a policy level*, the ontology of human beings which conceives of the relation Ego-Alter as an inseparable unit has practical and ethical consequences

(Marková, 2016): it requires a certain form of inclusive democracy. Indeed, the problem is not only to provide psychological support to those who struggle to meet the challenges of ageing, but also to develop a larger reflection about what makes social links possible in a heterogeneous and constantly changing society, and to provide a material and symbolic environment that afford significant activities and experiences to its older population (Söderström et al., 2025). This translates at three levels:

(1) *Include older persons in the decisions impacting their lives.*

Societies should develop deliberative practices regarding concrete policies that have implications for the life of older persons, e.g., regarding urban planification, housing, health care, etc. Ideally, older persons should have a voice when aspects of policies that concern them are discussed. When modes of housing for the older population are developed, when services for ageing in place are decided, when financial support can be obtained, older persons often have reasonably good ideas of what could be useful, or creative suggestions for ameliorations or alternatives to the existing. Including the older population in policy making is more than consulting them in a standardised questionnaire, or having a few politicians over average age to represent them: it is about creating spaces for discussion and debate. Associations of retirees, political movements as the Grand-Parents for the Climate, or participatory projects allow, in various countries, older people to speak up and be heard.

(2) *Revealing the social contributions of older persons.*

The very fact that older persons do often participate to the general economy by their contributions in time and expertise needs to be socially and publicly acknowledged. Older people are not only "costs"; they also participate invisibly in the general equilibrium of our societies: as carers for children from their families or neighbourhood; through their voluntary work in charities, associations, and in boards; through their initiatives in their own neighbourhoods—offering shared garden, taking informally care of the older than them; by transmitting their experience in oral, written form, through informal mentoring, etc. One of the objections to the increase of retirement age by a politician in Switzerland was that it would result in closing down the cheapest kindergarten of the country! In many countries, the financial equivalent of voluntary work has been evaluated; such numbers should be made public, and policy makers acknowledge explicitly this contribution to the collective.

(3) *Changing the social representations of ageing.*

These two measures should go together with a third one: a special care to the communication made by policy makers, administration, media, etc. about ageing: emphasising the costs of age feeds into ageist stereotypes, while the two previous points makes it clear that costs may be to some big extent compensated. In addition, as part of societal discourses on becoming older, it is important to promote voices that present alternative representations of age, the relativeness of age, and to support and diffuse cultural elements—films, artwork, theatre—that also may become symbolic resources for people, young and old, to reflect upon these issues. Therefore, it is an ethical requirement that we, as citizens and professionals involved in societal change, preserve the places and spaces where older persons can deploy their lives and experiences. Society at large needs to generate the forms of sociality where older persons' voices can be heard and become part of a general dialogue.

Second, our attempt to integrate sociocultural psychology and psychoanalysis has *implications for practitioners* working with older persons—carers, social workers, nurses, counsellors, psychologists, medical personal, etc. As it assumes that people have a need for self-continuity going beyond the limits of their skin that also depends on broader societal and interpersonal dimensions, and that knowledge and competence are situated, distributed activities, our work has two practical implications. On the one hand, many practitioners are required to evaluate a person's capacities before proposing support. The perspective developed in these pages invites to avoid assessing people's capacities—whether cognitive, linked to the daily activities and practical or social skills (Pedersen & Bang, 2015)—out of their living context. As we have seen, people think with tools, reason with their partners, remember with resources, feel well with others or their preferred objects or landscape. People are also different from one another, and have many different domains of experience, which evolve at different speeds; people have many ages simultaneously. All this calls for a careful assessment of older people's skills, knowledge, capacities. It is an invitation to consider people in their material, social and symbolic environment, including their weak ties. Of course, some regions encourage practitioners working on ageing to do such situated assessment and to acknowledge people's singular trajectory of ageing (Milligan, 2009; Plattet et al., 2018; Zittoun, 2026). But it is so easier to use a standard scale, test or a decontextualized evaluation before deciding what help people many need… On the other hand, practitioners and carers have to provide solutions for people who may have lost some mobility or autonomy. The perspective developed in this volume invites to reflect on solutions that take into account the environment in which they live. However, these solutions do not only depend on practitioners or carers as individuals, but also on the organization and creativity of the institutions that employ them. Without going into detail here, we will simply point out that certain psychoanalysts, René Kaës in particular (2007, 2012), have shown that institutions play a supporting role in the development of individuals, in other words they may act as "psychic envelopes (Bonnet & Louchard Chardon, 2024; Kaës, 2012; Zittoun, 2026). Hence, all the material, social and symbolic places that welcome older persons can be understood as offering external envelopes, together with means of social participation: places that afford volunteering, work, sharing experiences, as Old'up in France (Verdon, 2025); modes of housing that satisfy the needs and wishes of older person (Gfeller & Grossen, 2025); fostering landscapes of care enabling those who wish to remain at home with arrangements and a vital social network (Zittoun, 2025); or even hospitals or retirement homes with spaces allowing people to recreate a life of their own (Racin, 2025; Zittoun et al., 2021).

Finally, the integrative sociocultural and psychanalytical perspective proposed in these pages, together with the policy and practical implications, should also have consequences for the *practitioners' training* in various fields. Learning and development in older age should be part of curricula in psychology, educational sciences, adult training, etc. In domains where professionals are likely to work with older persons—nursing, medical domain, social work, medical studies, psychology and psychiatry—the emotional, social, psychological needs of the older population need to be addressed and, in our view, considered from a multidisciplinary approach which confront various theoretical trends. Moreover, the need and desire of older persons to keep learning and developing could be further explored by educational institutions. Many countries offer universities for the third age, with conferences and courses accessible to everyone. This is highly appreciated and even more when it is accompanied by reflection on the best modalities to teach older adults full of a rich life experience. This could be further explored, with special care for emerging interests and curiosities in old and very old persons. In addition, local initiatives facilitating older person's access to culture—museum, films, etc.—can only be encouraged—yet without forgetting that for many these are even more appreciated when they also allow to meet younger persons.

In other words, it is vital and of foremost importance to consider that older persons are exactly as much citizens as anyone else, and as such, that they need social recognition. They need to participate in meaningful relationships and dialogues, to access places where they can pursue their engagements and create new ones, enjoy life with all its complexity, and as such, participate in the transformation of a world that keeps moving. More specifically, the social, institutional, affective, symbolic nature of the environment in which older people live play a central role in the possibility of making sense of one's life and maintaining the pleasure of living. The chapters in this volume invite scientists, social actors, practitioners and policymakers, to create social spaces and promote discourses, dialogical spaces and artefacts which provide resources supporting the conditions of ageing in society with others.

This integrative theoretical proposal calls for a radically new stance in what regards the social and political handling of the older population. In this view, the so-called "problem of the ageing population" should not be posed solely in terms of healthcare costs, but also as a problem of othering older persons, with the risk of wasting their unique experience. It should thus invite us to imagine the social, material and relational environments which would better include older persons within current social and cultural dialogues, debates and activities. The gains would be shared; on the one hand, older persons engaged in meaningful activities would be supported in their living and developing movement; on the other hand, societies could benefit from older people's experience and perspective. Older people who may pursue or discover, perhaps with a little help, activities which are meaningful to them, which enable them to find pleasure in thinking, sharing, feeling—in living—would certainly help societies to find a better balance in the deep transformations of our current world. Hence, the development of older persons may paradoxically become the drivers of social renewal.

References

Angus, J., & Reeve, P. (2006). Ageism: A threat to "aging well" in the 21st century. *Journal of Applied Gerontology, 25*(2), 137–152. https://doi.org/10.1177/0733464805285745

Baltes, P. B., & Mayer, K. U. (Eds.). (1999). *The Berlin aging study: Aging from 70 to 100*. Cambridge University Press.

Beach, K. (1999). Consequential transitions: A sociocultural expedition beyond transfer in education. *Review of Research in Education, 24*, 124–149.

Bianchi, H. (2020). Travail du vieillir et 'travail du trépas'. In *Fragilité et force du lien* (pp. 35–43). In Press. https://doi.org/10.3917/pres.verdo.2020.01.0035

Bigonnesse, C., & Chaudhury, H. (2020). The landscape of "aging in place" in gerontology literature: Emergence, theoretical perspectives, and influencing factors. *Journal of Aging and Environment, 34*(3), 233–251. https://doi.org/10.1080/02763893.2019.1638875

Binstock, R. H. (2010). From compassionate ageism to intergenerational conflict? *The Gerontologist, 50*(5), 574–585. https://doi.org/10.1093/geront/gnq056

Bonnet, M., & Louchard Chardon, C. (Eds.). (2024). *Vieillissement et enveloppes psychiques*. In Press.

Butler, R. N. (1963). The life review: An interpretation of reminiscence in the aged. *Psychiatry, 26*(1), 65–76. https://doi.org/10.1080/00332747.1963.11023339

Caissie, L. (2011). The raging grannies: Narrative construction of gender and aging. In G. Kenyon, E. Bohlmeijer, & W. L. Randall (Eds.), *Storying later life: Issues, investigations, and interventions in narrative gerontology* (pp. 126–142). Oxford University Press.

Coleman, P. G., Ivani-Chalian, C., & Robinson, M. (2015). *Self and meaning in the lives of older people*. Cambridge University Press.

Cornish, F. (2020). Communicative generalisation: Dialogical means of advancing knowledge through a case study of an 'unprecedented' disaster. *Culture & Psychology, 26*(1), 78–95. https://doi.org/10.1177/1354067X19894930

de Beauvoir, S. (1970). *La vieillesse*. Gallimard.

Erikson, E. H. (1959). *Identity and the life cycle. Selected papers (1959th ed.)*. International Universities Press. http://www.archive.org/details/identityandtheli011578mbp

Erikson, E. H., Erikson, J. M., & Kivnick, H. Q. (1986). *Vital involvement in old age*. Norton.

Freeman, M. (2011). Narrative foreclosure in later life: Possibilities and limits. In G. Kenyon, E. Bohlmeijer, & W. L. Randall (Eds.), *Storying later life: Issues, investigations, and interventions in narrative gerontology* (pp. 3–19). Oxford University Press.

Friedan, B. (1994). *The fountain of age (original 1993)*. Vintage.

Gfeller, F., & Grossen, M. (2025). Moving house in older age: Challenges and resources for the sense of self-continuity. In T. Zittoun & F. Gfeller (Eds.), *Ageing, learning and development. Sociocultural and psychoanalytical perspectives on growing older*. Springer.

Gillespie, A., & Cornish, F. (2010). What can be said? Identity as a constraint on knowledge production. *Papers on Social Representations, 19*, 5.1–5.13.

Gillespie, A., & Martin, J. (2014). Position exchange theory: A socio-material basis for discursive and psychological positioning. *New Ideas in Psychology, 32*, 73–79. https://doi.org/10.1016/j.newideapsych.2013.05.001

Goffman, E. (1956). *The presentation of self in everyday life*. University of Edinburgh Social Sciences Research Centre. https://www.google.ch/url?sa=t&rct=j&q=&esrc=s&source=web&cd=1&cad=rja&uact=8&ved=0CB0QFjAAahUKEwiE4ISY5rTIAhXnEXIKHUQcBo8&url=http%3A%2F%2Fmonoskop.org%2Fimages%2F1%2F19%2FGoffman_Erving_The_Presentation_of_Self_in_Everyday_Life.pdf&usg=AFQjCNGS4CeIMuTuL8O_MCbI6E6ic8T1yQ&sig2=5JEE30GVM-fTA1GFsR6ORg&bvm=bv.104615367,d.bGQ

Golant, S. M. (2003). Conceptualizing time and behavior in environmental gerontology: A pair of old issues deserving new thought. *The Gerontologist, 43*(5), 638–648. https://doi.org/10.1093/geront/43.5.638

Green, A. (2005). *Key ideas for a contemporary psychoanalysis misrecognition and recognition of the unconscious* (1st ed.). Routledge.

Grossen, M. (2015). The diary as dialogical space. In B. Wagoner, N. Chaudhary, & P. Hviid (Eds.), *Integrating experience. Body and mind moving between contexts* (pp. 201–219). Information Age Publishing.

Grossen, M. (2021). When dialogism crosses the frontiers of psychology. In N. Muller Mirza & M. Dos Santos Mamed (Eds.), *Dialogical approaches and tensions in learning and development: At the frontiers of the mind* (pp. 13–32). Springer International Publishing. https://doi.org/10.1007/978-3-030-84226-0_2

Grossen, M., & Salazar Orvig, A. (2025). L'analyse dialogique du discours appliquée à l'entretien clinique, un point de rencontre interdisciplinaire. In L. Kloetzer & M. Dos Santos Mamed (Eds.), *Analyse du langage en psychologie: Approches dialogiques*. Antipodes.

Gubrium, J. F. (2011). Narrative events and biographical construction in old age. In G. Kenyon, E. Bohlmeijer, & W. L. Randall (Eds.), *Storytelling later life: Issues, investigations, and interventions in narrative gerontology* (pp. 39–50). Oxford University Press.

Habermas, T. (1996). *Geliebte Objekte. Symbole und Instrumente der Identitätsbildung*. Walter de Gruyter.

Hall, G. S. (1922). *Senescence, the last half of life*. University of California Libraries. D. Appleton and Company. http://archive.org/details/senescencelastha00halliala

Kaës, R. (Ed.). (with Fustier, P., Enriquez, E., Roussillon, R., & Vidal, J.-P.) (2012). *L'institution et les institutions—Études psychanalytiques*. Dunod.

Kaës, R. (2007). Du Moi-peau aux enveloppes psychiques. Genèse et développement d'un concept. *Le Carnet Psy, 117*(4), 33–39. https://doi.org/10.3917/lcp.117.0033

Lawton, M. P. (1985). The elderly in context: Perspectives from environmental psychology and gerontology. *Environment and Behavior, 17*(4), 501–519. https://doi.org/10.1177/0013916585174005

Lewin, K. (1943). Defining the 'field at a given time'. In *Resolving social conflicts & field theory in social science (original publication 1943)* (pp. 200–211). American Psychological Association (APA).

Lewin, K. (1951). Behavior and development as function of the total situation. In E. Cartwright (Ed.), *Field theory in the social sciences (original 1946)* (pp. 238–303). Harper and Brothers Publishers.

Lieblich, A. (2014). *Narratives of positive aging: Seaside stories*. Oxford University Press.

Linell, P. (2009). *Rethinking language, mind and world dialogically. Interactional and contextual theories of sense making*. Information Age Publishing.

Marková, I. (2016). *The dialogical mind: Common sense and ethics*. Cambridge University Press.

Milligan, C. (2009). *There's no place like home: Place and care in an ageing society*. Ashgate Publishing Limited.

Muller Mirza, N. (2025). Developmental processes and meaning-making in volunteering activity. In T. Zittoun & F. Gfeller (Eds.), *Ageing, learning and development. Sociocultural and psychoanalytical perspectives on growing older*. Springer.

Pedersen, S., & Bang, J. (2015). Youth development as subjectified subjectivity—A dialectical-ecological model of analysis. *Integrative Psychological and Behavioral Science, 50*(3), 1–22. https://doi.org/10.1007/s12124-015-9337-z

Plattet, A., Hugentobler, V., & Zwygart, M. (2018). 'Quartiers solidaires': Une méthodologie d'action communautaire. *Retraite et Société, 79*, 125–135. https://doi.org/10.3917/rs1.079.0125

Quinodoz, D. (2009). Growing old: A psychoanalyst's point of view. *International Journal of Psychoanalysis, 90*(4), 773–793. https://doi.org/10.1111/j.1745-8315.2009.00166.x

Racin, C. (2025). The dynamics of dependency in old age: Psychoanalytic perspectives. In T. Zittoun & F. Gfeller (Eds.), *Ageing, learning and development. Sociocultural and psychoanalytical perspectives on growing older*. Springer.

Radtke, H. L., Young, J., & van Mens-Verhulst, J. (2016). Aging, identity, and women: Constructing the third age. *Women & Therapy, 39*(1–2), 86–105. https://doi.org/10.1080/02703149.2016.1116321

Säljö, R. (2025). Cognitive adaptation, hybrid minds and ageing: Epistemic practices in cumulative cultures. In T. Zittoun & F. Gfeller (Eds.), *Ageing, learning and development. Sociocultural and psychoanalytical perspectives on growing older*. Springer.

Söderström, O., Zittoun, T., Gfeller, F., Ruggeri, A., & Kloepper, I. (2025). Designing landscapes of affordances for ageing in place. *Geographica Helvetica, 80*(1), 67–79. https://doi.org/10.5194/gh-80-67-2025

Tournier, I. (2020). Learning and adaptation in older adults: An overview of main methods and theories. *Learning, Culture and Social Interaction, 37*, 100466. https://doi.org/10.1016/j.lcsi.2020.100466

Valsiner, J. (2007). Developmental epistemology and implications for methodology. In W. Damon & R. M. Lerner (Eds.), *Handbook of child psychology* (Vol. 1, pp. 166–209). John Wiley & Sons, Inc. http://onlinelibrary.wiley.com/doi/10.1002/9780470147658.chpsy0104/abstract

Verdon, B. (2025). Taking care of oneself as an alederly person while being interested in the future of the younger generation: Incompatible concerns? In T. Zittoun & F. Gfeller (Eds.), *Ageing, learning and development. Sociocultural and psychoanalytical perspectives on growing older*. Springer.

Villa, F. (2010). *La puissance du vieillir*. Presses Universitaires de France.

White, J. (2013). Thinking generations. *The British Journal of Sociology, 64*(2), 216–247. https://doi.org/10.1111/1468-4446.12015

Winnicott, D. W. (1991). *Playing and reality (original 1971)*. Routledge.

Woodward, K. M. (2002). Against wisdom: The social politics of anger and aging. *Cultural Critique, 51*(1), 186–218. https://doi.org/10.1353/cul.2002.0024

Zittoun, T. (2009). Dynamics of life-course transitions—A methodological reflection. In J. Valsiner, P. C. M. Molenaar, M. C. D. P. Lyra, & N. Chaudhary (Eds.), *Dynamic process methodology in the social and developmental sciences* (pp. 405–430). Springer.

Zittoun, T. (2017). Modalities of generalization through single case studies. *Integrative Psychological and Behavioral Science, 51*(2), 171–194. https://doi.org/10.1007/s12124-016-9367-1

Zittoun, T. (2022). A sociocultural psychology of the life course to study human development. *Human Development, 66*(4–5), 306–324. https://doi.org/10.1159/000526435

Zittoun, T. (2023). *The pleasure of thinking*. Cambridge University Press. https://doi.org/10.1017/9781009039802

Zittoun, T. (2025). On being an oxymoron: A sociocultural psychology of development with older age. In T. Zittoun & F. Gfeller (Eds.), *Ageing, learning and development. Sociocultural and psychoanalytical perspectives on growing older*. Springer.

Zittoun, T. (2026). *Developing in older age—An integrative view*. Cambridge University Press.

Zittoun, T., Grossen, M., & Tarrago Salamin, F. (2021). Creating new spheres of experience in the transition to a nursing home. *Learning, Culture and Social Interaction, 28*, 100458. https://doi.org/10.1016/j.lcsi.2020.100458

Index

A
Achievement, 2, 21, 53, 56, 89, 143, 162
Ageing, 1–8, 10, 11, 19–32, 63, 64, 66–68, 75, 77–79, 85–103, 108, 109, 111, 112, 115, 117, 127, 129, 130, 137–155, 159–169
Alterity, 8, 47
Ambivalence, 45, 163

C
Care, 1, 3–5, 20, 21, 23, 32, 38, 44, 54, 64, 70, 76, 89, 112, 119, 137, 140–143, 150–155, 161, 166–169
Cognitive development in adult age, 25, 28, 43, 44, 87, 91, 147, 161, 163, 168
Commitment, 11, 38, 49–51, 54, 88, 92, 93, 103, 112
Creation, 44, 51, 63, 68, 109, 154
Cumulative culture, 19–32

D
Dependency, 8, 11, 121, 137–155, 161
Development, 1–11, 20–31, 42–46, 49–51, 64–68, 78, 85–103, 108, 109, 137–155, 159–166, 168, 169
Dialogism, 5, 91, 99

E
Engagement, 3, 9–11, 39, 41, 49, 50, 54, 67, 69, 72, 75–79, 86–88, 92, 99, 103, 109, 163, 165, 166, 169
Epistemic practices, 9, 19–32, 161

F
Fragility, 11, 38, 39, 41, 49, 57, 88, 89, 140, 146, 148, 151

G
Generations, 4, 9, 21, 22, 24, 27, 30, 31, 46, 49–54, 56–58, 60, 86, 89, 138

H
Help, 28, 30, 42, 55–57, 60, 69, 72–74, 76, 90, 92, 93, 111, 112, 123, 125–127, 138, 142, 143, 150–153, 155, 168, 169
Hybrid minds, 19–32

I
Identification, 7, 10, 40, 46–48, 50, 52, 139, 145
Institution, 1, 7, 11, 19, 20, 27, 30, 68, 94–97, 103, 141, 150, 155, 168, 169

K
Knowledge, 9, 10, 20, 21, 23, 27–30, 43–45, 47, 54, 65, 74, 75, 77, 86, 88, 94, 95, 98, 102, 103, 162, 168

L
Learning, 1–11, 19–32, 41–50, 65–67, 85–103, 108, 109, 137–155, 159, 161, 162, 165, 166, 169

T. Zittoun, F. Gfeller (eds.), *Ageing, Learning and Development*, Lifelong Learning Book Series 36, https://doi.org/10.1007/978-3-032-11057-2

M
Methodology, 24, 67–69, 163, 164

P
Pleasure, 38, 39, 41–44, 48, 56, 57, 59, 70, 76–79, 91, 97–98, 102, 103, 108, 109, 115, 139, 149, 152, 154, 160, 162, 163, 166, 169
Psychoanalysis, 5–9, 42, 43, 46, 59, 160, 163, 166, 168

R
Resistance, 7, 49, 51–54, 147
Resources, 2, 26–32, 38, 39, 46, 47, 58, 64, 69, 72, 74–76, 78, 85, 86, 88, 89, 92, 93, 95, 100, 102, 107–130, 138, 144, 148, 166, 168, 169

S
Self, 43, 60, 91, 108–111, 113, 119, 125, 141, 149, 154, 165
Semiotic processes, 8
Societal change and human development, 24, 32, 44, 46, 109, 142, 161, 162, 168
Sociocultural psychology, 5–10, 64, 90, 109, 160, 163, 168

T
Testimony, 38, 60, 165
Theory, 2, 7, 22, 85, 88–91, 109–111, 144, 163, 165
Transitions, 11, 32, 54, 66, 85, 86, 88, 90, 107–111, 113, 115, 116, 118, 122, 127, 128, 142, 144, 145, 148, 150, 162, 164, 166
Transmission, 86, 125, 154

V
Volunteering, 10, 85–103, 161, 168

MIX
Papier aus verantwortungsvollen Quellen
Paper from responsible sources
FSC® C105338

If you have any concerns about our products,
you can contact us on
ProductSafety@springernature.com

In case Publisher is established outside the EU,
the EU authorized representative is:
Springer Nature Customer Service Center GmbH
Europaplatz 3, 69115 Heidelberg, Germany

Printed by Libri Plureos GmbH
in Hamburg, Germany